THE
PEMBROKESHIRE
MURDERS

THE
PEMBROKESHIRE
MURDERS

STEVE WILKINS
JONATHAN HILL

THE PEMBROKESHIRE MURDERS

STEVE WILKINS
and JONATHAN HILL

SEVEN DIALS

First published in Great Britain in 2013 by Seren Books
This paperback edition published in 2021 by Seven Dials
an imprint of The Orion Publishing Group Ltd
Carmelite House, 50 Victoria Embankment
London EC4Y 0DZ

An Hachette UK Company

3 5 7 9 10 8 6 4

Image from *Bullseye* on p3 (c) ITV Studios.
Images on p1 & p2 Shutterstock.
All other images cleared and provided by the author.

Steve Wilkins thanks his wife Diane for her help, support and love
during the writing of this book.

Jonathan Hill thanks his wife for her considerable help in the making of
this book.

A CIP catalogue record for this book is available
from the British Library.

ISBN (Mass Market Paperback) 978 1 8418 8450 9
ISBN (eBook) 978 1 8418 8451 6

Typeset by Born Group
Printed and bound in Great Britain by Clays Ltd, Elcograf S.p.A.

www.orionbooks.co.uk

CONTENTS

ILLUSTRATIONS

CHAPTER I

'TAKE HIM DOWN'

It was the morning of the 26th of May 2011 and the jury at Swansea Crown Court had been out for two days considering their verdicts. The clock in the courtroom crept towards midday and I could feel the tension in the room. Why had they taken so long? Surely after nine weeks of evidence it must be clear to them that John William Cooper was guilty of the horrendous crimes that had cast a dark shadow over Pembrokeshire for a quarter of a century. It was a very strange feeling. For the last five years I had been in control of the investigation codenamed Operation Ottawa that had brought Cooper to justice. I had had the privilege of leading the finest team of police officers and support staff I had ever come across in more than thirty years of service but at this moment I had no control at all; it was in the hands of twelve ordinary men and women.

Detectives are resourceful individuals, trained to notice the smallest changes in human behaviour and I had a team of the very best. 'Today is the day, boss,' one of them said. 'The jury have got their "drinking gear" on. They'll be going out at lunchtime.' This was the best indication to me that the jury had broken from their regular pattern and not ordered lunch for the first time in nine weeks. Today was definitely going to be the day.

As I looked around the drab little side room which had been our home during the trial I could not help thinking that everyone who mattered was there: The Ottawa team; The Crown Prosecution Team, led by Tom Atherton; and The Crown led by Gerard Elias QC. Suddenly the door burst open and standing in front of us was the ample frame of Detective Sergeant Gareth 'Rambo' Rees. 'Verdict!' he exclaimed. The room burst into life. For me it was important that I spoke to the Ottawa team alone before we went into court. As the barristers dashed though the door we gathered in a tight circle. It felt right that we were together, as we had been since the very beginning. My words were simple. 'It has been my absolute honour and privilege to have led you on this journey, I could not have asked for more and you could not have done any more. Whatever the verdict here today we will receive and accept it with dignity. There will be no reaction from us. Good luck!'

The courtroom was packed and every seat was taken. To my right I could see the families and relatives of the victims who had waited so long for justice: Tim and Julie, the children of Peter and Gwenda Dixon, who had been murdered in cold blood whilst on holiday in Pembrokeshire some twenty-two years earlier. Next to them were the James family, cousins to siblings Richard and Helen Thomas, who had been blasted to death in their farmhouse in the mid-1980s. Unbeknown to most people in the courtroom the victims of a rape and robbery attack in Milford Haven were sitting in the viewing room behind a darkened glass window. They were all victims of one man – John William Cooper.

The press gallery was packed, as it had been throughout

the trial; they too had heard every piece of evidence and we were now moments away from its conclusion. I sat near Cooper's family who had attended court throughout the nine weeks and I could not help but admire the dignity they had shown throughout.

'All rise!' the court usher bellowed. Everyone stood. The judge, John Griffith Williams, walked briskly into the court resplendent in his red robe. Over the years I have never really suffered from nerves, pressure has always given clarity to my thoughts. Now though my mind was racing and I could feel my heart pounding against my ribs; in the silence of the court I thought I could actually hear it. My Ottawa team were in a group on the opposite side of the room, as one they all looked to the dock as Cooper was brought into court. He was wearing a grey suit with a pink striped tie, as he had done every day of the trial. He looked more like a crooked accountant who had been caught with his fingers in the till than the cold, calculating serial killer that I knew he was.

The judge looked down at the clerk. 'We have a verdict, I understand, please bring the jury in.' The jury door opened and the twelve members walked into the court but none of them looked at Cooper. For the first time I thought how young and innocent they looked and what a burden it must have been reaching such a decision. Some of the girls on the back row were holding hands, one was crying. They sat down quietly; the court was in total silence.

'Will the foreman please stand.'

One of the men in the front row stood up.

'Have you reached a verdict on which you are all agreed?' said the clerk.

'Yes,' he replied.

'Is that in relation to all charges?'

'Yes.'

I noticed other members of the jury were now crying.

'On charge one of the indictment, the murder of Helen Thomas, do you find the defendant John William Cooper guilty or not guilty?'

Without hesitation he replied, 'Guilty.' There was a gasp in the court.

'The murder of Richard Thomas, guilty or not guilty?'

Again he replied, 'Guilty.'

In my mind these were the two charges that I feared for the most as we had the least evidence. If the jury had convicted him of these murders then we must be home and dry, I thought. I turned to Assistant Chief Constable Nick Ingram, who was sitting next to me, and whispered, 'We've got him. It's a full house.' At that moment I could hear Cooper's family sobbing openly.

'The murder of Gwenda Dixon, guilty or not guilty?' continued the clerk.

'Guilty.' I could hear emotion in the juror's voice and I could see tears running down his cheeks. I was willing him to get through it.

'The murder of Peter Dixon, guilty or not guilty?'

'Guilty.'

Still no reaction from Cooper, he stood in silence staring straight ahead.

'On count five of the indictment, guilty or not guilty?' said the clerk.

'Guilty,' the foreman replied.

'Is that of rape or indecent assault?' he was asked.

'Rape,' came the reply.

Cooper snapped his head towards the foreman and

shouted, 'Rubbish! That's rubbish!' His face was contorted and angry. This was the first time he had shown emotion and I knew why. He was being consistent to the end because he knew what this conviction would mean. This was nothing to do with victims or the truth. He was now a convicted child rapist and, having spent eleven years in prison already, he knew how this particular crime would affect his treatment behind bars.

'On count six, indecent assault, guilty or not guilty?'

'Guilty!' again came the reply.

'This is a set-up. You haven't heard all of the evidence. Rubbish!' shouted Cooper. He now fixed the jury with his chilling stare.

The judge shouted at him, 'Mr Cooper, be quiet or I will have you removed.'

'On counts seven, eight, nine, ten and eleven, the offences of attempted robbery, guilty or not guilty?'

'Guilty!' said the foreman, one final time. He had made it, he had managed to get through, voice breaking with emotion and tears running down his face.

'Well done, well done,' I thought. By now the press were running from the court, some were texting or tweeting from their mobile phones, they all wanted to be the first to break the news to the world. Cooper's family now stood up. They were crying and I genuinely felt sorry for them, they looked broken. As they walked past the dock Phillip Cooper shouted to his brother, 'We are here for you, John!' They left the court and for a few seconds there was a stunned silence.

I looked across at my team, sitting together as one, not a shred of emotion on their faces but I knew that inside they must be screaming out loud. They had just made history as part of the team that brought John Cooper to justice. Keith Dixon, Peter's brother, who was also in court, looked at me and mouthed the words, 'Thank you'. I could feel a lump in my throat and had to look away from him.

The judge addressed Mark Evans QC, counsel for the defence. 'Mr Evans, it is my intention to pass sentence. Is there anything you would like to say?'

He stood and in a low voice of total resignation replied, 'My Lord, I fear that there is little I can say that will affect the inevitable sentence you must pass on these the most serious of offences.'

By now Cooper was contorted with rage. 'Rubbish, you have not heard all the evidence!' he shouted 'This is a set-up, look at the internet!' he continued to protest.

'John William Cooper . . .' the judge began, but Cooper continued to shout over him. 'John William Cooper,' the judge continued defiantly.

In my experience, the sentencing judge is less than tolerant over interruptions and would quickly direct the attending prison officers to 'take him down' whilst sentence is passed. There was no chance of that in this case and it was clear that Justice John Griffith Williams was going to sentence him whilst he stood before him in the dock so Cooper could hear his inevitable fate. In giving him four life sentences Justice Griffith Williams added the words I had wanted to hear: 'The murders were of such evil wickedness, the mandatory sentence of life, will mean just that.' Cooper would die in prison.

The more Cooper shouted and interrupted the more his voice twisted into anger and hatred. It was the voice heard by Sheila Clark, who had been so violently robbed at gunpoint in her home; the voice heard by the five innocent teenagers who went out to a field to play only to return broken and terrorised; the voice heard by the Thomases and the Dixons in their last moments. If the jury had needed any more proof, he had just given it to them. This was the *real* John William Cooper.

'Take him down,' ordered Justice Griffith Williams.

Cooper spun around and walked to the door leading from the dock to the cells and as he did he was still ranting, 'This is rubbish! Read the internet, you haven't heard the evidence!'

The door closed and he was gone. I had spent years looking at his picture and months staring at his face and now this would be the last time I would see him. There was a moment of silence.

The judge then went through the formal process of thanking the jury and discharging them from any future service; they had served their public duty to the best of their ability and would now return to everyday life, having sat in judgement over an evil man. Our paths would never cross again, but I felt proud of them and at the same time sorry that they had had to hear every single piece of evidence, a daunting responsibility indeed. The judge went on to commend the Ottawa team, paying tribute to their hard work, dedication and professionalism. Somehow, it just did not seem enough, considering all the commitment they had given for the last six years.

The jury filed out in total silence and the courtroom started to buzz with noise as twenty different conversations went on at the same time. I could see the Dixons and James family in an embrace, many tears being shed. The Ottawa team, disciplined to the end, sat in silence; I knew they must be bursting with pride and a fantastic sense of achievement and probably wanted to get back to the police room to let it all out. The press gallery was empty and I knew that in a short space of time I would have to face them and the TV cameras on the steps of the court. Prosecutor Gerard Elias QC and his junior counsel were in a huddle. They had been simply fantastic and it had been a privilege to see a master at work; it was fitting that this had been his last case.

I looked towards the darkened glass of the viewing room knowing that two of Cooper's victims from the Milford Haven sex attack were looking into the court. They were joined by the mother of Maria, one of the victims, who had died only a couple of weeks before the trial. She had never recovered from the attack by Cooper and had passed away without seeing her tormentor brought to justice. It was a source of great sadness to me and the rest of the Ottawa team. I couldn't see their faces through the glass but I knew they were there; I smiled and nodded towards the screen.

The conviction of Cooper for four murders was always going to grab the headlines because they were high-profile cases but for me the conviction for the attack on the children was the most rewarding. I had insisted on it being kept on the indictment because it was the mortar that held together the bricks of the Dixon and Thomas cases. More importantly I had visited the victims of the rape and indecent assault fifteen years after they had been attacked to tell them the next day we were to arrest Cooper. The impact was devastating, they had tried to move on and make new lives but the pain had never gone away. I was now telling them that they had to go through it all again and, if need be, go to court and face

Cooper to give evidence. The victim of indecent assault, Susan, was determined to do so, but her friend Jayne was reluctant, as her partner and children did not know she had been a victim of rape. I remember walking out of her house with Detective Chief Inspector Lynne Harries and we were both shaken by that conversation. Over the months building up to the trial the victims of the Milford Haven attack would go through many emotions and needed constant support. Up until the day they gave evidence I was not sure that they would go into the witness box. Helen Coles and Donna Thomas had been my family liaison officers and had managed to support, coax and cajole the girls to court to give evidence. Now here we all were, with Cooper convicted, and I was proud of them all. They too had been caught up in the moment and I was faced with a scrum of bodies in one mass hug. We shared a moment together that will remain private. My mind now turned to the media frenzy that was erupting on the court steps.

Leading up to the verdict I had done a number of television, radio and newspaper interviews to be used only in the event of a conviction. They had been difficult because I did not want to tempt fate. I had prepared some words for both a guilty and not guilty verdict. If Cooper was acquitted it had been my intention to resign from the police, accepting all responsibility for failure. I am a great believer that if you are willing to accept the bouquets for success, you should also accept the consequence of failure; this has always been my way. I knew as the jury walked back into court that this could be my last day as a detective. Now here I was standing on the court steps with the Dixon family ready to deliver my statement and thankfully the not guilty version stayed in my pocket.

The media had massed outside the front door of the court and Tim and Julie had agreed to give a statement on behalf of all of the families and victims. Over the years Julie had been a person of few words but today she was determined to speak and I was so pleased. Tim, her brother, was very suspicious of the press because of the way he was treated by them when his parents were murdered. The level of intrusion at his parents' funeral had been beyond belief; photographers had entered his home unannounced and uninvited, they had taken away photographs of his parents that have never been returned and they had caused the funeral cortege to stop so they could take photographs of the grieving family. Worst of all they had sneaked into the church and recorded the funeral service. Thankfully the press at court had behaved impeccably and the family understood that they needed to say something.

We now stood together on the steps of the court and Julie addressed the press.

'We, the family of Peter and Gwenda Dixon, are pleased with the verdict today. We are also pleased with the verdict in regards to the Thomases' case. While it can't take away our loss and grief we can now rest knowing the person responsible for these terrible atrocities has been served justice. To many Peter and Gwenda are just another two faces that happened to be in the wrong place at the wrong time. But to our family they are irreplaceable: there are no words that come near to explaining the impact this has had on us. An integral part of our family is missing. Peter and Gwenda were loving, gentle and loved people. They were also a charismatic couple that invested a lot of time and energy in the local community. They had wisdom, humour and were benevolent. Even after two decades their absence is noticeable.

'We would like to thank DCS Steve Wilkins, his team and all the officers over the years. The family of Peter and Gwenda, anyone else touched by John Cooper's violence and all the people of South West Wales owe a debt of gratitude to these officers. Because of their tenacity, dedication and hard work their communities will be that much safer after today. We now begin the task of getting on with the rest of our lives. Today's verdict gives us justice, but there is no sentence the courts could impose that could ever give us recompense for what we have lost and the impact the loss of Peter and Gwenda will have on the rest of our lives. We therefore ask the media to respect our privacy. There will be no further statements from any member of the Dixon family after today.'

It was now my turn and there was one message I wanted to give.

'Whilst attending court on remand, John William Cooper shouted to the community not to judge until after the trial. Over the last nine weeks, twelve ordinary people from the same community have listened to all of the evidence in this case and have found him unanimously guilty of all charges; I believe that is the right decision.'

The press and TV were satisfied. They had got their interviews and were now busy filing copy and broadcasting the news of Cooper's conviction. I just wanted to go home and be with my family. I slowly walked back to my car and sat in the driver's seat for fifteen minutes trying to take it all in. We had done it; we had convicted the most notorious killer in Welsh history and it felt fantastic. My phone started to ping like a demented microwave as message after message came in but one stood out, an email from someone I had never met. It simply said, 'Thank you, I have not walked the coastal path since the terrible murders. This weekend I will walk it again for the first time in over twenty years. God bless team Ottawa.' As I drove home the words of the judge, Cooper and of the Dixon family were ringing in my ears. It was the end of a long and difficult journey but it was one that I would never, ever forget.

CHAPTER 2

THE SCOVESTON PARK MURDERS

In the dying days of 1985, Pembrokeshire would witness a crime that triggered the extraordinary events that came to dominate my career and the lives of dozens of people who were drawn into this chilling case. The chain of events probably began with the striking of a single match.

It was a cold, wet and windy night as Anna McEwan and Lorraine Brown drove home chatting about their plans for Christmas. At 11 p.m. they passed through Steynton on the outskirts of Milford Haven and approached an area known locally as Scoveston Park. Heavy smoke was drifting across the fields and over the carriageway adding to the gloom. It rolled across the hedgerows from a small wooded area, set back from the main road. Local knowledge told them it was coming from the direction of Scoveston Park Farm, the home of brother and sister, Richard and Helen Thomas.

The pair were so concerned that they turned off the main road and drove down the narrow lane towards the farm buildings. It soon became clear that the Georgian farmhouse was well alight. The flames were already extending through the three-storey building and into the roof space. They could do little except raise the alarm. Minutes later the area was illuminated by blue flashing lights. It was obvious to the emergency crews that nobody could have survived such a ferocious fire. Through the charred timbers fire officers could see a body on the first-floor half landing and their priority now was to recover it. At ten past midnight on the 23rd of December, the body of a man believed to be that of Richard James Skeel Thomas was brought out and taken to the mortuary. A suspicious wound was evident on the right-hand side of his lower abdomen. One of the senior officers at the scene, Chief Inspector Chris James, requested an X-ray of the body. It was discovered that the wound contained lead shot. This changed everything. DCI James quickly informed the Head of CID, Detective Chief Superintendent David Davies, and then spoke to Superintendent Don Evans at the scene. Richard had been shot and every effort must now be made to preserve evidence.

Having brought the inferno under control members of the fire service began to search the debris for a second body, that of Helen Thomas. The fire had caused extensive damage and the wooden floors had burnt through, collapsing onto the ground floor. Sure enough while searching the ground floor a second body was found. It was very badly burnt and in a poor condition but it was indeed the body of Helen Thomas. Fire officers at the scene also noticed a strong smell of paraffin or another accelerant in the house. Had the fire been set deliberately?

The body of Helen Thomas was recovered and the scene preserved. Again X-ray examinations confirmed that she too had been shot; lead particles were discovered in the base of what remained of her skull. The discussion between DCI James and DCS Davies was simple, preserve the scene, inform the coroner and contact the Home Office

Pathologist. He needed to know what we had found and get to the scene as soon as possible. He arrived at 8 a.m. the following morning. Dr O.G. Williams was well known to the officers and a highly respected pathologist. His initial assessment was that of a murder and suicide with the fire being set to finish the job. The likelihood of a gang of dangerous criminals attacking Richard and Helen Thomas was totally out of context with the area and was not the kind of crime that happened locally. An examination of the bodies and a search of the scene were likely to provide the clues to what had gone on between the brother and sister on that fateful night.

Richard and Helen Thomas were regarded locally as the 'landed gentry', and owned a considerable amount of land and property in addition to Scoveston Park Farm. Richard also owned property at nearby Norton Farm and Scoveston Grove. He actively worked the land at Norton Farm, but the house to the farm was unoccupied. Richard was a quiet and reserved person who had followed in his late father's farming footsteps. His sister, Helen Thomas, was also quiet and reserved and took over the responsibilities of the house following their mother's death in 1975. She also owned two farms at Great Harmeston and Beaconing and their combined wealth was estimated to be in excess of £700,000. Even in the early stage of the investigation there were rumours of a rift between them. It was believed that Helen wished to spend money on improving their properties, whilst Richard was more cautious and intent on farming the land. Indeed the outward view of Scoveston Park was of an impressive country mansion; in fact most of the property was in a poor state of repair, adding to the rumour and speculation.

Both post-mortems were carried out at Withybush Hospital, Haverfordwest. Richard had a gunshot wound to the right side of his lower abdomen. The wound contained a complete column of a 12-bore cartridge containing an original loading of UK No.5 shot. The wadding was of compressed wood fibre that experts would identify as the shot from an Eley cartridge containing a Grand Prix loading. Although his body was badly burned some of his lower clothing remained intact. One of his brown leather shoes was missing, though his sock was relatively untouched by the intense fire.

Helen's body had been recovered from the debris on the ground floor room to the right of the entrance hall. She had apparently fallen through the ceiling from the bedroom above as she was found sandwiched between layers of debris. She was also dressed in her day clothes as a jumper and underwear could be defined. Beneath her body were items of bed linen and part of a foam mattress. Entangled in the body was a length of black-knotted rope. Around her neck was a heavily bloodstained shirt with the sleeves knotted tightly. As the examinations continued the murder and suicide scenario became less likely. The rope and shirt suggested that Helen had been tied up, gagged or blindfolded in a bungled robbery.

If a possible murder weapon could be recovered it would provide crucial evidence to add weight to the murder/suicide theory. On Christmas Eve a search of the building for a shotgun had proved negative and the chilling reality of the situation was all too clear to DCS David Davies. He was faced with a cold, callous double murder and as the Senior Investigating Officer he was the man who would have to lead the investigation. The crime was totally out of character for the area and he knew it wasn't going to be easy. As Christmas Day came there was little cheer in the local community or for the officers who found themselves drafted on to the grisly case.

North Pembrokeshire is dominated by spectacular coastline and countryside and the main source of income is from tourism and farming. The North and South of the county are divided by the Milford Haven Waterway, which also represents a major source of employment. The Dyfed-Powys Police area experienced on average two murders a year but they were predominantly domestic in their background. The core work was volume crime and it had one of the lowest crime rates in the UK. Fewer than 1,200 officers police an area covering two-thirds of Wales. It was a safe and idyllic place to live but now the force faced possibly one of the biggest and most complex investigations in its history.

An incident room was set up at Milford Haven police station using a paper-based system. Paper-based incident rooms were dominated by racks of files and rotating card index carousels. Incident room staff, known as indexers, would transfer and cross-reference data onto the cards. These cards were then placed in various categories agreed by the incident room staff. As a card was filled, another would be sellotaped to it and so the index would build up. Any large and protracted investigation will generate a mass of statements, reports, information, evidence and intelligence, all of which needs to be assessed, recorded and indexed to allow for it to be searched for clues. This information will generate actions that require officers to conduct enquiries, in order to verify the information. When completed, the action and associated documents are returned to the incident room where the process starts again.

As a Senior Investigating Officer, or SIO, you always feel the incident room is playing catch-up and it is important that it is properly resourced with a day and night shift in the early stages to try to keep pace with a fast-moving investigation. The incident room is only as good as its staff; it is certainly not a place to hide the weak and lazy and requires a good office manager with a strong detective background. DCS Davies knew this and ensured he had a good team for the challenges ahead.

Any investigation requires strong leadership; the SIO is the principle decision-maker and sets policy and the direction of the investigation. Because of the intense media coverage, the eyes of the nation were on this seemingly sleepy little force and decisions made by the SIO and his team would most likely be closely scrutinised and picked over by the media.

Search teams and scenes of crime officers together with forensic experts began the painstaking process of searching the scene and surrounding land and outbuildings. Large metal grilles were set up outside the burnt-out house and its contents were shovelled into them and searched by hand. In particular they were looking for a murder weapon and spent cartridges. They were helped in this arduous task by large industrial magnets, but despite a detailed fingertip search only *live* ammunition was found and an empty gun cupboard. The killer had taken away any firearms kept in the house together with the spent cartridges and set the building on fire to cover his tracks. This demonstrated a high level of forensic awareness.

On Boxing Day officers were conducting a search of a small outbuilding at the rear of the house when they discovered a pool of blood. Also found were two lead cartridge pellets in plasterboard and one bloodstained pellet embedded in the wall. Two cartridge waddings and a button were recovered; the button was later matched to buttons on the shirt of Richard Thomas. Again there were no spent cartridges at this scene. What was puzzling was that Richard's body had been found inside the house on the stairs lying on top of a blanket with what appeared to be bailing twine entangled in it. Why was there blood in the outbuilding?

Richard's Red Rover car was found in an open garage at the rear of the building. Witnesses had seen him driving it on the day of the murders. The door was open and the keys were missing. Had Richard returned to Scoveston having been away during the day, leaving his sister alone, and disturbed the offender? Had a struggle taken place in which Richard was shot? Was it likely that he had been shot outside and then dragged into the main building? On New Year's Eve the Forensic Science Laboratory initially told the SIO that the blood in the outhouse was not Richard Thomas's, later changing their findings to confirm it was unlikely to be anyone else's.

On the 2nd of January 1986 pathologist O.G. Williams re-examined the bodies. It was at this point he discovered what he described as a 'raking shot' to the left side of Richard's head. An X-ray revealed that only 20 per cent of the shot remained in the wound, confirming that the blast had only glanced him. The pellets recovered from Richard were of UK No.5 shot, whilst those recovered from Helen were of UK No.4. This would later prove to be significant.

Now that the post-mortem results and initial forensic findings were in, DCS Davies was troubled by the motive for this callous and cold-blooded double murder. Was the killer local or did a team of travelling criminals target the location in the knowledge that Richard Thomas had money and wealth? Because of the damage it was impossible to say what, if anything, was missing from the house other than shotguns. Why kill them if they could not recognise their attackers? Many aspects of the crime did not make sense. If it was a robbery that had gone wrong, why was Richard found with £75 in his jacket pocket? There was a local rumour that in the past Richard had disturbed intruders on his land and threatened them with a shotgun. He had also told one of his farm labourers that he had set up an early warning system in case they returned.

This was by now the largest inquiry in the force's history. Vast amounts of information came into the incident room, and teams of detectives flooded the area following up actions to trace and eliminate persons of interest and establish the movements of Richard and Helen Thomas leading up to the murders. From these enquiries it was established that Richard had been seen on a number of locations in the area and had certainly visited Norton Farm. Of great interest were a number of sightings of a Land Rover vehicle which appeared to be following Richard's vehicle, the driver was described as a bearded fat man: was this Richard's killer stalking him before he attacked? In all, nine witnesses reported seeing the Land Rover on a stretch of road between the Horse and Jockey Public House and Sentry Cross, just a short distance from Scoveston Park, between 11.30 a.m. and 11.55 p.m. on the 22nd of December.

Another witness who passed the scene described a vehicle parked opposite the entrance to Scoveston Park, it was described as a saloon car, probably a Ford Cortina Mark IV.

Efforts were made to trace all Land Rover and Ford Cortina owners in the area, a massive and resource-intensive task. All houses and farms in the area were visited and the occupants spoken to. It was important to establish their knowledge of the victims, together with their own movements on the night. Road checks were set up in the area at which all vehicles were stopped and the occupants questioned as to their knowledge of the victims or whether they had ever met them or visited Scoveston Park. A substantial reward, £25,000, was offered for information about the murders, along with a request for information regarding the blue Ford Cortina and Land Rover together with the 'fat man' who was driving it. It all came to nothing.

DCS Davies needed a break and he was about to get it. On the 28th of January he received a call from the Forensic Science Laboratory informing him that an anal swab taken from Richard Thomas contained semen and it must have been there around the time of his death. Because DNA technology was very much in its infancy, the scientist could give little more detail other than the blood group.

This information together with the witness accounts placing Richard's vehicle in proximity to the Land Rover and description of the 'fat man' driver presented a real line of enquiry to the SIO. Did a gay lover, who then tried to cover his tracks by killing Helen and setting fire to the house, murder Richard? Was Richard actually killed at Scoveston Park? One of his shoes was missing and was never found. The 'fat man' lead could also fit in with other information that Richard had visited a local cinema to watch pornographic movies in the company of such a man. Extensive enquiries were made into the local gay community in an attempt to secure information about

Richard and his private life. Very little was known about him and Helen, though it was clear that neither had taken a partner. After months of investigation and appeals there was not one shred of evidence that Richard had indeed had a gay lover or was in fact gay.

The police had acted on dozens of tip-offs including a suggestion that the killer had been wounded and was hiding in a housing estate in the Swansea area. All appeared to be credible but came to nothing. Ten months into the investigation over 70,000 documents, reports, index cards and statements had been entered into the incident room. More than one hundred people had been traced, interviewed and eliminated. Eight people were actually arrested; of these six were eliminated. The remaining two men were not eliminated but there was no evidence to suggest they were connected to the murders.

By the spring of 1986 the team had worked tirelessly for months on end with little reward; DCS Davies did not favour the theory that a gay lover had killed Richard, though there was some forensic evidence to support this hypothesis. He was more inclined to believe it was a bungled robbery on a lone female by criminals from outside the area who had killed Richard when he had disturbed them; Helen, as witness to this, then simply had to die. Whatever the truth, they were no closer to finding the answers.

CHAPTER 3

THE COASTAL PATH MURDERS

Tim Dixon arrived at Birmingham airport to pick up his eighteen-year-old sister Julie, who was returning from her holiday in Cyprus. It was the 3rd of July 1989 and their next stop was Witney in Oxfordshire, the home of their parents Peter and Gwenda Dixon. They were looking forward to a family get-together as their parents had been on their annual summer holiday to the beautiful coastal village of Little Haven in North Pembrokeshire, a place they loved and had visited for the past fifteen years. To their surprise the house was empty and there was no sign that their parents had returned from Wales. More worrying was the fact that Peter had not returned to work as expected.

Margaret Davies was the proprietor of Howelston Farm Caravan Park at Little Haven and was surprised to get a concerned telephone call from Tim Dixon enquiring about his parents Peter and Gwenda. They were popular visitors to the area and well known by the locals. Over the years they had spent hours walking and exploring the miles of breathtaking cliff tops and hidden coves that made up the coastal path of Pembrokeshire. Now Margaret Davies made her way across her campsite in search of their pitch. Their tent was still there, as was Peter Dixon's red Ford Sierra car. This was very unusual as she was aware they were due to leave on the 29th of June and they had not indicated an intention to stay or paid the additional site fees.

It was quickly established that Peter and Gwenda Dixon had last been seen on the site on the morning of the 29th of June, when they had spoken to fellow camper Richard Lines who had pitched his tent immediately next to theirs. Peter had indicated his intention to return home at midday and that he and his wife were to take a final walk along the coastal path towards St Brides to allow their tent to dry out. Indeed a number of people saw them leave the site in the direction of the coastal path. The reports suggested that the Dixons seemed happy and were enjoying the last few hours of their holiday.

Immediately Tim Dixon knew something was wrong. His parents were considerate people and would never have overstayed without telling someone or without paying their fees. On the 3rd of July 1989, Tim Dixon reported to police that his parents Peter and Gwenda Dixon were missing. Very quickly police were mobilised in a search of the area near to Howelston Farm Caravan Park, helped by the National Park Wardens and the Coastguard. As the long summer evening faded the sound of a helicopter rang out along the coastline. The search continued at first light and was now bolstered by police dog handlers and a helicopter from RAF Brawdy supported by the inshore lifeboat. The search for the Dixons was declared a major incident and there were now very real fears for their safety. Many believed the couple might have fallen and injured themselves along the cliff path, but with every passing hour hope of finding them alive faded.

The terrain was difficult and dangerous and on the afternoon of the 4th of July, dog handlers were tasked with searching an area known as Borough Head. This was a wooded area near to the edge of the sheer 200 ft cliffs; one careless step would mean disaster. It meant that progress was slow and again the fading light made it impossible to finish searching this area of pathway. The search teams would return the next morning to continue the task.

This was hot and dangerous work with only sea breezes bringing occasional relief from the heat. It was shortly after 3.30 p.m. when PC Mike Callas, a dog handler, noticed something was not right as he searched near to the cliff edge. There were swarms of flies in an area below him and a pungent smell which experience told him was the stench of death. He followed what appeared to be an animal run made by either foxes or badgers, fully expecting to find the carcass of an animal. Instead, he was confronted by the decomposing bodies of Peter and Gwenda Dixon.

Their bodies lay in a heavily wooded and overgrown area of the coastal path approximately 800 yards from the Howelston Farm Caravan Park where they had been camping. They were concealed behind a screen of broken branches, which were pushed into the ground and interwoven with ferns and vegetation. Crucially the bodies were completely hidden from the view of anyone walking along the coastal footpath. For Superintendent Don Evans this was his worst nightmare. He had been one of the first at the scene of the Scoveston Park double murders and now he was attending a second double killing. For Don it was impossible to comprehend. This idyllic corner of Pembrokeshire was yet again about to become the centre of national attention.

The scene could only be accessed by an ill-defined, overgrown path, which led to a small plateau and clearing. Beyond this plateau the cliff fell away to the shore below.

Gwenda Dixon was found lying face down near the edge of a precipitous drop of some 200 feet, with her head pointing towards the sea. She was naked from the waist down apart from her socks. Her trousers and underwear were a short distance away. The trousers had been turned inside out and her pants were entangled in the trouser legs indicating they had been removed together, either hurriedly or forcibly, and discarded. Her walking boots were nearby. Her bra had been pulled down towards her waist. Her jumper and blouse had been rucked up exposing her breasts. In addition to being partially hidden by the screen of branches, other efforts had been made to conceal her body by covering it with brambles, uprooted plants and other vegetation. The position and condition of Mrs Dixon's body was clearly indicative of a sexual assault. Peter Dixon's body was found a few feet away from his wife's at the extreme edge of the cliff. He was also lying face down with his feet facing towards the sea. His body had in fact started to slide over the edge of the cliff top. Mr Dixon was fully clothed with his hands tied behind his back with a single length of grey three-ply polyethylene rope binding him.

As with any major crime, the scene and any associated locations are potentially rich with evidence and must be properly preserved. Following the discovery of the bodies, scenes of crime officers taped off a common path to the bodies, established inner and outer cordons and started a log, providing a continuous record of those officers and other persons who entered or left the scene. Little Haven and the surrounding area was a very popular tourist destination and this was high season. The investigation team had to move quickly and obtain details of the local holiday parks and visitors to the area before they returned home.

Preserving the bodies and their clothing was now the key objective but a proper examination would be extremely dangerous because of their proximity to the cliff edge. The conditions were unique and initially the pathologist and forensic scientists were reluctant to carry out any examinations of the bodies where they lay because of the very real risk of falling. Professor Bernard Knight, the Home Office Pathologist, arrived at the scene at 8 p.m. on Wednesday the 5th of July and carried out a brief initial examination of the body of Gwenda Dixon, but he was unable to examine the body of Peter Dixon due to its precarious location. Doctor John Whiteside, a scientist from the Home Office Forensic Science Laboratory in Chepstow, also attended the scene the same day and found it an equally difficult and dangerous examination to undertake. The assistance of HM Coast Guard was required to secure the body of Peter Dixon by tying it to a tree to stop it sliding over the cliff edge. All those working at the scene had to be secured with ropes and safety harnesses. Despite being hampered in his work, Professor Knight suspected even at this early stage that Gwenda Dixon had been shot. At 9.30 that evening her body was removed from the scene and, due to the obvious dangers, DCS Clive Jones also gave instructions for the body of Peter Dixon to be removed the same night. Ideally he would have wanted more time with them at the scene, but its unique and dangerous location made this impossible.

The coastal path between Little Haven and Borough Head was thoroughly searched with all undergrowth being removed fifty yards each side of the crime scene and down to the rocky shore below. The plateau was fingertip-searched and divers were brought in to comb the bay below. The searches were thorough and methodical although nothing of any obvious evidential value was found other than the personal belongings and clothing of the couple and the contents of their rucksack. These had been strewn around the scene and included a waterproof jacket and trousers that were heavily bloodstained. There was also a camera case, walking stick, binoculars and a key ring. The blood on the clothing would suggest that the rucksack was searched before the Dixons were shot. It was soon established through Tim Dixon that his father carried a wallet in which he kept cash and his bankcards including a NatWest cash card. The wallet and its contents were missing.

Both bodies were taken to Withybush Hospital at Haverfordwest where the post-mortem examinations were carried out by Professor Knight. The examination of Gwenda revealed two shotgun wounds, one in the centre of the back and one in the right breast. There were other marks and injuries to her body consistent with rough handling. She had also received a substantial blow to the left side of her head with a blunt instrument, enough to cause unconsciousness. The shotgun wound to the chest had passed through the blouse and jumper and not the bra, which was undamaged by the blast.

Peter Dixon suffered three gunshot wounds. One in the back, a second to the right side of the chest and a third to the head, which Professor Knight believed was delivered when he was still alive, blowing away the central part of his face and brain. Both the victims had died as a result of these gunshot wounds. From examination of the wounds it was established that the fatal shots had been delivered from a double-barrelled sawn-off shotgun. It was also concluded that the wound on Gwenda's back and the head and back wounds to Peter were fired from the same barrel and the chest wounds sustained by both were fired from the other. In essence the killer must have reloaded the gun twice. Two plastic cartridge cups and cork wadding were recovered from the body of Gwenda. Three plastic cartridge cups, two cork waddings and a quantity of shotgun pellets were recovered from the body of Peter Dixon. The type of wadding recovered suggests the cartridges were manufactured by one of three Italian firms: SMI, Maionchi or Martignoni. Doctor Renshaw, the ballistics expert, observed that the weight of the pellets corresponded with No.5 shot, but he could not exclude No.4 or No.6. Similar shot had been used at Scoveston and at both scenes no spent cartridges were recovered.

Detective Chief Superintendent Clive Jones needed to establish a time of death and this was proving difficult. Both bodies were heavily infested with maggots, samples of which were examined by Doctor Zakaria Erzinclioglu of Cambridge University's Department of Zoology. From examination it was concluded that the time of death was on the 28th or 29th of June 1989. This can be explained by the feeding habits of the maggots. As they eat they excrete a fluid, which in turn keeps the body in a condition most suitable to feed on. Another vital piece of evidence came from a witness who, at about 11 a.m. on the 29th of June was walking on the beach below the coastal path and heard five shots: two blasts followed by two more and then a final shot. All of this, together with the sighting of Peter and Gwenda Dixon at Howelston Farm Caravan Park on the morning of the 29th of June led DCS Clive Jones to believe that the shots heard by the witness were those that had killed the Dixons. The position of Mrs Dixon's clothing suggested that her body had not been moved after the fatal gunshots had been delivered. The hole in the back of her blouse was circular and the same size as the wound whereas the hole in her jumper was considerably elongated, indicating it had been creased or 'rucked up' at the time the shot to the back was fired. The shot to the chest had not passed through the bra, indicating it had been moved exposing her breast before the shot was made. The 'plateau' was indeed the murder scene and the time of death was the morning of the 29th of June.

The brutality of the killings sent shock waves through the beautiful coastal village of Little Haven and spread into the wider community of Pembrokeshire and beyond. This was now the second double shotgun murder within just a few miles and a Major Incident Room was established at Haverfordwest police station. The investigation was already generating a vast amount of information all of which had to be evaluated and logged.

A few years earlier, following the Yorkshire Ripper inquiry, the standard procedures for recording information in a large investigation had changed. That investigation had been hampered by the sheer volume of paper, all of which had to be sifted and indexed by hand and recorded on card systems for research and retrieval. When Peter Sutcliffe was eventually arrested it would emerge that his name had featured several times in the inquiry but the significance of his connections to the crimes had never been picked up. Investigators had become bogged down in paperwork.

Now in 1989 the MIRSAP (Major Incident Room Standardised Administration Procedures) had become the bible. The old Rotadex and paper-based systems used at Scoveston Park had been replaced by the Home Office Large Major Enquiry System, or HOLMES, computer. Dyfed-Powys Police had just taken delivery of such a computer system and the Chief Constable decided to use it on the Dixons inquiry. Unbeknown to him this decision would seriously hamper the investigation with some simple searches taking almost 45 minutes to return a result.

Dyfed-Powys Police was yet again at the centre of a major crime investigation that was attracting national interest and was facing awkward questions about its ability to investigate another double shotgun killing after the failure of the Scoveston Park inquiry four years earlier. It was clear that DCS Clive Jones needed a strong line of enquiry and fast. The stolen cash card belonging to Peter Dixon provided it. The investigation revealed that it had been used on four occasions following the murders. The first transaction occurred in Pembroke town centre, some fifteen miles from Little Haven, at 1.36 p.m. on Thursday the 29th of June 1989, when £10 in cash was withdrawn from the NatWest Bank service till. Prior to this withdrawal a void transaction took place indicating that the card may have been used by someone who was inexperienced with the procedure of taking out money or the amounts that could be withdrawn. The second transaction occurred at the same cashpoint at 4.09 p.m. on the same day. The correct PIN number was entered, a balance enquiry was made and a printed slip was given, showing a balance of £122.59. The withdrawal option was taken; again a wrong amount was entered before a withdrawal of £100 was made. The third transaction occurred at 2.59 p.m. the following day, the 30th of June 1989, at the NatWest in Carmarthen town centre, some thirty miles east of Pembroke and Little Haven. On this occasion the correct PIN number was used at the first attempt and a balance enquiry made. Again the offender requested £100 that was dispensed. The fourth and final transaction occurred at 7.14 a.m. the following day, Saturday the 1st of July 1989, at the NatWest in Haverfordwest; in effect whoever was using the card had returned the twenty-five miles to Pembrokeshire. Again the PIN was entered correctly at the first attempt and a balance enquiry was made before £100 was requested and dispensed.

In order to access the cash machines the killer had to have been in possession of Peter Dixon's PIN number. This meant he either knew it, found it written on some piece of paper belonging to them, or most likely he had forced them to divulge it prior to their murder. It is difficult to imagine what they must have been subjected to in the moments before their death. Minutes earlier they had been enjoying a summer's walk and the next they were being confronted by a gunman. It is likely one of them saw the other murdered in cold blood, knowing they were to face the same fate. Even for hardened detectives it was very poignant. This was a callous execution for little gain.

The focus of the investigation now switched to the location of the cashpoints in Pembroke, Carmarthen and Haverfordwest. It was vital that anyone who might have used the cashpoints or been near them at the time of the transactions was traced. Detectives had to move quickly because at this time of the year the area was full of tourists who would be returning home. Teams of officers flooded the area. Radio, TV and press appeals were made. The swift action paid off and soon a picture and suspect began to emerge. A number of witnesses in Main Street, Pembroke, described seeing a man at the time of the transactions hanging around the town centre. He was twenty-five to thirty-five years old, six feet tall with light brown scruffy collar-length hair and wearing knee-length khaki shorts, hiking boots and he had two to three day's growth of beard. Other witnesses gave a similar description and included the fact that the man had a straight-handled bicycle with him. At 7.15 a.m. on the 1st of July 1989, Nicholas Elliot was driving his car along High Street in Haverfordwest when he looked towards the NatWest. He always did this as he passed because his girlfriend worked in the bank. At this time in the morning it was very quiet, and his attention was drawn to a lone man using the cashpoint. Nicholas Elliot described the man as five feet ten inches tall, late thirties to early forties with dark brown collar-length hair that was slightly bushy. He looked unshaven sporting a slight beard and moustache; he looked tanned as if he spent time outdoors. He was wearing ankle-length boots with almost knee-length khaki to brown shorts and was carrying a rucksack. He also noticed a bicycle with straight handlebars leaning against the wall.

Each confirmed sighting produced an artist's impression and this left DCS Clive Jones with an important policy decision to make: should he go public with this, and if so which one? Experience told him that the release of an artist's impression could overwhelm the investigation because well-meaning members of the public will in good faith report sightings from one end of the country to the other. This could divert valuable resources away from the case on fruitless enquiries. His decision was helped by one simple fact in the sighting by Nicholas Elliot in Haverfordwest:

the killer had chosen to use the cashpoint very early in the morning to no doubt avoid being seen. This he believed was significant. This single isolated transaction and sighting by Elliot had fixed him as the person using Peter Dixon's cash card; the time that the bank gave for the withdrawal could be matched to the time of the sighting. With this in mind, DCS Clive Jones went public with the Elliot artist's impression of the dishevelled man on the bike and it became the main line of enquiry for the investigation. Trace the wild man!

The artist's impression was released into the public domain on the 10th of July 1989 and featured on the BBC programme *Crimewatch* and as predicted possible sightings came from far and wide. There were in excess of six hundred and thirty calls from the public naming persons as being identical to the artist's impression. These calls would almost double in two days. A number of possible sightings appeared to be promising and attracted considerable media coverage and police resources, but came to nothing. The release of the artist's impression together with the poor performance of the HOLMES computer almost ground the investigation to a halt.

Sightings of persons fitting the artist's impression in the Pembrokeshire area were from as far back as the first week in June, the majority of which were in an eight-mile radius of the scene. In all there were twenty-six sightings at or near the three cashpoints used by the killer during a three-day period from the 29th of June up to and including the 1st of July 1989. This was clearly the main line of enquiry for DCS Clive Jones and his team. Another line of enquiry was to establish the origin of the rope used to tie the hands of Peter Dixon. Doctor Whiteside, a Home

Office forensic scientist, described the rope as being thirty-strand three-ply polyethylene cord, greyish in colour and approximately four millimetres in diameter, Z twist with right hand lay. It was also expert opinion that the rope was likely to be connected to the fishing industry and a knot expert observed the knot used as being non-specialised, nondescript and very loose. Again substantial resources, time and effort were put into tracing the possible origin of the rope. National and international suppliers were contacted, boats and boatyards were checked: the task was daunting.

After extensive enquiries it was established that the rope was probably sourced from Portugal and used in the fishing industry, the only identical rope recovered for comparison was found in the rear yard of the Lobster Pot public house at Marloes, only a few miles from Little Haven. The licensee of the pub, Alan Simpson, had found it whilst beachcombing with his son sometime between 1983 and 1988. That part of the Pembrokeshire Coast has many small coves and beaches and many are littered with ropes, lobster and crab pots and other equipment either lost at sea or ripped loose by the spectacular storms that batter that part of West Wales.

It was clear that the offender could easily have found the rope rather than have purchased it from a store. This line of investigation had run its course, the most interesting outcome being the possibility that the offender was local and frequented the area. Likewise, hundreds of shotguns were examined and test-fired in order to compare the waddings and distinct striation marks left on them as a result of the wadding exiting the barrel of the gun once fired. Doctor Renshaw, Head of Firearms at the Home Office Forensic Science Laboratory, was of the opinion that the fatal shots had indeed come from a double-barrelled sawn-off shotgun and the process of sawing the barrels had damaged the muzzle of the gun leaving distinct scratch marks on the wadding as it was fired. What was clear was that the killer had removed the cartridges from the scene believing that he was covering his tracks.

The investigation then took a sinister twist when in November two sites were found which contained Semtex explosives, firearms and other devices associated with terrorism on the coastal path near Newgale, some seven miles from Little Haven. At this time the UK mainland had been subjected to a number of terrorist attacks linked to the IRA. It was clear that the authorities had stumbled onto an arms stash belonging to one of its active service units.

A covert investigation was quickly put in place between Dyfed-Powys Police and the Anti-Terrorist Branch of the Metropolitan Police, code name 'Operation Pebble'. This involved rendering the stash harmless and at the same time deploying armed covert surveillance teams in the knowledge at some time the terrorists would return to recover their weapons. The question troubling DCS Clive Jones was the possibility that the Dixons had stumbled across the terrorists resulting in their execution-style killing. He now needed access to the evidence quickly in order to implicate or eliminate them.

Peter Dixon was a visitor to Ireland when he worked for a company called Antiference Ltd that promoted the sale of security systems including tilt switches, a favourite component for terrorists at the time in the manufacture of car bombs. Could there be some connection?

In December 1989 the trap was sprung and two men were arrested after being caught red-handed with the arms cache.

They were also in possession of a SPAS 12-bore pump-action shotgun, with full-length barrels and a Smith and Wesson 12-bore pump-action sawn-off shotgun. Both men were totally uncooperative with the police investigation. Very quickly the shotguns were test-fired and eliminated as the guns responsible for the murders. Furthermore, the 'Elliot' artist's impression and the killer's actions during and after the murders did not sit well with it being a terrorist-related attack. It was also established that both men had a cast-iron alibi showing they were not in Wales at the time of the killings. To some Operation Pebble might have provided a convenient peg on which to hang the offence; the reality was somewhat different, there was no evidence at all to link the two incidents.

The police investigation was massive; there were hundreds of sightings of the 'wild man' between Little Haven and the Pembroke NatWest Bank, none of them presented the police with a name or tangible connection to the killer. Likewise the detailed investigation into the origin of the rope and murder weapon came to nothing. As with any undetected murder a team was identified to review the investigation. During this review the team noticed that the Personal Descriptive Form completed in respect of Peter Dixon showed his twenty-two-carat gold wedding ring was missing, a ring he always wore. It was clear that the killer had also stolen his wedding ring. Six months after the murders a new line of enquiry was identified to trace the gold wedding band.

As with the rope enquiry, significant resources were directed towards identifying jewellers and possible places of disposal for the wedding ring. After extensive investigation, it was identified that only two wedding rings had been sold in West Wales during the relevant time. The first had been sold at Burgess Jewellers, Carmarthen, not far from the NatWest cashpoint, by Mr David Evans from Cardigan. Detective Constable Dudley, an experienced officer who had worked in the Milford Haven area for many years, visited Mr Evans; he had with him the 'Elliot' artist's impression for comparison. DC Dudley concluded that David Evans, a sixty-one-year-old man, did not resemble the artist's impression and he was quickly eliminated from the investigation.

The second had been sold at Pembroke Jewellers on Main Street in Pembroke on the 5th of July 1989, the same day the bodies of Peter and Gwenda Dixon were found on the coastal path. This shop was fifty yards away from the same NatWest cashpoint used by the killer on two occasions on the 29th of June. The owner of Pembroke Jewellers, Mr Raymond Smith, kept records and receipts of transactions for his purchase of second-hand jewellery. One such transaction referred to a twenty-two-carat gold wedding ring, which he had bought from a Mr J. Cooper, 34 St Marys Park, Jordanston, Milford Haven for £25. DC Dudley went to speak to him but Cooper told the officer that he had in fact sold his *own* wedding ring and his wife Patricia verified this. The officer, who was familiar with Cooper, unfortunately concluded that the man in front of him did not resemble the artist's impression and he too was eliminated from the investigation.

Over the months hundreds of people had been put forward as suspects or persons of interest by members of the public. Local police officers had also suggested names of local villains who had shown some of the same characteristics in their offending. These are known as MO

(Modus Operandi) Suspects. The review and tracing of MO Suspects raised problems for Clive Jones, as again he knew this would use up valuable resources, but at this point he had little choice. Hundreds of men were interviewed and eliminated, thousands of hours were committed to these enquiries and it all came to nothing. The trail went cold and the murderer was still at large.

CHAPTER 4

THE MILFORD HAVEN ATTACK

The Pembrokeshire town of Milford Haven is situated on the sheltered estuary of the same name and has a population of around 13,000. In the first half of the twentieth century it was a prosperous fishing town. It's now more famous as a deep-water port giving large oil tankers facilities to unload crude oil at the refineries that cluster around the Haven. It houses pockets of council estates including one known as The Mount. The Mount Estate is located on the edge of a wood, on the periphery of Milford Haven near to an area known as Steynton. The estate is a warren of densely packed houses interspersed with a series of interconnecting walks and alleyways. Children play freely in this relatively crime-free area.

On the pleasant spring evening of the 6th of March 1996, the light was fading quickly, and the lives of five children were about to be changed forever as they ambled through the fields near Milford Haven. (The names of the victims have been changed to protect their identity.) Jayne, at 16, was the eldest; Maria and Susan were both 15; and two brothers, David, also 15, and Steven aged 14, made up the rest of the group. They were all good friends, having grown up together. That evening they had decided to go for a walk in the fields at the rear of The Mount.

The fields fenced with barbed wire to protect livestock and crops were somewhere that the children had navigated before. Once in the open they headed for the woods – privately owned woodland near a tidal estuary. The same woods then opened out onto land adjacent to Scoveston Park. One of the trees in the wood had a rope swing which in the past had provided them with hours of fun, as it did this evening. Maria and Jayne were rolling around on the floor laughing and enjoying themselves, getting very dirty. The others joined in, cutting themselves on the brambles during the process. Making the most of the spring evening they then planned to cross over the river through a location known as Black Bridge, following a route to North Road and towards the comfort of home. However when they got down to the river it was high tide and David was the only one wearing wellies so he bravely tested the depth of the water by putting his foot in. To the delight of the others David's boot filled up with water and they realised it was too deep and so decided to retrace their steps going back into the woods and through the field. David and Maria took a short cut through another section of barbed wire, whilst Jayne, Steven and Susan took the longer route. Moments later they all met up in the lower part of another field adjacent to their school. Susan decided to take a moment and lit up a cigarette. Unwilling to wait for their friend, David and Maria got up and started to walk off towards their home on the nearby Mount Estate. Susan, not wanting to be left behind, got to her feet to catch up. Within a few steps they were all back together talking and laughing about the evening's tomfoolery. As darkness fell, little did they know that their childhood was about to be taken from them. Suddenly they heard a noise and footsteps behind them in the shadows of the hedgerow. The children then saw a bright light coming across the field so they all turned around and were dazzled by its intensity. Susan, thinking it was someone that she knew, naively shouted, 'Oh shine the light in my eyes, why don't you?' David then said, 'Oh it's Wayne,' thinking Wayne, a friend of theirs, was out lamping or shooting rabbits. They continued to believe it was their friend, until David in a nervous voice said, 'I don't think that's Wayne.' Again he called out, 'Wayne!' but as the figure got closer his shadow became clearer and the children could see that he was wearing a balaclava and pointing a sawn-off shotgun at them. Then in a gruff voice he snarled, 'Do I look like Wayne?'

David, terrified by the balaclava and the gun, started to cry. Thinking it was a farmer he pleaded, 'Oh I'm sorry, farmer, we'll get off your field now.' The man then shouted, 'Get back down there!' Fearing they would be shot and now under the control of this frightening character, they were made to walk a few yards further down the field towards the edge of the woods. 'Get down on your stomachs, put your face on the grass,' he demanded. He then hit David on the head with the butt of his gun, ordering him to shut up and stop crying. Jayne became worried for Steven as she could hear his chest wheezing. The man however showed no such concern telling him to shut up, as he walked around, shining the light upon them. Again he demanded that they be quiet, offering them the small reassurance that none of them would get hurt. They were all frozen to the spot, shaking and frightened of what was going to happen. He then grabbed Jayne by her hair. Grasping her in this painful manner he dragged her away from the others and then told her to lie on her stomach;

petrified, she complied. 'Don't look behind!' he shouted to the rest of the children. He then repeated his previous instruction, 'Don't look up and no one will get hurt.' The man then instructed Jayne to turn around and while he was saying this he shouted to someone or something, 'Oi!' He then whistled and the children believed it was a dog he was calling to. Neither Jayne nor the others ever saw the dog, although Maria and David stated that they could hear and sense a dog moving about. Jayne then heard the attacker doing something with his shotgun; she believed he was loading it. He then ordered her to get on her back; again she did as she was told, trembling with fear. The masked man told her to stop crying and that he wouldn't hurt her. Putting the gun down by her side, he proceeded to pull her polo neck over her mouth; one assumes to stop her from shouting. He then pulled her top up and started caressing her breasts. Undoing her trousers he told her to take one leg out, which she did, and while she was doing this he a gruffly told the rest of the children to shut up and not to look behind. The attacker then took out a knife, which Jayne believes was from an inside pocket of his jacket and put it against her and said, 'Stop crying, stop making a noise.'

Jayne *was* crying though and calling Susan's name, unsure of why she was shouting for her. The man then raped her before telling her to get dressed and not to tell anyone.

Jayne later described the offender to the police as 5'9" and of skinny build. The jacket he was wearing had a lining that was white with green checks and the knitted balaclava was tight fitting. He had light blue jeans and his gloves were green knitted ones, and he spoke with a deep Welsh accent. Steven also stated that the man's jeans were tucked into black combat boots and he wore a wax jacket. He described the balaclava as black with its eyes and mouth cut out and that the attacker had bushy eyebrows.

Maria's statement agreed that he wore a black balaclava and that he must have cut out the eyes himself because the holes were big. The gun she described as being double-barrelled, black, and approximately twelve inches long. He was carrying a lamp in his left hand which Steven had described as a Black Eye make, connected to a twelve-volt battery in a box about eight inches wide, similar to a car lamp. The knife was described as possibly a flick knife.

After raping Jayne he turned his attention to the rest of the group, asking them if they had got any money. Then he spotted another female in the group – Susan. Whilst she was lying on the ground face down he put his hands underneath her and started to feel her breasts through her jumper, doing this for about thirty seconds. He then held her by the side as if he wanted her to turn over, so she turned over on to her back and he put his hands up her top. He pushed her bra up and he started feeling her breasts again, doing this again for about thirty seconds. He then put his hand down her trousers on top of her pants and started touching her and then he went back up to her breasts, fondling them again. He repeated this sexual assault before finally pulling her bra and jumper down and saying to her, 'If you tell anyone I'll kill you and I know who you are and I'll kill you. Don't tell anyone.' While he was assaulting her, he kept covering her eyes with his fingers, so she wouldn't look at him. But she could see that he had some sort of sack, or something like it, pulled over his head and it looked like the eyes were cut out. Having been on his knees, he now got to his feet and instructed the other four to get up and start walking up the field, again threatening them not to tell anyone because he knew where they lived and he'd come and get them. At this time he was controlling and holding Jayne by her jumper and the others were about six or seven feet away. He then pushed her and said, 'Don't look back.' He started to walk off, again threatening the children with the words, 'Remember what I said, don't tell anyone because I know where you live and I'll come and get you.' He then fired the gun into the air. The noise terrified the children and understandably none of them looked behind.

The group made their way as fast as they could to the stile which gave them access into the council estate. Maria, concerned for Jayne, asked her what had happened. Jayne burst into tears and the boys were asked to run up to Maria's house. The children once in the safety of Maria's home telephoned the police and within minutes the area was flooded with local police officers and detectives. This was a cold and callous attack on five innocent children. It was a chance encounter with a man who was prowling the fields, masked and in possession of a loaded double-barrelled sawn-off shotgun. He was clearly confident in controlling multiple victims. Robbery and sexual assault were evidently the motives for this attack. Very quickly an incident room was set up at Haverfordwest police station; the SIO was Detective Superintendent Aldwyn Jones, a top detective who was hugely respected by his team.

Over the next few months Aldwyn Jones directed the investigation. His approach was thorough and meticulous, and a number of suspects were identified, interviewed and eliminated. It was not lost on him that the same area had been plagued with a number of burglaries and robberies which had taken place at isolated properties with lone females becoming victims in their own homes. Another significant and worrying fact was that this latest attack was within sight of the scene of the two brutal and undetected murders at Scoveston Park. After months of hard work the trail went cold leaving this quiet rural part of Pembrokeshire with yet another dark secret.

CHAPTER 5

CAREER DETECTIVE

I was born in Liverpool in 1959, thirty years before the Dixons were murdered, and was the youngest of four children. My father worked in the docks before going to sea as an engineer. In the early sixties his work took us to the Midlands and then on to Cheshire in the early 1970s. In 1976 my parents took over the Caledonia Inn public house on High Street in Pembroke Dock. Then the town was a bustling place with plenty of work at the nearby oil refineries and power station. Like many teenagers I didn't really have any idea about what I wanted to do. In spring and summer I would work on local farms making hay or potato picking; it was instant cash and provided beer tokens for the social side of life and my first love, which was sport. I was a wild young man who enjoyed playing rugby for Pembroke Dock Harlequins and Pembrokeshire County Youth and cricket for Pembroke Dock Cricket Club. My sporting claim to fame was playing in a half back partnership for the County with Peter Morgan who went on to play for Wales and the British Lions.

Eventually I found more regular employment with GKN Engineering as a tool setter and then at Jenkins and Davies Engineering as a welder's mate. It was hard going but for an eighteen-year-old it was good money and the workplace was full of characters and fun. Something was missing though and I could not see myself doing this for the rest of my life. One of my best friends at the time was Billy Horne, who had joined Dyfed-Powys Police and was doing very well. He would later retire as Assistant Chief Constable for Gwent Police. He was a huge influence on me and I admired him greatly. In 1978 came the moment that changed my life. I had been out in Pembroke after playing rugby and had consumed a considerable amount of best bitter. On the walk home I decided it would be a great idea to remove the lovely orange flashing beacons from a zebra crossing as a souvenir of my day's exploits. Carrying my trophies I walked the two miles home. Suddenly I was aware of a police car pulling up alongside me and before I knew it I was in the back and on my way to Pembroke Dock police station where I was interviewed, photographed and fingerprinted before being released and told to return the following day.

The worst part of the whole episode was telling my parents. They were proud law-abiding people who had never had contact with the police. The next day I was marched into the police station by my mother and eventually given a caution by the local chief inspector who was a very serious and surly character. As I left his office I offered my hand to him, he looked at me and said, 'No, I will not shake your hand as I will probably see you again.' My mother was disgusted and could not believe his response. For me it was the turning point in my life. I was determined that he would not see me again. The whole experience had fascinated me and from that day on I wanted to be a police officer and nothing else.

My next move was to contact Billy Horne and tell him what I wanted to do. He was not convinced that

I had made the best start for my intended career, but as usual gave me sound advice. Within a year I found myself sitting the entrance exam for Dyfed-Powys Police at their Carmarthen headquarters. I failed and was devastated but remained determined that one day I would achieve my goal. I was now twenty and desperate to start a career. Both my brothers had left home at sixteen and joined the Royal Marine Commandos. They had seen the world and had had many great experiences and adventures. I had a simple choice, follow them into the Marines or try another police force; I decided to try my luck with Cheshire Police.

In late 1979 I travelled to Cheshire and after a full day of exams and selection interviews I was accepted as a probationary police officer. In July 1980 I arrived in Warrington for ten weeks of basic training before being posted to Winsford. Although I was in uniform I harboured dreams of joining my plain-clothed colleagues in the CID. I wanted to be a detective and in 1982 after a six-month attachment I was posted as Detective Constable 1612 Wilkins to Winsford. It was a very busy town consisting of a number of large housing estates that were the product of the overspill from Merseyside. If you closed your eyes and stood in the town centre you would swear that you were in Liverpool and it was a fantastic place to work for a keen young detective.

In December 1985 my parents were still living in Pembrokeshire and I was shocked to hear the news that there had been a double murder of a brother and sister just outside Milford Haven. I knew the area well and the murders seemed totally out of context for this rural community. From what I could glean the investigation was focused on tracing a large bearded man seen driving a Land Rover. It was also rumoured that Richard Thomas was involved in a gay relationship that might hold the key to the murders.

The following year I was posted to the Serious Crime Squad and spent a number of years in Cheshire investigating among other things terrorist arms stashes, murders and a large number of armed robberies that had plagued the North West of England in the 1980s. I had also married. Because of my workload I didn't really keep in touch with the Milford Haven investigation, but I was again shocked when in 1989 I saw the news that there had been another double murder in the area, this time on the coastal path at Little Haven. Two double murders within a few miles of each other in one of the most picturesque places in the UK was a devastating blow to an area that relied heavily on tourism. To make matters worse the latest murders had happened in high summer when the area was bustling with visitors. The solution appeared to present itself when a few months later a terrorist arms cache was discovered a few miles from the scene. As the months passed I lost touch with the case and the new focus of my life became the challenges of fatherhood with the birth of my first child Emily.

Family life was good and in 1991 I passed my promotion exams to sergeant but was less than impressed when Cheshire decided there would be no promotion for at least two years. At the time I was still with the Serious Crime Squad, working the case of a murdered prostitute in Chester, when I noticed an advertisement by Dyfed-Powys Police offering promotion on transfer. Six months later I was a uniformed sergeant in the beautiful seaside town of Tenby in South Pembrokeshire.

Dyfed-Powys was a totally different working environment to Cheshire and the North West. Chief Constable Ray White was very proud of the force's detection rate. The Head of CID Detective Chief Superintendent Jeff Thomas was a tough, uncompromising character who had a strong grip on all matters to do with serious crime. All appeared to be well in the force and Pembrokeshire was a fantastic place to work and live. That said the force still had a dark cloud hanging over it with the two unsolved double murders. It was like having a troublesome relative that no one liked to mention or talk about. Although I had enjoyed my first eight months in the force in Tenby, I was desperate to return to the CID and the opportunity finally presented itself when a post as detective sergeant became available on the Fraud Squad. After twelve months I was transferred to Milford Haven CID where I spent probably the happiest eighteen months of my service. Crime there was low level and mainly committed by a small group of hard-core persistent offenders to fund their drug habit. In Milford Haven you always knew where you stood with people. They were straight-talking, direct and would not use ten words when one would do.

In the new post my three detective constables were all fantastic characters. Fred Hunter, Glyndwr Henry Jones and Jeremy Davies all worked hard and we had tremendous fun. My office looked down the Haven and on my first day I was admiring the view using a pair of binoculars left on the windowsill. Fred came into the office and said, 'Sergeant, we need you downstairs to speak to a shop-lifter.' I was less than impressed that my new team could not deal with a shoplifter on their own but, wanting to make a good impression, I went to the interview room.

The female prisoner looked at me like I had three heads and while I went into my best persuasive patter she just stared at me and laughed. 'Young lady, this is no laughing matter,' I said. 'I am not laughing at that,' she replied, 'it's just that I have never been interviewed by a bloke wearing black mascara before.' The laughter outside the room was a good indication that I had been set up, and to my horror when I looked in the mirror I had panda eyes from the fingerprint ink strategically placed on the eyepieces of the binoculars I had so willingly used to survey the view. I had been caught, hook, line and sinker!

Whilst I was at Milford Haven, this part of North Pembrokeshire was plagued by a number of burglaries where cash and jewellery were stolen; they were all in isolated rural locations and backed onto fields. In certain cases fences were cut, some were to gain access, others were left strategically to injure anyone who gave chase across the fields and hedgerows. North and South Pembrokeshire are divided by the Milford Haven waterway. The offences were taking place in a small cluster to the north of the county, which suggested someone with a good local knowledge was committing them. Despite the best efforts of detectives we never caught the person responsible for the burglaries and I left Milford Haven, promoted to head up Dyfed-Powys' surveillance unit and Specialist Operations Team for the next four years. The new detective sergeant in Milford Haven was Steve Matchett, a very able young officer who quickly latched onto the series of undetected burglaries in the area and began a review. He was of the opinion that the offender was responsible for dozens of offences as far back as 1983. Significantly it was also noted that in North Pembrokeshire there had been two robberies on properties where women had been at home alone at the time. The properties were in similar locations to those targeted in the burglary offences and backed onto open fields. Could the same man be responsible?

A major incident room was set up and the investigation headed by detective Superintendent Aldwyn Jones, a popular and capable detective who was also an absolute gentleman. His investigation skills were meticulous and I would learn a great deal from him over the years. At the time I was a detective inspector in Carmarthen and I was drafted in to assist with the investigation. One local man in particular was interviewed a number of times as a suspect but he had a cast-iron alibi and sadly after a period of intensive investigation the trail went cold. We did not have to wait long though before the attacker struck again!

On a dark winter's night in 1996 Sheila Clarke was alone at her home in Sardis near Milford Haven when an intruder attacked her. She lived in an isolated bungalow, Westwinds, on the outskirts of the small hamlet. As she watched television she was confronted by a man wearing woollen gloves, a balaclava and brandishing a double-barrelled sawn-off shotgun. He quickly overpowered her with excessive violence, hitting her about the head and body with the butt of the gun before tying her hands together with rope. He forced her into her bedroom before searching the rooms for cash and jewellery. Sheila Clarke knew her husband was about to return and she managed to activate a personal attack alarm. The man ran off but as he made his escape he was confronted by Sheila Clarke's neighbour. The gunman threatened him before disappearing into the night across the fields.

This was another terrifying attack on a woman at home

alone. A large police investigation was launched and the surrounding fields were searched. In the hedgerows officers recovered a number of items that had been abandoned by the attacker as he ran away. Significantly they found a double-barrelled sawn-off shotgun, a balaclava, gloves, a rope and a woollen fleece. The police launched Operation Huntsman. It focused on the burglaries and robberies in North Pembrokeshire. A team was dedicated to this investigation and after a great deal of painstaking work and effort they arrested a local man who was in possession of property stolen from a number of the burglaries. His name was John William Cooper.

By this stage I had returned to Headquarters and was involved in a number of covert operations aimed at heroin traffickers and only took a passing interest in the arrest and prosecution of Cooper. It was clear that the Huntsman team and in particular Detective Sergeant Matchett and Detective Inspector Jim Morris had done an excellent job. As he was led into court Cooper told waiting journalists that he had been fitted up but in the end he was convicted of thirty burglaries and the robbery of Sheila Clarke at Sardis. The judge described Cooper as a one-man crime wave and sentenced him to sixteen years imprisonment.

Because Cooper had used a sawn-off shotgun and attacked women who were at home alone he was considered to be of interest for the Scoveston and Pembrokeshire Coastal Path murders. Indeed it had even been suggested during his trial for burglary and robbery that he was the killer. Cooper was questioned, but with little more than speculation to connect him to the crimes he admitted nothing. It was clear, if the police wanted to take it any further, they would need substantial evidence to link him to the murders and at that point in time they simply didn't have it, or at least they didn't *know* they had it.

In 2002, I had been promoted to superintendent in uniform at Police Headquarters in Carmarthen but in my heart I knew that I really wanted to return to the CID as a detective superintendent and I didn't have to wait long before the opportunity presented itself. I noticed that the National Criminal Intelligence Service (NCIS) was advertising for the post of head of region for the Northwest of England. Just a few months later I was sitting in my new office in Manchester having moved my family back to Cheshire. Again I enjoyed working in the North West; it was a great challenge with a significant amount of serious crime and dangerous offenders. As a national organisation we provided intelligence on the very top tier of criminals and I had a good team working for me. I had made up my mind that if the opportunity arose I would remain in the North West for the rest of my service. This however was a period of great change with the NCIS. The National Crime Squad and parts of HM Customs and Excise merged to create the Serious and Organised Crime Agency, SOCA. It was clear that many seconded police officers would return to their original organisations and I had to decide what I was going to do. My decision was made easy because by now I had been asked to run the South East Regional Office working out of Spring Gardens in London and New Scotland Yard. I commuted on a daily basis from Cheshire and it was killing me. As the plans unfolded for the new organisation for the first time in my police career I was disillusioned with my job. I was spending an increasing amount of time away from my family: this was not for me.

At the end of 2004, I had decided to return to Dyfed-Powys and had already started to make enquiries with the force. The opportunity presented itself when the Head of CID retired and I applied for the job as Detective Chief Superintendent, Head of CID. I was unsuccessful, but more than happy to return to the force as Detective Superintendent, Deputy Head of CID. My boss was Steve Mears, a friend, and someone I knew well with a similar career background to myself. I was really looking forward to returning home.

I was now part of a new Headquarters CID team in Carmarthen and soon found that many things had changed since I had been away. The force was entering a period of transition and renewal, and the new boss quickly organised his team. It was clear to us that standards in some areas had dropped and in other areas had stood still. The fix was relatively easy; it was about getting a grip on things and attention to detail. Within a short space of time, performance had started to rise again and we were soon back at the top of the league table. However, one statistic didn't read well at all – serious undetected crime in Pembrokeshire. The two unsolved double murders continued to haunt the force's otherwise impressive record.

It was a sunny afternoon in the summer of 2005 and the boss and I were sitting in his office in Carmarthen chatting when the subject turned to the future of the department and what still needed to be done. One area of weakness was Major Crime Review. We had a number of historic offences that were serious and still unresolved but unlike much larger forces we did not have the resources to deploy a dedicated team to investigate old cases. What's more, the police service had become preoccupied with performance league tables and specialist squads for just about everything and it was taking up a huge amount of time and resources. When it came to investigating major crimes, such as murder, our response was to bring together officers from Headquarters and the local divisions. This worked well to a certain extent but tended to draw people away from other key tasks and caused some tensions with local commanders. We both knew that this position was becoming increasingly difficult to sustain and both felt that in an ideal world we would have one Major Crime Team that could investigate the most serious crimes and double up in a reviewing capacity. As we talked we felt that if we were to ever justify such a move we would need the evidence to make our case. Two crimes jumped out at us; the double murders at Scoveston Park and Little Haven. We were agreed that whatever the future looked like, we needed to have a closer look at these crimes. Little did we know at that stage just how important this discussion would prove to be and how events would unfold.

CHAPTER 6

THE ELEPHANT IN THE ROOM

There had been a great deal of publicity over the years about legacy cases being reopened and then solved using the latest forensic science. The neighbouring South Wales force had had some notable successes including the identification of serial killer Joseph Kappen. In Dyfed-Powys there had been some selective attempts to submit certain exhibits from historical unsolved cases for forensic review but they were mainly focused on trace DNA and heavily influenced by the Head of Scientific Support. There were also periodic appeals for information and witnesses that had revealed precious little. Other larger forces may have had more resources to dedicate to such investigations but for me the position was clear: we had two unsolved double murders in Pembrokeshire and if we didn't seize the initiative and investigate then who would?

There was also another pressing issue that would exercise Steve Mears and me. During Operation Huntsman John William Cooper had been interviewed as a suspect and he was now eligible for parole. What was his involvement, if any? There were many unanswered questions and it was agreed that at this initial stage I would try to get some basic answers and make recommendations in a report to our chief officers. The Association of Chief Police Officers

(ACPO) recommends that undetected murder offences should be subject to a formal review every two years. There is a considerable amount of guidance and best practice available to assist reviewing officers, borne out of years of experience. In essence there are two types of review process: a full paper review, which examines the investigation in detail from start to finish, and a thematic approach, which concentrates on certain elements of the investigation.

The Senior Investigating Officer (SIO) is normally a senior detective officer who leads and is also the principle decision-maker in any murder investigation. The vast majority of murders are domestic, where the offender is known from the outset and are therefore relatively simple investigations. From the outset the SIO is aware that their investigation is to be reviewed after seven and twenty-eight days and is prepared for this. It is a supportive process and not designed to delay or interfere with the investigation. The review team can be from the same force in the case of a seven-day review or from an outside force for the twenty-eight-day process and more formal reviews. External reviews provide a transparent and objective examination of the investigation and make clear recommendations.

The term 'cold case' has been attached to historic cases that are in some instances many years old and have been subject to a number of these reviews. Effectively they are 'case closed' because experience has shown that they are unlikely to benefit from simply re-examining the incident room documentation. Recently developments in forensic science have been the single most important factor in successful cold case reviews providing new opportunities for investigators. The scientist works on the principle that every contact leaves a trace and as science has developed, the recovery of trace evidence has become extremely sensitive, resulting in some spectacular successes across the UK.

The recommendations to ACPO were, for me, quite simple; we had a public and moral duty to conduct a formal review of the Pembrokeshire offences. The Cooper issue was more complex. If he was in fact responsible for the murders (and it was a big if) we had to know what work had been done in the past to implicate or eliminate him. Detective Inspector Jim Morris, who'd worked on the Huntsman case, was of the view that he was a prime suspect and had placed his thoughts on the record, but little had been done to really test this view or interview Cooper in any meaningful manner. The reason was quite simple. During Operation Huntsman, even faced with some damming circumstantial evidence, Cooper had refused to make any sort of admission. Based on this, the heads of CID at the time, Detective Chief Superintendent Jeff Thomas and then Detective Chief Superintendent John Lewis, had decided that there would have to be substantial evidence, probably forensic, to connect him to the offences.

Over the years a number of items had been sent for examination for trace evidence, in particular DNA, but the process for selecting these items appeared to lack any external objectivity and involved people who had worked on the original investigations. There were still items in storage including forensic slides that had not been examined for fear that the process would destroy any potential evidence. I entered initial discussions with the Forensic Science Service and they were of the view that it was unlikely that there would be any significant advances in forensic science over the next five years, particularly in relation to DNA. I decided there was no logical reason to delay a review. In August 2005 I submitted a report to the chief officers recommending we undertake such a thematic forensic review on undetected serious crime in Pembrokeshire including the two double murders at Scoveston Park and Little Haven. Most importantly we needed to establish what material we had, where it was stored and what condition it was in before any attempts were made to recover it. The Chief Constable at the time was Terry Grange, a very serious man for whom I had a great deal of time. If he thought you were in the right he would support you through thick or thin. His view was clear: 'Whatever it takes, I want it done properly.'

The initial action was to engage members of the National Centre for Policing Excellence, NCPE (latterly known as the National Police Improvement Agency, NPIA) to establish national best practice and a clear way forward. I have always learnt more from studying investigations that have made errors than from looking back at perfect inquiries seen through rose-tinted spectacles. From our meetings it was clear when a historical case came to court, based on forensic evidence, the integrity of the physical evidence was always the focus of attack for the defence. Unfortunately some review teams in their haste to submit material for examination had not paid enough attention to the provenance of their evidence and had subsequently been savaged in court. I suspected that in our case the exhibits from the offences were likely to be stored and deposited in many locations. It would be vital that we established exactly what we had before any efforts were made to recover it for forensic evaluation and examination.

At the back of our minds like a ticking clock was the realisation that Cooper could soon be released. I sat for many hours with my boss Detective Chief Superintendent Steve Mears and considered what we should do next. There was a pressing need to identify an SIO and small team to carry out the initial scoping of the review. During this initial fact-finding process, a so-called 'sterile corridor' needed to be maintained between the review and Cooper; I did not want to be accused at any stage in the future of having tailored an investigation towards a single individual. The forensic review needed to be impartial in its search for evidence and at this stage we decided we would do no more than monitor John Cooper through the Pembrokeshire Division. I was comfortable in the knowledge that this process was being handled on a local basis by Superintendent Euros Lewis who was probably the most committed police officer I have ever known: his working hours were simple, light o'clock until dark o'clock every day. Superintendent Lewis sat on a multi-agency group that considered and managed the risks that dangerous offenders posed to the public. There was no doubt that he would do his job with his customary enthusiasm and attention to detail.

Detective Chief Inspector Andy John was identified as the officer to lead the initial phase; I would act as a mentor. Andy was a quiet unassuming man, a gentleman who always delivered high-quality work. I knew he would be ideal for the task. At this early stage it was essential that he had clear terms of reference. This is what I drafted:

- To trace all non-documentary exhibits in respect of the undetected investigations into the murders of Richard and Helen Thomas and Peter and Gwenda Dixon.

- To establish what, if any, exhibits are missing and to conduct searches as necessary to retrieve any out-standing exhibits.
- To review the submission of items to date and to make recommendations on any further forensic submissions that should be considered in view of advancement in forensic techniques.
- To make recommendations on the submission of items for forensic analysis which have not previously been submitted.

On the 17th of January 2006 Assistant Chief Constable Andy Edwards agreed the terms of reference. The review was given a code name and Operation Ottawa was born.

A force the size of Dyfed-Powys does not have a massive pool of resources and many of our officers carry out a number of different functions. Our team would be small but dedicated and it was essential that none of the officers had ever been involved in the original investigations or previous reviews. The reason for this was simple; I did not want Ottawa to follow the path of any previous work or be influenced by any previously held views. We needed a fresh, untainted approach. Those involved in previous investigations would at a later stage be very important to Ottawa as a way of testing previous hypotheses and to provide context when appropriate. Andy John still had a busy day job as a senior detective and he needed a deputy, someone who he could trust to get into the detail, someone who was organised and committed, and we had just the perfect man. Detective Inspector Lynne Harries was head of the West Coast Ports Offices that policed the ferry terminals of Pembroke Dock and Fishguard.

He was a local man and an office manager for major incident rooms. Lynne was an experienced detective and knew his way around complex investigations. He was supported by DS Glyn Johnson, another local officer who had an exceptional knowledge of IT systems. He could create the computer programmes to record and track data. They were an ideal pairing but to support them we needed someone who had the corporate memory of the murders but was not too close to be influenced. Detective Constable Nigel John was also trained in HOLMES computerised incident rooms and would be just what we wanted. Finally we needed a workhorse, someone who could be tasked to dig deep and find things and Detective Constable Steve Rowe was the obvious choice to complete this small but perfectly formed team. At this stage I wanted to keep the first phase very low key, away from public gaze and local police interest. Our first home was to be Fishguard Port Office, an empty suite of rooms owned by the Port and occupied by HM Customs and Excise. They were grey, unwelcoming offices with little character but they were out of the way and provided the perfect solution. Ottawa was up and running and it was time to get down to work.

CHAPTER 7

OPERATION OTTAWA

The police's attitude towards the media has significantly changed over the years. I had policed in a time when they were treated with total mistrust and kept very much at arm's length. Thankfully this view has changed and there is now a far more sophisticated working relationship based on the fact that we need one another. I can remember being the SIO on a murder case when a chief officer made it clear that I was not to engage with one particular TV station because they had criticised the force. I asked him to sign my incident policy book to this effect as it went against my media strategy and would result in certain parts of the public not hearing my public appeal; a decision we might need to explain if reviewed. As you can imagine he quickly reconsidered and I never did get a signature and we did engage with the TV journalists. The decision not to involve the media in Ottawa at this stage was more tactical: any news release would need to be controlled to achieve maximum impact. Now was not the right time.

By February 2006 the team had made arrangements with their line managers and I had informed them that this would probably be a six-month project; little did we know then that six months would in fact become six years for some of them. The first job was to upgrade the office security and then allocate the rooms for the review. Some would be used to store exhibits after they had been recovered, another would become the briefing room and the largest would be our incident room. The small team quickly got to work and created a pictorial timeline around the walls with copies of original scene photographs and plans. The pictures we had of Richard and Helen Thomas and Peter and Gwenda Dixon dominated the room and gave us a clear focus. The images of the Thomases were grainy, black-and-white photos and had obviously been taken at a family gathering. Richard looked smart in collar and tie and Helen was wearing her Sunday best. Further along the wall of the office were the imposing images of the burnt-out remains of Scoveston Park. The gunshot wounds on the bodies were clearly visible in the photographs, as was the rope that had been used by the killer to tie them up.

In contrast, the images of Peter and Gwenda were in colour and the couple looked happy and relaxed. They had been snapped outdoors, probably on a country walk, something that they loved doing so much. Both were casually dressed with shorts and walking boots and they gave off an appearance of contentment. They seemed comfortable with each other and very much in love. For me, looking at the photographs was the first time I had had a personal connection to the victims; before they had just been names. Now though they became real people, full of life. A life cut short. Then something struck me about the pictures of Peter Dixon's body. He was dressed almost exactly as he was in the lovely photograph with Gwenda, only this time he was lifeless, murdered in cold blood.

In the incident room, computers, shelving and creature

comforts such as a kettle had now been installed. Like any good police team we quickly identified the best and cheapest place to eat. A small cafe looking out over Fishguard Harbour became our unofficial HQ, hosting many team meetings and debriefings. At this stage we needed to get to grips with the scale of the task in hand and the initial steps would require careful consideration in order to avoid potential pitfalls at a later date. The SIO leads the investigation but they should consult widely and be receptive to sound advice. Our style in Dyfed-Powys CID was to discuss and talk through problems in a trusted environment making everyone feel valued and able to contribute. Ottawa would be no different and at the first management meeting we all agreed the way forward.

It is of vital importance that the first steps and actions on a major crime review, particularly in those where a considerable time period has passed, are made with the mindset that the process will end up in a court of law. This might appear to be an obvious statement to make, but in some cases those leading an investigation can start from a negative viewpoint of just going through the motions. This approach is doomed to fail because the investigator tends to look only for those elements that support their view. In thirty-two years' service I have never been involved in an investigation in which I have not been convinced that we will find the truth and prove or disprove the offence. The influence of the SIO on his or her team cannot therefore be underestimated; they can be a positive or negative force. My approach was simple: if you do not believe we will find the truth, wherever it lies, then you have no place on my team or the right to represent the victim or their family.

I knew that both my boss Steve Mears and my colleague

Andy John thought the same; this was a thematic forensic review, a forensic assessment of all available material in order to potentially identify an offender or offenders. If it was going to end up in the Crown Court, or 'Big House' as we affectionately called it, we needed even at this early stage to imagine where the attacks on the evidence were likely to come from. The answer was simple; it would be the integrity of the original material on which those forensic conclusions were based.

Accepting this view made the first decisions easy. Having located the material and assessed how and where it was stored, we needed to recover it in a methodical manner, under forensic conditions. When recovered it would then need to be assessed in order to establish its provenance, what had happened to it, what forensic examinations it had been subjected to and what new forensic opportunities were available. DCI Andy John was deliberate in his policy and clear in his direction, the process required a detailed forensic strategy for each location and this needed to be constructed in such a way that it provided protection from any future attack by defence lawyers. These strategy documents needed to be crafted by an experienced Crime Scene Manager and we had the ideal person. Glan Thomas was a jolly character marked out by his total commitment and he relished the opportunity to join the Ottawa team. I knew him well and once sold him a car for his daughter. Doing him a favour, I told him he could have the car for at least £700 below its book price.

We met in a car park near to Laugharne Castle.

'Do you like it, Glan?' I said.

'It's lovely, boss, just what she wants and at such a good

price,' he replied.

'Let's do the deal then, Glan,' I said.

'I will if you knock £50 off,' he replied with a big grin on his face.

How could I refuse!

Each location where relevant exhibits had been stored was treated like a crime scene. Invariably the exhibits were still on police premises but the areas concerned were sectioned off and all those who entered did so with full and appropriate protective clothing. The strategies produced by Glan Thomas were highly detailed and meticulous, leaving nothing to chance. The recovery of each item was recorded and photographed, including its proximity to other exhibits, how it was packaged and its general condition. They were taken from their individual locations to a more permanent store. In addition the areas used to photograph, record and repackage the items were forensically sterilised. I wanted to be confident that from the minute the Ottawa team identified the location of an exhibit the handling and continuity thereafter was beyond question. If there were to be any flaws in the integrity of any exhibit I wanted to know about it, assess its value and impact on other material. If any exhibit were to be contaminated we would have to accept it and ensure *we* were the ones to find and reveal any frailties. I didn't want any surprises in court! There is nothing worse than having the defence drive holes through the integrity of a key exhibit or forensic process; it completely undermines a jury's confidence in the police. This is particularly destructive when it is clear the police have not done their job properly or have failed to disclose a weakness. Andy John and the team needed to implement a process that allowed us to record each exhibit and its history. It would then be up to Lynne Harries and Glyn Johnson to provide the answers.

Lynne Harries 'did detail', he was painstaking in his approach. Never a man to cut corners, he was the ideal person to oversee the recovery phase and when paired with systems man Glyn Johnson it was a winning combination. In addition to this Lynne was careful with money as he was from Cardigan in West Wales. Tradition suggests that men from Cardigan have long pockets and short arms; this would come in handy when challenging escalating forensic costs. Of course in reality Lynne is a generous man, he just hasn't realised it yet.

In any major crime investigation it is very important to audit trail the decision-making process. Complex cases require oversight arrangements to support the SIO at a strategic and tactical level. In this case strategic oversight came from the 'Gold Group' chaired by Deputy Chief Constable Andy Edwards. It helps take pressure off the SIO and provides accountability. The Operational Management Group, chaired by my boss DCS Steve Mears and including myself, DCI Andy John, DI Lynne Harries and Glan Thomas, also provided practical advice and guidance to the investigation team.

Andy John and his team were now up and running and quickly started to locate relevant material and in turn Glan Thomas prepared detailed documents that allowed their forensic recovery. The items were handled in a professional and transparent manner and then stored in rooms at Fishguard Port. The team started to meticulously record the life and times of each item on the custom-made electronic spreadsheets and so the process went on. Recovering all of the incident room material was a mammoth task. It was massive and it felt like we were ancient explorers uncovering all sorts of treasures. As the team sifted statements and reports, the time difference between the offences and the present day hit home. It was like being in the TV series *Life on Mars*!

We were now into March 2006 and it was becoming increasingly evident that exhibits and material from Operation Huntsman were becoming more and more relevant to our review and needed to be considered alongside material recovered from the murder scenes. (Operation Huntsman was of course the investigation into a series of burglaries and robberies in the Milford Haven area that resulted in the conviction of John William Cooper.) As we scrutinised the case a very interesting picture began to emerge. From the early 1980s up to 1996, a number of burglaries were committed at homes within the Milford Haven area. In addition to this a small number of robberies were also committed within the same tight geographical area in North Pembrokeshire. There was an obvious cluster around Milford Haven, Neyland, Rosemarket and Llanstadwell. Research indicated that there were in excess of sixty burglaries that fitted the same modus operandi or MO. Persistent offenders usually have a trademark; it is their 'thumbprint of offending' which they repeat because it works for them. They will display consistent behaviour at scenes, select similar types of property to attack and steal similar items from each of them. The location also provides good clues about how an offender targets a property; how they approach the scene, gain entry and how long they remain at that location. Geographical profiles also provide clues on the likely area that an offender comes from, do they travel by foot or in a vehicle, and do they have links to an area that gives them a degree of comfort because they know their surroundings?

In addition to the vast number of burglaries, there were also four robberies. The first was in 1985 and from then on, the level of violence increased, culminating with the Sardis robbery in 1996. It had been noted that the robberies were very similar; lone women in isolated rural properties. Prior to the Scoveston Park murders the robberies did not involve a firearm, just excessive violence to control the victims. The offender was alone and always instructed the women to cover their heads with clothes or bed covers. Significantly, robberies committed after Scoveston Park always involved a sawn-off shotgun. In April 1985, a robbery occurred at an isolated house called The Briars at Crossways in Milford Haven. The telephone was disabled, the occupant, a lone female, was threatened with violence and jewellery was stolen. The property was later recovered at Scoveston Fort, a disused military structure from the Napoleonic wars, very close to Scoveston Park Farm. In September 1985 there was a second robbery at a similar house called Primrose Hill Cottage in Rosemarket. Entry was gained to the house and a lone female was threatened with violence. Her hands were tied behind her back with rope that the attacker had brought with him. Jewellery was stolen. In September 1994, nine years after the murders of Richard and Helen Thomas, an armed robbery occurred at an isolated house at Westfield Cottage, Sardis. A lone female occupant was threatened with violence and blindfolded. Her hands were tied behind her back with rope brought to the scene. The offender was wearing a balaclava and was armed with a shotgun. He disabled the telephone and jewellery was stolen from the house. Then in November 1996 came the armed robbery at Westwinds in Sardis, when Sheila Clarke was confronted by a man wearing a balaclava and carrying a double-barrelled sawn-off shotgun. It was a carbon copy of the other robberies. Significant research was carried out on burglaries and it was considered the MO was very similar in most of these offences:

- Properties were approached across fields
- Evidence of surveillance by the offender
- Hedge line had been used as cover
- Stolen items had been discarded along the hedge line
- Wire fences had been cut on the route taken by the offender
- Keys had been stolen from the houses

In the case of the robberies that had been committed in this area, the properties were very similar to those targeted in the burglaries but in addition:

- Use of a shotgun to control the victim was evident
- Victims were lone females
- Hands of the victim were tied behind their back
- Rope was brought to the scene by the offender and then taken away, if possible

On a number of occasions police dogs had tracked the offender across fields and hedge lines. Fences were cut to allow easy escape at locations only known to him. Also, at some of these locations, he had left the top strand of wire intact, only cutting the lower strands; no doubt to injure any would-be chaser, unable to see it in the dark. It was also clear to the officers who investigated these escape routes that the North Pembrokeshire night sky was illuminated by many significant landmarks. The oil refineries, which lined the Milford Haven waterway and the Pembroke Power Station stack, provided beacons on the horizon on which he could fix his location at any one time; this was someone who knew the area like the back of his hand.

Back in 1998, Cooper had fallen into the parameters of the Huntsman house-to-house enquiries and was required to give a voluntary sample of his DNA. He refused and was obstructive but remained an 'interesting' character and when the various dog tracks and cut fences were reviewed it was clear that he lived at the very epicentre of the criminal activity. On one occasion in March 1996, dog handler Mark 'the bark' Jenkins had followed a track from a burglary at Castle Pill Crescent, Milford Haven which took him to the entrance of a field opposite Cooper's home and he had actually spoken to him. This offence took place a few days before the Milford Haven sex attacks and was within sight of the scene. Detective Sergeant Steve Matchett and Detective Inspector Jim Morris were suspicious and went to his home. Cooper was uneasy, and then officers noticed property in his house, including videotapes, that were identical to items stolen in a number of the burglaries. In January 1998, following months of research and planning by the Huntsman Team, John William Cooper was arrested at his home address of 34 St Marys Park in Jordanston. His house, surrounded by fields, sat at the hub of the circle of offences. Fingertip searches were carried out at both his house and at the homes of his relatives as well as on the surrounding land including the tracks that the various dog handlers had previously followed towards his home address. It was a huge operation lasting more than thirteen days involving earthmovers and dozens of officers. In all, more than three thousand eight hundred items of property and exhibits were found in and around Cooper's home. These included:

- ROPES Numerous pieces of rope were recovered, some of which appeared to have been constructed to be used as a hand restraint
- JEWELLERY A range of items were recovered from his house, attic and hedges. Items were also found at the homes of his relatives which were later identified as coming from the burglaries and robberies. Some of these items had been burnt and discarded probably with a view to preventing forensic testing and identification.
- AMMUNITION Two shotgun cartridge boxes and another box containing various loose cartridges were found under a duck run in the garden. The cartridges were similar to the types of cartridge that the ballistics experts had indicated were involved in both the Scoveston and Dixons murder inquiries. (Eley and Maionchi/SMI). One of the boxes contained an old-style cardboard-cased cartridge, which again appeared to be similar to the type recovered from Richard Thomas's gun cabinet back at Scoveston in 1985.
- SHOTGUN A well-oiled shotgun with its stock sawn off was found under the duck run at his home covered by over a foot of soil. This had been preserved by being soaked in gun oil, placed in black bin bags and then enclosed in a sewage pipe. This was later identified as being stolen during a burglary at Castle

Pill in Steynton on the 1st of March 1996.

- GUN PARTS Components of a shotgun were found discarded in the hedge at 34 St Marys Park; one firing mechanism could be described as belonging to a hammer-action shotgun. In the Scoveston inquiry, it is suspected that Richard Thomas's gun or guns were stolen from the house and even though he owned a gun cabinet and other associated shotgun items, no shotguns were ever found.
- KEYS Over five hundred keys were recovered from Cooper's possession, many of which were found in a cesspit on his land. Some of the keys would later be matched to mortise keys stolen from some of the burglaries. It's important to note that the keys belonging to Richard Thomas's Rover car were missing when police arrived at the scene of the house fire at Scoveston.

During the investigation Cooper was linked to seventy-two offences of burglary and robbery. However, following early liaison with the Crown Prosecution Service, he was eventually charged with thirty-four offences consisting of thirty burglaries, one burglary with intent and three robberies. When he was questioned about the Scoveston and coastal path murders the officers were wrongly advised that Cooper would respond to their authority. Instead he refused to answer any questions and the interview lasted just thirteen minutes. What the officers didn't know at the time was how important to me those interviews would become almost twenty years later in influencing our approach to Cooper.

We were now at a stage where we wanted to move

evidence from the Huntsman inquiry into the new Ottawa investigation without formally naming Cooper as a suspect. The investigation was growing into a hybrid of a thematic forensic review and re-investigation of crimes over a twenty-five-year period in North Pembrokeshire. We were required to go through a formal linking process and review the terms of reference for Operation Ottawa. It was decided because of the scale of the investigation and in line with ACPO policy that I would take over the role of SIO with Andy John as my deputy. We were now totally immersed in the investigation and I could not have been happier leading this exceptional group of officers and support staff.

In line with our decision to take an objective and independent approach Andy and I agreed to engage a new forensic service provider to carry out any examinations. The original material and exhibits had been examined by the Forensic Science Service, which at the time of the original offences had the monopoly on forensic examinations. The intention was to submit the final schedules to an experienced scientist who would review the schedules and give advice on any further examinations or forensic opportunities. The National Centre for Policing Excellence (NCPE) provided the ideal person in the shape of Joanne Ashworth, head of physical science. Joanne was well known in the homicide arena and had been instrumental in developing many approaches to the recovery of trace evidence in major crime investigations. The examinations were to be carried out by LGC, a private company which had a growing reputation after their groundbreaking work on cases such as the murder of Rachel Nickell on Wimbledon Common.

With the Huntsman exhibits now of great interest to

Ottawa all the exhibits needed to be found and logged in the same way as the other material. The issue of Cooper being named as a suspect had to be addressed as Ottawa and Huntsman were now so intertwined that I felt it needed transparency. There was another school of thought that suggested naming him would leave me open to accusations of tailoring the investigation to fit. This held no fears for me because I was sure that the forensic review process was not directed at any one individual and would either implicate, eliminate or identify another suspect. On the 18th of December 2006 the decision was made to name John William Cooper as a suspect in Operation Ottawa.

CHAPTER 8

THE PRIME SUSPECT

With Cooper named as a suspect I was able to focus on his long history of offending and include in my review all the forensic evidence from Operation Huntsman. It was clear by now that we were in for the long haul so I decided to tap into the expertise of Des James from the National Centre for Policing Excellence, NCPE. I had known Des for years; he was a retired detective superintendent from Gwent Police and very experienced in major crime investigations. Des was a gentleman and had a lovely way about him; he could make a suggestion in such a way that you felt it was your own idea. By now we had put together a presentation that showed the Ottawa crimes overlaid with Cooper's convictions; it was crude but a great briefing tool. Des came to Carmarthen for an initial chat and we showed it to him. He watched in total silence and at the end I looked at him and said, 'OK, Des, in your professional opinion as the Regional SIO advisor, what do you think?' Des looked at me and pondered his answer, 'He's fucking done it, Wilkie!' I must say that I was hoping for something a bit more scientific, but this was the start of an excellent relationship with Des, who became a good friend and advisor to the team.

The terms of reference for Operation Ottawa needed to be adjusted to include Cooper as a suspect and my policy book named him as such. The changes to the terms of reference were simple:

- Investigate further lines of enquiry identified during the forensic review.
- Progress new investigative opportunities in respect of the suspect John William Cooper.
- Prepare for an interview with the suspect John William Cooper or any other person identified from the evidence gathered.
- Exploit any advances in investigative techniques and legislative changes in an effort to gather any other admissible evidence that would support a prosecution of the offences under review.

The last point was unusual and would significantly impact on the investigation and court process. There had been a change in the law that allowed Bad Character Evidence to be admissible as part of the prosecution's evidence of guilt. It has been a great source of frustration to the police, and I believe the general public, that during a trial they are not made aware of certain information about the defendant when it is directly relevant to the case and tended to show that the defendant had a propensity to behave in a certain way. In simple terms prior to 2005, a defendant's bad character would only be admissible in certain very narrow circumstances when they made the character of another witness a point of issue, and then only with the leave of the court. As you can imagine, defence lawyers steered well clear of such a position. In 2005, the Bad Character provisions changed for the better allowing the prosecution to include a defendant's bad character to be introduced through so-called 'admissibility gateways'. In essence if a career criminal demonstrated through previous convictions that they carried out certain behaviour during offending or committed certain types of offences, the gateways allowed these facts to be given as evidence to the jury.

In terms of the exhibits, we needed to keep it simple. My initial thoughts were to build up comprehensive schedules of material and physical evidence and establish the provenance of each item, assess and consider its relevance and importance to the investigation and identify a system of prioritisation before submitting for forensic examination. We created a 'one-stop shop' database of information relating to forensic exhibits that meant that we could view the original reports immediately. The database also contained images of the exhibits, whether it was an original photograph or a more recent image prepared during Ottawa.

This method of recording information gave the team a comprehensive research capability to interrogate the system. It also served another purpose in allowing the team to start to build up continuity schedules for the exhibits, mapping the journey each one had made. It was established that all investigations except the Scoveston Park review which had been done on a card index system, had been recorded on the HOLMES computer system. Many versions of HOLMES had been developed and we experienced considerable challenges in trying to convert the old systems into the new. The work done by Glyn Johnson to crack this problem was exceptional and would become national best practice. I was very impressed.

All the recovered exhibits were eventually transferred to the forensic laboratories of LGC in Oxfordshire where they would undergo fresh and independent examinations.

A corresponding inventory was then recorded by LGC on receipt of the items to ensure continuity of the exhibits. It was also likely that some exhibits had been destroyed, returned to their owners or indeed lost. It was therefore important to establish if any exhibits were missing and to conduct the necessary searches to retrieve any that were outstanding. Any such searches needed to take place in forensic conditions and by specialists. The services of Police Search Advisor (POLSA) Inspector Nigel Hayes as well as search officers were used to ensure that the main historic storage venue, the firearms range in Haverfordwest, was clear of all relevant exhibits relating to our review. Again the forensic integrity of any exhibit was maintained and recovered in line with the original strategy.

It was soon apparent that many exhibits had been destroyed with the authority of the then SIO, because forensic opportunities, especially DNA, were very limited. To review the submission of items to date and to make recommendations on any further forensic submissions the team needed access to various source documents to understand the 'forensic' history of each exhibit as well as its provenance. These documents included:

- Major Incident Room documents
- Scientific support submission forms
- Scientist General examination records
- Original photographs
- Exhibit books

The original scientists' notes from the FSS gave the team the opportunity to gather considerable and reliable information on the exhibits, some of which would have not been reported back to investigators at the time. The notes were light on the significance of the fibre evidence because at the time gathering it was very expensive and time-consuming. Some of the clothing belonging to the Dixons had gone missing within the Forensic Science building at Chepstow only to resurface later when it was found in a storage bin. The exhibits were divided into the following categories:

- Firearms/Shotguns
- Ammunition
- Ropes
- Keys
- Clothing
- Jewellery
- Sexual elements
- Forensic samples
- Miscellaneous exhibits

Further research on the Eley ammunition threw up an unexpected contact. Graham Morris, who had been managing director of the Eley Hawk company, was able to provide information on the dates of manufacture of certain cartridges as well as indicating the type of wadding and shot they contained just by looking at them. Some of the ammunition actually dated back to the 1940s. There follows a summary of the significant findings:

FIREARMS/SHOTGUNS

It is suspected that a shotgun(s) was stolen from Scoveston Park and possibly used as the murder weapon. Both Richard and Helen Thomas suffered shotgun wounds as did Peter and Gwenda Dixon. Ballistics experts indicated that the murder weapon used during the Dixons' attack was likely to be a double-barrelled sawn-off shotgun. Significantly during Operation Huntsman, various shotguns and component parts were recovered from Cooper's home address in Jordanston. A well-oiled shotgun was concealed under a duck run. This shotgun was identified as having been stolen from a local burglary in March 1996. The stock of the gun had been sawn off and a screw placed in the stock with a small washer attached. Other sections of older shotguns (barrels, trigger mechanisms) were also recovered from a hedge at Cooper's home. In 1996 during the Sardis robbery for which Cooper was convicted a sawn-off shotgun was discarded. It had been modified including the introduction of a rope lanyard attached to the stock and barrel by metal clips and screws. A missing screw from this shotgun was eventually matched to a screw recovered from a container in Cooper's garden shed. A similar robbery happened in the Sardis area in 1994, in which the victim was tied up, and which involved the offender brandishing a sawn-off shotgun.

Research during the Huntsman inquiry into the death of pensioner Flo Evans, who lived a short distance from Cooper's house, identified that Flo's late husband possessed a number of shotguns. Enquiries revealed that they had not been handed down to other family members and yet they could not be found at her home. It is suspected that they also had been stolen at some time. During the Dixons and Huntsman inquiries, a number of shotguns were found concealed or abandoned at various locations in the general area of Milford Haven and the geographical area of Cooper's offending. Some were hidden in black bin bags (as was the gun under Cooper's duck run). Of particular interest was the discovery two weeks after the Milford Haven rape and robbery of sawn-off pump action Winchester shotgun in a hedge in Freystrop together with a cartridge belt and ammunition. This shotgun still remains unidentified.

AMMUNITION

Various types and rounds of shotgun ammunition were recovered from rooms within Scoveston Park but on examination it couldn't be confirmed that they contained wadding similar to that which was found in the bodies of the victims. No spent cartridges were found at the various scenes that could be linked to the shotgun injuries. Officers spent days at Scoveston Park sifting by hand mounds of burnt debris as well as using powerful magnets to detect metal cartridge heads but to no avail. On the coastal path no spent cartridges were recovered in the immediate vicinity of the bodies. However scientists identified that wadding found in the Dixons' bodies probably had come from an Italian-made cartridge (Maionchi/SMI/Martignoni) and were of No.5 shot size. During Operation Huntsman, a number of boxes of shotgun cartridges were recovered from Cooper's home at the same location as the concealed shotgun under the duck run. These were found in cardboard boxes that related to Baikal and Maionchi makes. These contained various size cartridges and makes including Eley and Maionchi. Also an old Eley ICI cartridge with cardboard casing was found with apparent brown staining on the casing. Huntsman enquiries identified that Cooper had held a shotgun certificate back in early 1980s. Again it was noted that during the Sardis robbery for which Cooper had been jailed, two Maionchi cartridges were discarded near the address. Furthermore, after the rape at Milford Haven, a shotgun cartridge belt, together with the shotgun, was found in a hedge at Freystrop. This belt contained Maionchi cartridges as well as old Pembroke County cartridges. This is the make that Cooper used to buy when he possessed a shotgun certificate.

ROPES

During the post-mortem of Helen Thomas, a piece of knotted rope was discovered amongst her burnt clothing. In addition a skirt appeared to have been used as a gag or blindfold but unfortunately it has since been lost. It was suspected that she had been tied up as part of a robbery that had gone wrong and that Richard Thomas had been shot dead in the outbuildings and dragged, on a blanket, into the house. This blanket had been tied with the remnants of orange bailer twine. Different samples of bailer twine appear to have been recovered from various locations within Scoveston Park. As a matter of interest during searches at Scoveston Fort in 1998 remnants of bailer twine were found in various rooms within the Fort complex. Peter Dixon was found on the coastal path with his hands tied behind his back. The rope that was examined by the FSS was also submitted to knot expert Geoffrey Budworth to compare against the knots found on the Scoveston rope. Images of Gwenda Dixon's body indicated that one of her hands was positioned to the rear of her back. Could it be that she was also tied up but the offender removed the rope from the scene? When Cooper's home was searched during the Huntsman inquiry sixty sections of rope were recovered. During examinations some of them had what could be classified as 'handcuff contrivances' with obvious restraints present. Both the sawn-off shotgun and threaded tool, discarded during the Sardis robbery, had ropes attached for use as lanyards. Also recovered was a longer section of similar rope. The victim of the robbery had rope tied around her wrists that according to examinations was not dissimilar in nature to other ropes recovered at Sardis. Our researches revealed that there were a number of 'tie-up' robberies in the Milford Haven, Neyland and Sardis areas, where vulnerable females were restrained by ropes before property was stolen. The offender then removed some of the ropes from the scene. Our experts concluded that the existence of various knots in all the significant ropes should warrant further examination because of the complexity of some of the knots.

KEYS

During the original Scoveston investigation, one of the lines of enquiry was that a set of keys belonging to Richard Thomas's Rover car had been stolen. When police arrived, Richard's car was parked in the yard with the doors open and the keys missing. This fuelled a belief that he had arrived home and had disturbed the offender during the robbery. During the search various sets of keys were recovered including one found behind the larder in the kitchen at Scoveston. This key has been 'connected in some way' to the Rover car. On this key, which is still in police possession, there are serial numbers visible that would normally be hidden by the plastic key fob. It would appear that these numbers have not been considered for further analysis. During the examination of Cooper's home a set of Leyland/Rover car keys were recovered. These have been shown to a mechanic who worked on Richard Thomas's Rover car who described them as being of similar description. Another set of keys also contained one that was similar in all aspects to one used on a Rover car. Unfortunately of course, Richard Thomas's Rover was disposed of some years ago prior to 1998. The searches for Operation Huntsman resulted in excess of five hundred keys being recovered on Cooper's property, mainly hidden in his cesspit, several of which have been matched to the burglary scenes. One key has been forensically matched to Norton farm, which was owned by Richard Thomas in 1985. Another key recovered from Cooper's home was linked to the burglary in Freystrop in October 1985 where keys, a chequebook and a card were stolen. The card was used at the NatWest cashpoint in Haverfordwest the following Sunday at 7.45 a.m. This was identical to how Peter Dixon's cash card was used at the same service till just after 7 a.m. days after his murder.

CLOTHING

Obviously there was a lack of information available from the murder inquiries regarding the suspect's clothing. However the artist's impression as compiled by the witnesses who saw the man using the cashpoint card indicated he was wearing a pair of dark shorts and walking boots. During the

Huntsman inquiry, a pair of olive green shorts was recovered from Cooper's home. These appeared to be dirty and old with some staining. The description of the suspect in some of the 'tie-up' robberies was of a man wearing a balaclava and gloves. This matched the description of the offender in the Milford Haven rape. Similar items were discarded during the Sardis robbery. During the search of Scoveston Fort, in one of the turret rooms, officers found a piece of old brown leather boot with eyelets. It looked as though an attempt had been made to dispose of it. A shotgun was also found during the Huntsman searches in a bin bag at St Brides. The bag also contained a very distinctive fleece jacket. This fleece had never been examined or publicised in order to find the owner, which in turn may then identify who the shotgun belonged to.

JEWELLERY

Richard and Helen Thomas were reclusive with no close family and it was therefore impossible to establish what property had been stolen from Scoveston Park. Enquiries did reveal however that shotguns were missing from the property but their make and model was not known. Some jewellery items were found in the fire debris outside and it was concluded that other items of value might have been stolen. It was established that Peter Dixon's wedding ring had been stolen as well as his wallet and cashpoint cards. Significantly, it was ascertained back in 1989 that a man identified as a one J. Cooper sold a man's wedding ring at a jewellers in Pembroke Dock a few days after the Dixons' disappearance. The searches in Huntsman resulted in significant quantities of jewellery being found in fields and along a warren of hedgerows surrounding Cooper's home. Jewellery was even found in his attic, some of it had been burnt. Jewellery that was not identified by the victims of crime was returned to the Cooper family. Some of it still remained with the police however because the owners couldn't be traced, indicating that it was probably stolen property.

SEXUAL ELEMENTS

An important line of enquiry in the Thomas murders was established during the post-mortem examinations. An anal swab from Richard Thomas was found to contain the presence of semen. A sighting of him with a fat man in a Land Rover on the day of the fire was scrutinised by police, and the suggestion that Richard might have been homosexual was extensively investigated but never confirmed. Experts were convinced that there had been a sexual element in the murder of Gwenda Dixon. They believed her bra had been moved before she was shot and all her lower garments had also been removed. Injuries were also observed on her inner thigh. Pages from two pornographic magazines were recovered on the coastal path, not at the scene but in the vicinity; this appeared to be more than just a coincidence. A pornographic magazine was also found in Scoveston Fort during the Huntsman searches. Nearby was property from a robbery for which Cooper had been convicted. In the Milford Haven attack the offender tried to rob the children of valuables before one was raped and another sexually assaulted. This attack occurred just six months before the Sardis robbery for which Cooper was convicted. The two scenes were only a short distance apart and the victims' descriptions of the attacker were similar. For us this was hugely significant.

FORENSIC EXHIBITS

During the Scoveston Park inquiry, various forensic exhibits were recovered in the course of the post-mortem, including blood and hair. Blood grouping techniques were very limited at the time and significant problems were encountered in establishing the origin of certain blood samples not taken from the bodies. A pool of blood was located within an outbuilding as well as wadding. Various interpretations were made as to the sequence of events that had occurred that night. No grouping profile was raised from Helen Thomas. Several of these exhibits were still stored in the laboratories at the Forensic Science Service. The presence of sperm heads within the anal swab taken from Richard Thomas had been evaluated and but since only one slide was left from this sample, the decision to re-examine this had been deferred until DNA techniques were sufficiently sensitive to ensure success in raising a suitable profile. During the Dixons inquiry in 1989, the same problems were encountered in establishing a standard DNA profile for the deceased couple. In accordance with crime scene investigative procedures in 1989 various tapings were taken from both bodies; in effect a strip of sticky tape is pressed on to any significant surfaces to collect microscopic debris. Particular attention was paid to Gwenda Dixon because of the suspected sexual element to the murder. No speculative

DNA swabs were taken from the surface of their bodies, as would be the case today. During Huntsman, Cooper had refused to give a blood sample hence a sample of his head hair was taken and used to develop a DNA profile. The Mitochondrial DNA technique was used to develop this sample to link it to discarded exhibits during the Sardis robbery including the balaclava and gloves. We believed that in order to progress the inquiry it would be essential that DNA profiles of all four victims and Cooper were developed to the standard modern specification.

MISCELLANEOUS EXHIBITS

The Scoveston Park scene had produced several exhibits that were initially submitted to the Forensic Science Service to confirm or discount the presence of accelerant. The exhibits included the samples of debris that had been sifted to locate any spent ammunition. A significant item was a blanket suspected of being used by the offender to drag the body of Richard Thomas from the outbuilding into the house itself. Part of this blanket was recovered on the landing as well some remnants outside the house. It was established that the fire officers had removed Richard's body from the half landing and taken it outside before it was realised that he had been murdered. The recovery of a button in the outbuildings led the inquiry team to believe that there had been a scuffle between Richard Thomas and his attacker. Richard's jacket had a button missing even though the button found was different to other buttons on the jacket. These items could be of significance because they had possibly come into contact with the offender, however because fire damage and their deterioration some detailed decisions would have to be made on what would be sent for further examination.

During the Dixons inquiry, general samples of tapings were taken from the bodies as well as surrounding soil and vegetation. The scene was concealed with broken branches and it was noted that the force required to break them would potentially result in DNA, or even blood being deposited on the branches, if the offender grazed or cut himself. Fibres may also have been left. Items from the rucksack belonging to the Dixons were strewn in the area, again indicating that the offender had rooted through looking for valuables, supporting the theory that a robbery had occurred. A number of items initially returned to Tim Dixon, Peter's son, had been recovered for further, more sensitive DNA techniques in 2001. This prompted police to recover further items from the Dixon family in 2006. These items were subjected to fingerprinting and at least one mark of value was developed on a camera instruction booklet that has been entered on the National Finger Print database (NAFIS) and on the Serious Crimes Cache. With the advent of digital photography, this is another area where potential marks left back in 1989 could now be cleaned up, enhanced and searched on the databases. Also found on the coastal path scene was a crumpled-up cashpoint receipt relating to Peter Dixon's account dated a few days prior to his death. Tim Dixon said that his father would have taken out cash and placed the receipt in his wallet. Since the wallet and cash cards were stolen there was every possibility that the offender may have handled this receipt while he searched the wallet. This has been subjected to various fingerprint treatments but with negative result. Various fibres were also recovered including a thick white fibre. Significantly there was a connection between white fibres and the various burglaries of which Cooper was convicted. White cloth had also been found at various points of entry at the properties and under Cooper's duck run with the shotgun and ammunition.

The artist's impression of the man using the stolen cashpoint card in Haverfordwest indicated a specific type of bicycle. During Huntsman, a 'sit up and beg' bike was recovered from Flo Evans' address at Thornhill Farm. Even though Florence Evans had died in February 1989, this bicycle had been left at the property. It had been subjected to fingerprint analysis and two marks had been located on the underside of the handlebars. It had been documented that Cooper had been a friend and visitor to Flo Evans and her husband Artie prior to their deaths. An investigation into another 'tie-up' robbery in 1994 identified that the victim had also been burgled in February 1989. It had been noted by police at this time that bicycle tracks were found in the field at the rear of the property. This again was at a time when Florence Evans's home would have been vacant due to her death and her bike would have been easily accessible. This would also have been the case in June 1989 when the Dixon's were murdered. It should be noted that Thornhill Farm backs onto the scene of the Sardis robbery.

During a search of Cooper's home an old common prayer book was located which was examined by an antiques dealer who stated it was Victorian and would have belonged to a 'well-to-do woman'. It was known that on the day of her death, Helen Thomas had attended church and so her prayer book would have been readily accessible in the house. This item had since been returned to Mrs Cooper at her request. A building trowel was recovered during the Huntsman searches at Cooper's address. This trowel on closer examination had the initials engraved on it 'RST'. Richard Skeel Thomas perhaps?

There was a wealth of information, data and material that had to be assessed in order to present it as admissible evidence in court. It was important that we were able to determine fact from fiction. Experience has shown me that important and serious crime investigations attract legend and myth and cops are the worst for exaggerating. Some of this myth and legend can attach itself to investigations and influence decision-making. I needed to send out a clear message to the team that this would not happen on my investigation. The television room at Fishguard Port office became our briefing room; I would bring the cakes and biscuits and discuss the case. One Friday afternoon as we munched I set out the ground rules, 'We deal only in evidence and fact, we don't do myth and legend. When we have identified and isolated the relevant material and information I want to know who will stand in a court of law and give it as evidence, if we cannot identify this person, it isn't evidence, simple.'

For instance, it was suggested that Cooper whilst in custody for the Sardis robbery had taunted the investigation team regarding the murders, but there was no evidence whatsoever to support this claim. It was also said that he had asked for a book and circled page numbers corresponding to Peter Dixon's PIN number for his NatWest card; this again was nonsense. The trowel recovered from Cooper's house with the initials RST engraved on it (Richard Skeel Thomas) was a red herring. It did have RST on it but this was the manufacturer's name and it was stamped on and not engraved. A main line of enquiry for the original Scoveston Park murder team was the sighting of a blue Ford Cortina seen parked opposite the entrance to Scoveston Park. This sighting was included in an appeal that offered £25,000 for information linked to its owner and the murder. No one ever came forward with such information and the owner of the vehicle on the night was never traced. During the Huntsman investigation it was suggested that the vehicle belonged to the Cooper family and had been parked in a lay-by opposite the entrance whilst its occupants had a heated argument. During this argument it was suggested that one of the occupants saw John Cooper walking out of the lane leading to Scoveston Park. This would have been significant if true; alas it was not. The vehicle did belong to the Cooper family, which was interesting in itself because they had never come forward despite the significant publicity, but the sighting was myth. It made us aware of how important it was to only deal in fact.

At this stage the most frustrating news was that Richard Thomas's Rover car was missing and no one knew where it was or what had happened to it; or rather no one was admitting to disposing of it. For years it had been parked up at the back of Milford Haven police station covered in bird droppings, disappearing under a layer of moss with a small tree growing out of its front windscreen. The order had been given to get shot of it and it had probably now been recycled into baked bean tins. The loss was not the car but rather the locks and ignition. We had keys, recovered from Cooper's cesspit, which may have fitted it. Only a mechanical forensic fit would do because back then a Rover or Leyland key would probably have started a number of cars, such was the crude nature of the locks and ignition. Hindsight is a wonderful thing but the decision to get rid of the car was a great source of frustration to the team.

CHAPTER 9

A LEAP OF FAITH

By March 2007 we were more than twelve months into the review and by now numerous exhibits and relevant material had been forensically recovered, recorded and forwarded to LGC Forensics for examination. For the team it was a waiting game while the initial assessments were completed. Indications, from the lead scientist Maggie Boyce, were that we would receive the first news by April 2007, but in truth I felt this was a little optimistic. Whatever the timescale it was clear to me that with the circumstantial case starting to build up, together with the changes to the provisions of Bad Character Evidence, we needed at some stage to put the allegations to Cooper.

There was also the question of linking the offences, which I had not formally done, for good reason. Following discussions with Des James, my SIO advisor, I decided to employ the services of Neil Traynor, a geographical profiler, and Paul Lobbe, a behavioural profiler, both on the books of the National Policing Improvement Agency, NPIA. I had worked with Neil before and he was a very knowledgeable individual. I wanted them to look at the Ottawa offences and use their findings in my linking process.

Surprisingly we did not have a full DNA profile of all of the murder victims and it was important that we had them for identification and elimination purposes. LGC was tasked with raising such profiles for all of our victims, and after a considerable amount of time and effort this was finally achieved. During the post-mortem examination of Richard Thomas, anal swabs indicated evidence of semen but, due to the limited development of DNA, all the scientists could do was provide a blood group. The theory that Richard Thomas might have had a murderous gay lover was born and became a major line of enquiry. After thousands of hours spent trying to unlock a potential motive or suspect, there was not a shred of credible evidence that Richard Thomas was involved in such a relationship or had a secret life. Back then this caused Detective Chief Superintendent Davies many sleepless nights and it was clear that he too had his doubts over the value of this lead.

Now more than twenty years on developments in forensic science had given us another opportunity to investigate the theory. There was one semen slide left, together with the original swabs and container. Previous SIOs had been reluctant to open the slide because it was sealed and they had been advised that the process of separating the glass might well be destructive. I was quite clear that we had to open it and unlock any potential evidence as I had already been told that it was unlikely that there would be any advances in DNA science for at least five years, which would justify delaying the procedure. The results were conclusive and silenced any rumours; the swab, container and slide revealed a full DNA profile and it belonged to Richard Thomas himself: the semen was his own. Many theories were then put forward for this, including the suggestion that a natural reaction for a man who has been shot is to ejaculate: we never found any expert to confirm this. I was of the belief that while Richard Thomas was lying on his back during the post-mortem, semen had drained through his severely burned lower abdomen tissue and into his anus, which had then been swabbed during the examination; it was clearly a contamination issue. This was significant because it explained the lack of evidence at the time to support the suggestion that a gay lover had murdered Richard. This result again focused the team on the belief that Helen had been the victim of a bungled robbery and Richard had returned to the house and confronted the intruder, resulting in a struggle and eventually their murders.

I wanted to get the best advice in relation to any future interviews with Cooper. We had to ensure that we had the best and most appropriate interviewers and a clear strategy of engagement given the previous experience of the Huntsman team. Gary Shaw was the National Interview Advisor and he had been involved in developing best practice. He would give me tactical advice on how to build a plan. On top of that I needed to know Cooper the man, who was he, how did he think and how might he react to situations and people? I had access to a number of assessments that had been carried out on Cooper while he was in prison and they were fascinating. He was a man who wanted control; he always had to have the final say, would lie but convince himself that he was telling the truth and he would justify the means to an end however unreasonable his actions.

The assessments revealed an interesting contradiction to how he behaved in his previous interviews. Here was a man who enjoyed talking about himself and painting a picture of a superman who was everyone's friend. In reality he was a very unpopular man who was given a wide berth by anyone who came into contact with him. His working life had been a series of failed ventures, built on poor planning, usually his. When challenged he tended to take the questioner on a journey that gave him time to assess and respond with another lie. It was this type of insight that we needed and it would prove to be critical in our preparation.

Dr Adrian West is a prominent and highly respected forensic criminal psychologist who has worked with some of the significant and dangerous criminals in British jails. I wanted to engage Dr West at an early stage and get his view on how to approach Cooper. They were old acquaintances if you like because Dr West had been involved in the Huntsman investigation and had been very interested in Cooper's profile. Des James arranged a meeting with him at Fishguard Port Office. I liked Dr West immensely, he is quietly spoken and his gentle Merseyside accent always reminded me of home.

We sat for hours in the television room talking about how to approach Cooper. I needed to get him talking while not giving him a chance to take the interviewer off on a tangent, as he had done in Huntsman. This would need careful planning and special interviewers. They needed to be physically and mentally robust, able to focus, retain information and have bags of courage. Their knowledge of Cooper needed to be extensive, detailed and accurate. They needed to know more about Cooper than he did himself. Unfortunately we did not have a shred of forensic evidence and the interview would be solely based on circumstantial evidence and bad character. After discussion with Dr West I wanted to have a male, female combination, because of the response it might provoke from Cooper.

Most of his offending had involved extreme violence against women. We both agreed that it could be a masterstroke or a disaster stroke. Whatever the outcome, I wanted to have the option available and a clear strategy of when and when not to use it.

As we were finishing for the day I asked Dr West a simple question. 'Adrian, how would you best describe Cooper as an offender?'

He thought for a few seconds then replied, 'There are two people who I have come across in my professional career, who if I awoke in the middle of the night to find them in my bedroom I know I would have to kill them to survive, one is Donald Neilson, the so-called Black Panther,* and the other is John William Cooper.'

His simple but explosive response made the hairs on the back of my neck stand up; it underlined the enormity and importance of the task the Ottawa team was facing. I knew that even if we came to a point where we did not have any forensic evidence I needed to interview Cooper. Although my forensic review was not targeted at any one suspect, the Cooper element troubled me greatly. Whatever the outcome, in my mind, I needed to be in a defensible

---

* *Donald Neilson, born Donald Nappey on the 1ˢᵗ of August 1936, and given the criminal name 'Black Panther', was a multiple murderer and armed robber. During three attacks on sub-post offices between 1971 and 1974 he murdered three people. His fourth victim was heiress Lesley Whittle whom he kidnapped and demanded a ransom from her family of £50,000. Following bungled attempts by the police to pay the ransom through her brother, her body was discovered at the bottom of a drainage shaft near Kidsgrove, Staffordshire in 1975. Neilson was captured and sentenced to life. He died on the 18ᵗʰ of December 2011.*

position if Cooper came out of prison and killed again. I had to be able to explain that we had done everything possible. Dr West's words would give me many sleepless nights.

Deputy Chief Constable Andy Edwards had already chaired a number of 'Gold' oversight groups and made it clear that Operation Ottawa was not an investigation to be resourced from the Pembrokeshire Division alone; it was a force responsibility, a priority investigation and its key players would be drawn from throughout the force area. The interview team would need to come together early and start to absorb the masses of information and data held in the incident room. I needed a team that would not be intimidated, who could remain calm and cool under pressure and not be sidetracked by Cooper. After careful consideration a team was selected: Detective Sergeant Colin Clarke as interview advisor, Detective Sergeant Gareth (Rambo) Rees, Detective Constable Nigel Jones and Louise Harries. All were experienced and I knew that they would be more than a match for Cooper. Colin was an excellent interview advisor and able to produce detailed interview strategies; Gareth and Nigel, both famous for their superhuman feats of eating, were larger than life figures who would not be intimidated, while Louise was developing an excellent reputation and gave me the option of having a female in the mix.

The disclosure of evidence was another key issue that I needed to consider. It is the responsibility of the investigating authority to disclose to the defence issues and material that might assist them or undermines the prosecution case; this is done in conjunction with the Crown via the Crown Prosecution Service or CPS. The first stage is for the police to review all material and to schedule it into different categories and then to reveal it to the CPS, who then consider its relevance and make a decision as to whether or not to disclose it. It's a massive responsibility and has been the graveyard of many good and high-profile investigations. It was clear that with all of the material involved, disclosure would be a huge piece of work. At the start of Ottawa we had 80,000 documents with some containing hundreds of pages and by its conclusion the investigation had amassed some two million pieces of paper.

The problem we faced was quite simple; disclosure would normally take place post charge. At this stage we had not even interviewed Cooper and the forensic review might well throw up another suspect. We had consulted with another team in West Yorkshire who had carried out a high-profile cold case review of the murder of a young girl called Lesley Molseed. In this case the SIO had started the disclosure process post charge and had to employ a team of over twenty officers for six months. We just did not have the resources to do this in our case; instead we needed to start the disclosure process now, fully understanding the risks of reviewing material without knowing the significance of the evidence and what was relevant.

By this stage Andy John had moved on to another post. It was a decision which weighed heavy on him, but the correct one for his career. Andy is an excellent officer and a very good friend and I have no doubt he will go far. His contribution to Operation Ottawa at the start was significant and planted the seeds of success. Together with Lynne Harries and Glyn Johnson I considered the disclosure conundrum and after many hours of lively debate we agreed a way forward which included bringing a small team of officers together to start the process. Many of the problems with disclosure relate to the quality of schedules. They should contain enough information to make a clear assessment of their relevance. Some are far too brief, allowing vital documents to slip through unnoticed, only to resurface again, ambushing the Crown's case during a trial. I wanted to avoid this at all costs. The disclosure team for Ottawa would pay particular attention to the quality of the schedules and ensure they contained enough detail to allow us to review them post charge and reassess the material, if we ever got to this stage. The downside was it might be a totally unnecessary exercise if we did not charge. There was, however, another advantage to this approach in that the disclosure team would develop a detailed knowledge of the case and any pitfalls, while possibly identifying new evidence for the investigation team.

Dyfed-Powys is a small force, and everyone knows everyone else. I believe being a 'family force' with strong community links is a strength, which has helped keep us at the top of the performance table for many years. The flip side is of course that it's impossible to have secrets and keeping Ottawa under wraps would be a significant challenge. We needed to have an internal communication strategy in place and this job was given to our press office. I was even more concerned about any interest from the media, which was something I wanted to avoid at this stage. I knew that eventually I would want to go public, but at a time of my choosing to maximise any tactical advantage; in essence, if Cooper was my main suspect then I needed to make sure during any news coverage I could monitor his response. This was my strategy but then out of the blue

I received a telephone call from ITV that I didn't want.

In the spring of 2007, Jonathan Hill, a journalist and presenter of ITV Wales's nightly news programme, contacted the force. For the last ten years he had fronted a series called *Crime Secrets*, which told the stories behind some of Wales most notorious murder investigations. For many years the force had refused to take part in any filming but Jonathan still wanted to meet me. The producers were interested in running a piece on the murder of Welsh backpacker Kirsty Jones in Thailand in 2000; it was a case I was closely involved in. It's fair to say that the force had at times had a difficult relationship with another journalist at ITV Wales and I knew my bosses would be nervous about getting involved. Their current affairs series had accused a former Head of CID of being less than competent in investigating a major crime, at the same time pointing to the Pembrokeshire murders as another example of poor detective work. This issue was still reverberating around the ACPO corridors and I did not want this to derail my plans. I decided to make some of my own enquiries with detectives at other Welsh forces who had worked with Mr Hill. Their response was positive but it was time for me to make up my own mind. I have always had a good relationship with the press because I respect what they do and in my experience most of the time they do a pretty good job; yes there are some who abuse their position, but I have also worked with police officers guilty of the same charge. I was curious to know more about what Mr Hill wanted from us so we arranged for him to come to Headquarters in Carmarthen.

Over a coffee we talked about the Kirsty Jones case and we decided to do it. After seven years the case needed some publicity and his interest seemed genuine. I agreed that a colleague and I would do some interviews and we would liaise with Kirsty's family to get their consent. Job done! Then came the bombshell. Mr Hill was also very keen to make a programme about the Pembrokeshire Coastal Path murders and the killings at Scoveston. Totally unaware of Ottawa and how the operation was developing, Jonathan intimated that the researchers already had enough material to make a story and they would like us to take part but it was not essential; the programme would go ahead with or without our help. He also revealed they had extensive archive footage of the crimes from the time. We were in a tricky situation and I had to make a leap of faith. If the programme went ahead it could compromise much of the good work that had been done and it would alert Cooper before we were ready for him. I closed the door and fixed Jonathan with a stare. I paused and then said, 'Your programme would make it very difficult for us.' He looked puzzled as I continued, 'I am going to trust you and if you break that trust then I will have nothing more to do with you.' It was a thinly veiled threat. Jonathan believed that the murders were cold cases but I was about to cut him into the Ottawa secret. 'The murders of Helen and Richard Thomas and Peter and Gwenda Dixon are not a cold case but very much active.'

He looked stunned as he realised he might have stumbled across one of the biggest stories of his career. I told him that I wanted to strike a deal. If they abandoned plans to cover the Pembrokeshire murders in the forthcoming series of *Crime Secrets*, then I would give him first bite when I was ready to go public. I paused and the full implication of what I had just said sunk in. It was a calculated risk on my part but I had few options. After some careful consideration Jonathan agreed to drop the story for now. I explained that we would have to take it one step at a time and if he kept his side of the bargain I would keep mine. We shook hands and he headed back to Cardiff. I hoped my faith in him would not be misplaced.

CHAPTER 10

GOING PUBLIC

By the spring of 2007, the team had become so familiar with the exhibits that I could mention any one of them and they would in an instant blurt out the police reference number and its full history. In particular Lynne Harries and Glyn Johnson were becoming exhibit number anoraks. Lynne had also developed an uncanny knowledge of all things to do with shotgun cartridges and started to speak a language that none of us understood. Mid conversation, and without warning, he would introduce words such as Eley, Maionchi and Martignoni and any other manufacturer he could think of. It provided many humorous interludes and alleviated some of the intense pressure we were all under.

Certain exhibits jumped out as a priority and were quickly submitted for examination, some were even fast-tracked. We then had to find expert witnesses via the NPIA. There were also many exhibits such as fibre and body tapings together with the record of their examination, which were still located in the Forensic Science Service. Crucially they had never left the custody of the FSS. The examinations fell broadly under the following categories:

- DNA
- Ballistics including shotguns and ammunition

- Rope/knot analysis
- Forensic locksmith
- Fibres
- Handwriting analysis
- Fingerprints
- Pathology

The description of the exhibit is preceded by its police reference number:

Scoveston

- BM/64 – Anal swab from Richard Thomas
- BM/12A – Rope from Helen's body
- BM/1 to 5 – Clothing of Richard Thomas
- BM/14 – Watch taken from Helen Thomas
- LC/35 – Button from outhouse
- OGW/4, LC/92, MJR/2 – Shotgun wadding

Dixons

- JAW/106 – Rope used to bind Peter Dixon
- JAW/15 – Bra belonging to Gwenda Dixon
- JAW/2 to 5, 16 to 18 – Tape lifts from Dixons' clothing
- JAW 7 to 8, 102 to 104, 112 – Clothing of Dixons
- LHD/12 and 17 – Clothing and boots of Dixons
- GWJC/9 – Boots of Dixons
- GWJC/3 – Handkerchief from Peter Dixon
- JAW/100 to 101 – Tape lifts from bodies of Dixons
- JAW/113, 114, 116 – Shotgun wadding
- BK/9 and 10 – Shotgun wadding
- LHD/1 – NatWest bank slip found at scene

- LHD/21 and WDGJ/23 – pornographic magazines found on coastal path

Huntsman

- AJM/216 /6 to 8 – Shotgun cartridges and boxes recovered from under duck run
- AJM/158/176/177 – Parts of a firearm found at 34 St Marys Park
- AJM/165 – Green shorts found in bedroom of John Cooper
- JR/19 and MDS/1 – shotgun cartridges discarded at Sardis robbery
- PH/2/2A – Shotgun and lanyard discarded at Sardis robbery
- MTJ/5/7 – Gloves discarded at Sardis robbery
- HPC/7/11 – Tape lifts from Milford Haven rape victim
- BKG/9/10 – Tape lifts from Milford Haven rape victim
- PAS/1/2 – Shotgun and cartridge belt found in Freystrop (after rape)
- Large quantity of ropes found at 34 St Marys Park, Jordanston.

Several other exhibits were the subject of the initial assessment but following advice from scientists were set aside for future consideration at a later date if necessary.

As far as the exhibits were concerned we needed to gather expert opinion on what we had. The original enquiries had identified the specific makes of shotgun cartridges used in the murders. At Scoveston Park wadding found in the bodies pointed to an Eley-type cartridge. In the case of the Dixons they were identified as being of Italian origin. There was a potential link with the cartridges found under the duck run at Cooper's home in 1998. Ammunition expert Graham Morris had significant knowledge of the Eley cartridge company after a thirty-three-year career which saw him finishing as managing director. As far as the Italian-manufactured cartridges were concerned, Brian Carter from Worcestershire was identified as someone who used to work for a company called Mediterranean Shooting Supplies back in the 70s and 80s that imported the Italian cartridges into the United Kingdom. Both these experts were invaluable in establishing the potential connectivity between certain cartridges and the two murder investigations. A local contact was Mr Neville Pryce Jones from County Sports shop in Haverfordwest. He had been spoken to during the original investigations because he was one of the main suppliers of ballistics in the county of Pembrokeshire. His wealth of knowledge again proved to be invaluable to the Ottawa team.

Research indicated that there were a number of unidentified fingerprint marks available from the Ottawa cases. The original documentation was held at the Fingerprint Bureau at Police Headquarters in Carmarthen. At the time of the murders the Western Criminal Records Office (WCRO) existed in Cardiff and all examinations relating to fingerprints were carried out at there or at the Serious Crime Fingerprint Unit within the Metropolitan Police force. When the WCRO closed in 1992 local forces created their own Fingerprint Bureaus and all existing documentation was transferred back to the local areas. Over subsequent years, various staff within Dyfed-Powys Police

Scientific Support Unit carried out analysis on outstanding fingerprints using the techniques available to them. These included Automated Fingerprint Recognition (AFR 1992) and the National Automated Fingerprint Identification Service (NAFIS). The latter was renamed as IDENT 1 in 2005. In addition, NAFIS saw the introduction of the Serious Crimes Cache that holds the unidentified marks gathered from a number of serious crime scenes in the UK. Certain marks from the Scoveston and Dixons scenes were stored within this cache and automatically searched against any new fingerprints taken across the whole of the UK. As part of the Operation Ottawa review, the services of Mrs Esther Neate of Neate Imaging Services in Chippenham were used in March 2007. Using the new technique of 'digital cleaning of fingerprints', she was able to enhance certain marks but disappointingly no formal identifications were made; another door had been closed on us.

As the saying goes, just as one door closes another one opens. We had engaged the services of handwriting expert Hilary Pritchard, from Llangrannog in West Wales. We wanted her to examine the writing on two ammunition boxes recovered from under Cooper's duck run. One was a Baikal ammunition cardboard box (AJM/216/6). The other was a MAX 5s box with 'MAXIMUM 5s' written on it in biro to indicate that a different type of cartridge had been added to the box. Research into the FSS case notes from Scoveston indicated that Richard and Helen Thomas owned similar shotgun cartridge boxes, which had writing on as well as owning a BAIKAL ammunition box. The suggestion was that Cooper might have stolen the ammunition boxes on the night of the murders and later hidden them under his duck run.

Unfortunately the actual boxes from Scoveston had been destroyed but we still had the examination notes of the handwriting. It was decided to use samples of Helen Thomas's handwriting that had been preserved from Scoveston together with the forensic notes to see if there was a connection. Samples of Cooper's writing were also used. The evidence, provided by Hilary Pritchard, was that the handwriting on the cartridge boxes recovered from Cooper's duck run could not have been written by John William Cooper or Richard Thomas, but could have been written by Helen Thomas. The evidence was interesting but not conclusive as the comparison samples were too brief to provide further evidence.

During Operation Huntsman a number of keys had been recovered from Cooper's cesspit but in 1998 they were unable to say whether any of them were connected to the missing keys from Richard Thomas's Rover car. One witness, a Mr Edward O'Brien, was revisited in 1998 and he confirmed that the bunch of keys referred to as GAL/96/1 were similar in all respect to keys used by Richard Thomas. We decided to look at this again with the help of forensic locksmith Ron Cliffe. Unfortunately, without the car itself and with Rover and British Leyland long gone, there were few manufacturing records left and he was unable to prove a link between the keys and Richard's car. I did consider a media appeal to find the car but decided against it.

The original pathologists back in the 1980s were Dr Owen Glynn Williams on Scoveston and Professor Bernard Knight on the Dixons. They were both living legends with decades of experience and we needed to talk to them. Bernard Knight was still an active man who had taken up writing in retirement and was a published author. The passing of time had diluted his memory somewhat but I was confident following my visit that he would be able to give evidence if required as long as he could have access to his original notes. Doctor Owen Glynn Williams, affectionately known as O.G., was considerably older and lived alone on the outskirts of Swansea. I visited him with Lynne Harries. O.G. greeted us at the kitchen door wearing his dressing gown and slippers, we introduced ourselves and he invited us in. As he shook hands with Lynne, he said, 'I have been thinking, that fracture to Richard Thomas's skull could have been as a result of a sharp blow to the head rather than caused by the shotgun blast.' This was unsolicited and struck a chord with both Lynne and myself. Gwenda Dixon had been struck to the head, probably rendering her unconscious, the victims of the Milford Haven Robbery and rape had also been struck about the heads with the butt of a shotgun; of course we knew that during his robberies Cooper had used the butt of his gun to strike his victims. We spent a couple of hours with O.G. and he was a fascinating, lovely man full of memories but I thought that he was too frail to give evidence in court.

Regular Gold Group Meetings chaired by DCC Andy Edwards were receiving updates from myself and deciding on logistical support and finance. This was all well and good but we were now in the summer of 2007 and had nothing to show on the forensic front. There was also a storm building. I had been notified that Cooper had applied for parole and a possible release date was September 2007. The pressure was on for the interview team to be ready before this date. His possible release and future management in the community would need a so-called multi-agency approach between the Probation

Service and the local police. The forum for managing dangerous offenders is called Multi Agency Public Protection Arrangements (MAPPA). In accordance with MAPPA guidance Cooper was identified as a Level Three Offender, the highest risk.

The local police, together with all the relevant agencies, had done all the groundwork in readiness for Cooper's release. Superintendent Euros Lewis was in charge of the process and for me this was great news. Euros was a living legend and one of the very best cops I had ever known. I loved working with him, as he was great fun. I recall one instance during a murder investigation when he wanted to bug a location where a suspect was going to be and possibly give away vital conversations. I was in charge of the force surveillance unit and responsible for producing the detailed applications for such activity for consideration by the Chief Constable. Euros was the SIO and phoned me to say, 'Wilkie, get your arse down here, boy, I want you to do the application so I can brief the deputy chief constable.' I hotfooted it down to Pembroke Dock and wrote the application. Euros said, 'Right, Wilkie boy, sit there and I will put the phone on loudspeaker, if the DCC asks a difficult question I will repeat it out loud and you give me the answer.' 'OK, Lew, it sounds a good plan,' I replied. Moments later the phone rang, it was DCC Keith Turner and Euros launched into his briefing. Every now and again he would look at me and nod, or shake his head. I responded by mirroring his actions. At the end of the conversation he put the phone down, rubbed his hands excitedly and said, 'Wilkie boy, job sorted.' I looked at him and said, 'I haven't got a clue, Lew boy, I am a scouser and you have been speaking Welsh for the last twenty minutes.' We rolled about laughing as we did many times working together. The other side of Lew was a dedicated, thorough and highly professional police officer, who I believe did not get the recognition he so deserved. I knew that if he represented us at MAPPA we could not have a better person.

Also at the forefront of our minds was the fact that we might soon have to interview Cooper. Over the years the public have seen many television programmes, from the *Sweeney* to *Life on Mars*, showing detectives quizzing suspects. All too often the detective is depicted as a bumbling, ill-prepared fool. I can promise you that a good interviewer is a highly skilled and professional individual. My team were well prepared with detailed and comprehensive strategies and it was time for them to start the build-up for the most important and challenging interviews of their career. The plan also included interviewing Cooper's family about his background. The question was, after all this time, would they be willing to speak?

Before the interviews with Cooper I wanted to unlock his family secrets. There was a feeling amongst the Huntsman and Ottawa teams that his family had knowledge and information that would help us understand the man and his habits. The view of the Huntsman team was that the family would come so far in disclosing information but feared him more than the police; they had made certain disclosures in 1998 but had not been able to see them through in court. It was important that the team gave every opportunity to the family to reveal any information or suspicions regarding the murders. With this in mind the interview team came together and started to prepare to face Cooper.

By now the process of submitting exhibits for examination was pretty slick, but the examinations themselves were revealing precious little. One Friday evening I spoke with Lynne and Glyn at Fishguard Port Office and each of us presented a persuasive argument as to what we believed had happened at each scene. Lynne was becoming increasingly more concerned that the scientific work lacked innovation. Invariably, he explained, it was the Ottawa team suggesting ideas to the forensic scientists about examining exhibits rather than the other way around. In particular two exhibits vexed us: surely if the rope used to secure the hands of Peter Dixon belonged to Cooper then there would be some DNA trace evidence? Low copy number DNA was now so sensitive it was difficult to imagine not getting something. It was at this point that Lynne started to talk about 'twenty-eight and thirty-four cycle DNA processes'. I had only just got my head around the cartridge manufacturers! The rope was crucial, as was one of the cartridges found under the duck run at Cooper's home. It was a pre-war cartridge with a cardboard finish casing and identical to cartridges found in the larder at Scoveston Park. It had a dirty brown stain on the casing, which had given an indication of blood; could it be the blood of one of the victims?

It was at this time that LGC informed us that a new process called Mini Filer was available but had not been validated in the UK. It was designed to develop degraded DNA. The problem we had was the time gap between the recovery of the exhibits and their examination; over time DNA degrades and can potentially be lost. Mini Filer therefore presented us with a fantastic opportunity. Previous tests on the cartridge had proved negative for blood but could the new process provide another chance?

Not long after this we had our first significant lead from the forensic tests. We were certain that the rope used to tie the hands of Peter Dixon (JAW/106) had been brought to the scene by the killer. This meant that at some stage he must have handled it in such a way that we could recover DNA evidence. LGC Forensics had worked hard on this item and tried every avenue open to them. They had raised a partial profile and some mixed profiles. Some DNA elements matched the profile of Cooper but the discriminating value was low, less than one in every three hundred of the population would have the same elements. It was interesting, but not enough for us to get excited about. LGC were suggesting that the new Mini Filer process might enhance the profile and could also be used on the shotgun cartridge shell that had at one stage tested positive for blood. Good news in one sense but we were six months off the process being validated and being admissible in our courts. I desperately wanted to interview Cooper before he was released into the community but by now his parole application was looming; the problem for us was that other than the circumstantial evidence we had precious little.

The Prison Service too was doing little to ease my concerns. Due to an administrative mix-up Cooper had been moved to an open prison. Superintendent Euros Lewis, yet again, saved the day when he noticed the error. This oversight was very quickly resolved and we were informed that Cooper had failed in his parole application. His next chance wasn't until September 2008; the pressure was off us for a little while at least.

Then followed some long discussions with DCS Steve Mears and DCC Andy Edwards and we agreed that the interview would be postponed whilst we awaited the validation of Mini Filer and the results from LGC on key exhibits. I could not believe that with all the hard work, it would not break in our favour. I had had a good feeling about Ottawa from day one and I needed to ensure that the team could see that I had not lost faith. I informed the team of our decision to delay the interviews and continue the forensic submissions and assessments. The interview team was stood down and we were again working hard on trying to find what I described as the 'golden nugget' of forensic evidence. By the autumn of 2007 it was becoming increasingly difficult to protect the confidentiality of the investigation and I did not want it leaked into the public domain. Lynne Harries and Glyn Johnson were my confidants and I trusted their judgement. We therefore agreed that now was the right time to go public. It would clearly make headline news both in Wales and around the UK so we wanted to observe how Cooper would react. Having kept his side of the bargain and sat on the story I knew that I had to keep our part of the deal with ITV Wales, so I called Jonathan Hill, who had maintained the news blackout we needed, and told him we were ready to go live. Clearly the force wanted the maximum publicity but ITV Wales had gone the extra mile in keeping up the contact over the months since our first meeting.

Trust is at the heart of any relationship and I was now beginning to trust Jonathan, he was someone I could do business with. We arranged to meet again to plan how we could get the maximum coverage. It was October and the country was gripped by speculation that Gordon Brown would take advantage of his lead in the polls and call a general election. Jonathan advised me that we should avoid the potential election date of the 8th of November. In the end the Prime Minister decided against and early election and we therefore decided to go for the 7th of November. The date was set and we filmed a series of special reports for the evening news programme. ITV said they would devote the bulk of their programme to the story, and we agreed that they would break the news. It was obvious that once the story was out there a feeding frenzy would follow. The Ottawa team and the local police commander would hold a news conference at Haverfordwest police station the morning after the news broadcast, to make sure that everyone got the story and we got the best possible coverage.

On the night of the 7th of November I met Jonathan on the coastal path just yards from where the Dixons had been murdered. It was a wet and blustery night and the narrow path was no place for the faint-hearted. Our location had been lit and we were preparing to go live when out of the gloom came a distressed old lady who asked if we had seen her dog. I could hear the producer counting down, forty-five seconds.

'Willy, where are you?' came the shrill voice from the darkness.

I could see the look of sheer horror on Jonathan's face. Oh shit, I thought, this is not what we planned and also who the hell would be walking along a coastal path in winter with an undetected double murderer still at large. With thirty seconds to air I was now slightly unnerved, but no sooner had she come around the corner of the path than she disappeared back into the sea mist. At exactly six o'clock we went live and Jonathan broke the news to

Wales. The programme carried a very emotional interview with Keith Dixon, the brother of Peter. I couldn't help thinking that he had been murdered in cold blood just yards from where we were standing. It was a very moving moment but I was keen to get the message across to the public and to Cooper, who I believed would be watching from his prison cell.

'We believe the answer to what happened all those years ago lies in this community,' I told the audience. It was a statement directed at Cooper but we did not know how he would react. I was careful not to formally link the Dixons' murder with the Scoveston case but I emphasised that the murders were being investigated side by side; the inference was clear, we believed the murders were connected and that the killer was a local man. The main thing I wanted to get across was that I felt forensic science would have a significant influence on the investigation. As we closed the broadcast I was desperate to know if we had received any calls and how the news had been received in the local community. Above all I wanted to know if Cooper had seen it but I would have to wait until 2008 when he was finally interviewed to discover his extraordinary reaction.

CHAPTER 11

'LET'S GET HIM TALKING'

It was ten years since Cooper had first been confronted with the accusation that he had been responsible for the murders. The interview had taken place during Huntsman, but was very brief and Cooper had heard nothing more since. I had made a point during the television appeal on ITV of directing my comments to him. 'I believe that forensic science will have a significant say in the outcome of this investigation,' I predicted and I hoped he would hear those words. The incredible advances in DNA have been well publicised in the media and during the broadcast on ITV I had reminded the audience, and of course Cooper, that on a national basis all successful cold case reviews had been detected by forensic science.

It was clear that the broadcast had also had an impact on the viewers. Within hours members of the public had contacted us and even my mother had been approached with information. While at the hairdressers, another customer, who knew I was her son, told her she had seen the man in the artist's impression on the day the Dixons' cash card was used in Pembroke. She had never come forward because she saw that other people had seen him and did not think her sighting was significant. A team was dispatched to see her immediately and she made a full statement; I had little doubt she had seen the man. She described walking along the coast path near Pembroke Dock with her son and pet dog. Walking the other way she saw a scruffy unshaven man pushing a bicycle and wearing shorts. He was carrying something over his shoulder secured by a strap or lanyard. As he walked towards them her pet dog started to bark at the man. She then described how he gave them a look that almost turned her to stone, his eyes were piercing but he said nothing and carried on walking. She was so frightened by his stare that she immediately went home with her son and locked the door. This sighting also triggered the question of identification. We had a number of witnesses who had seen the man at various locations, and in particular at the cashpoint. I could put together an album of images including a passport photograph taken of Cooper around the late 80s. Rules of evidence tell me that I should not consider photographs if the suspect is readily available to put in an identification parade, which of course he was. His appearance had significantly changed though, and any identification either way would be of little value. After further discussions, with Crown Prosecution Service lawyer Maggie Hughes, I was happy not to go down this route, although it had been fascinating to see that even after eighteen years there were still new witnesses coming forward.

The forensic strategy was now focused on those exhibits that we felt had the most potential for the DNA-enhancing Mini Filer technique. Glan Thomas concentrated on the ropes recovered from the scenes and from Cooper's house together with the stained, pre-war cartridge. The Forensic Management Group chaired by DCS Steve Mears was now well established and working well. Steve was able to probe some of the decision-making from an objective viewpoint. One exhibit of particular interest was a pair of shorts that had been recovered from Cooper's home during the Huntsman searches. They were found in a drawer in his bedroom and were described as khaki shorts (Police exhibit number AJM/165); could they be similar to those pictured in the artist's impression? The forensic spreadsheets were now a work of art. Glyn Johnson and Lynne Harries had developed a process which would later be identified as national best practice. We were able to electronically view all recovered exhibits, photographs and original documents from the comfort of an office in Headquarters. When we viewed the original photographs of the shorts, the disappointment was tangible. They looked more like blue/green silk shorts and nothing like the khaki shorts from the artist's impression. The style was similar, but the colour was not and we were of the opinion that they were of little value to the case.

As we stared at the pictures, Glan Thomas looked puzzled.

'What's troubling you, Glan, you look unhappy?' I said.

Glan knew his stuff and he was clearly less than convinced by our conclusion.

'Well boss, I have seen AJM/165 and they look nothing like the colour they are in the photo.'

Glan now had our full attention.

'You have to be careful if you make decisions based on the original photographs,' he said, 'the colour can be distorted by the quality of lighting and skill of the photographer.' By now we were hanging on his every word. 'AJM/165 are khaki shorts, I am sure of it and I can show you accurate photographs.'

Glan soon returned to the meeting with new photographs and yes they were indeed khaki and very similar in style to the artist's impression if not a little shorter. He showed us photographs of the shorts taken under a range of different lighting conditions and they all looked different in colour. The decision was now an easy one to make.

'Send them off for blood and DNA trace evidence right now,' I insisted.

Little did we know how important this decision would be. The experience also ensured that we would never make a decision based on original photographs of an exhibit; something we have shared nationally with our police colleagues.

We were now celebrating our second Christmas together and had organised a number of team building events, but 2007 had come and gone without a forensic breakthrough and it was tough. In early 2008 the Mini Filer forensic technique to enhance DNA was validated, allowing us to concentrate on a handful of exhibits that had shown promise, including the ropes and dirty old cartridge from under Cooper's duck run. The ropes were also subject to a separate strategy looking at knot evidence and forensics. The rope used to tie Peter Dixon's hands behind his back had a slipknot and looped end, but apart from that it was very nondescript. It appeared that the offender had slipped the loop over one of his wrists, tightening it before wrapping the rope around both wrists to secure him. Ropes recovered from Cooper's home had a similar set-up but were not of any evidential value; it was still interesting though.

Lynne Harries was in contact with LGC forensics on a daily basis and it was becoming clear that Mini Filer was not enhancing any previously raised profiles and the dirty brown stain on the cartridge had not tested positive for blood. Other key exhibits had revealed nothing to suggest they had been in contact with the murder victims of or the youngsters involved in the Milford Haven sex assaults. Other key exhibits had been extensively examined but to no avail: the khaki shorts had been tested for blood but with a negative result; the sawn-off shotgun and lanyard PH/2 and PH/2A, discarded by Cooper after the Sardis robbery had also been tested for blood and DNA, again with a negative result. At this stage fifty-six significant exhibits had been identified, twenty-eight had been forensically assessed and of these, eight had undergone the Mini Filer process without success. The forensic costs were already over £160,000 and it seemed we were back to square one.

The team were clearly disappointed and I needed to pick them up and refocus their efforts. With the excellent individuals I had working for me it was not difficult. We went out for lunch together, followed by a brainstorming session in the briefing room at Fishguard Port Office. Without exception we shared the view that as long as we kept faith in our process of recovery, assessment and submission something would come good. We believed the evidence was there, we just needed to find it. Lynne, however, was becoming increasingly uncomfortable with the forensic support from some experts; he felt that it was the Ottawa team suggesting examinations rather than the specialists. I felt LGC were in an awkward position because the Forensic Science Service had been heavily criticised in police circles and so the new forensic providers, like LGC, were understandably trying to maintain independence and impartiality. It was a fine balance, but Lynne had a point and I needed to keep an eye on it.

We were now entering the spring of 2008 and Cooper would be eligible for parole in September. I wanted to interview his close and extended family to unpick Cooper's complex life, explore his bad character and the circumstantial evidence. I needed to get the interview team back together to prepare. As ever DCC Andy Edwards and the chief officers were very supportive through the Gold Group. As long as I justified any additional resources, I knew that I had the full support of the force and Police Authority, represented by Councillor John Davies.

Colin Clarke had considered the strategy for the interviews with both witnesses and the suspect. His documentation was detailed and high quality and placed witnesses in certain categories, which would dictate how they would be dealt with. Everyone from hostile witnesses to vulnerable adults and children had to be considered and an appropriate strategy developed. Members of Cooper's immediate family would be key witnesses and needed their own specific strategies.

Constantly ticking in the background, like a grandfather clock, were the preparations for Cooper's release. The MAPPA team required information about his background to inform their decision-making but there was a risk of duplication and more importantly I needed to maintain a sterile corridor between the two processes to avoid any conflict of interest. The interview team was reconvened by May 2008 and started their detailed preparations. At the same time I needed to consider the impact of Cooper's previous interview and arrest in 1998 for both double murders. Potentially, Cooper's time in custody back then could reduce the interview time available to me this time around, unless I could produce fresh evidence that wasn't available to the Huntsman team. I didn't want to be a position that we had interviewed him only to find I had fallen foul of the Police and Criminal Evidence Act 1984 (PACE) and the interviews were inadmissible in court. CPS lawyer Maggie Hughes knew the case intimately, as she had been involved in providing advice to the Huntsman team. Maggie was greatly admired in police circles in Pembrokeshire; she was an awesome force in court and was a highly professional, committed lawyer. I asked Maggie to consider the issues I was facing and she responded quickly. Case law was unclear, but she was of the opinion that there was unlikely to be any major consequences from interviewing him whilst he was still in custody, as the provisions of PACE were designed to ensure police questioning was carried out fairly and expeditiously in order to secure an individual's release as soon as possible. The position would have been different if he was not already in prison.

I now needed to get a view from the CPS Complex Case Unit on the bad character, similar fact and circumstantial evidence. It was time to reveal our hand to them. It was arranged for us to present our case so far to the CPS at Police Headquarters in Carmarthen. Little did I know that this would be the start of a fantastic partnership that would become the cornerstone of our success. Jim Brisbane was the new Branch Crown Prosecutor, he was a very gently spoken Scotsman who had transferred to the area with a reputation of being a very helpful and practical man, and I was not disappointed. Tom Atherton was a proud Lancashire man, head of the Complex Case Unit, and I would come to like this man immensely, as would my team. Suzanne Thomas was a lawyer from the same unit and would be assisting any case preparation; she was a very sharp woman who would remain with the team until the very end.

Together with Lynne Harries and Glyn Johnson I presented the case so far. It was a fascinating story with some very interesting circumstantial links, but it lacked the forensic golden nugget. Tom was the most challenging. In his opinion the first obstacle would be the severance argument: the case relied on keeping both double murders and the Milford Haven robbery and rape together, as the behaviour and location of the Milford Haven offence pulled in the double murders. I was convinced that the murders were the bricks of the case but the Milford Haven attack was the mortar. Tom was of the view that we had an interesting case, but it would not get past severance and if they were split up the links would disappear. I feared this position but came to understand that it was Tom's way to challenge us, and I would grow to love it. He would become the voice of reason on my shoulder. Together we would agree common ground or find an alternative route to take, based on sound professional considerations.

'It's an interesting case, Steve,' he said, 'and would be overwhelming if you had some forensics in the middle, someone like Gerard Elias QC would love this, I might just speak to him early doors.' Tom was already thinking of who would be the best silk to prosecute for the Crown, both the team and I needed this support.

Cooper was now in a 'Category C' Prison and I needed to speak to the Head of Prison Security to make them aware that I would be looking to produce him from prison for interview. Following a letter to the governor, I had a personal meeting at Parc Prison in Bridgend and briefed them; this was just out of courtesy to allow them to plan. I was not expecting what happened next. Within days Cooper was re-categorised to Category A and moved to the high-security prison at Long Lartin. The full impact of this would not become clear until we developed our plans to produce Cooper for interview. It was less than helpful.

We were informed that Cooper would be brought from prison for interview on the 30th of June 2008, and I needed a detailed plan. At the same time I had to consider the disclosure tactics because there was a wealth of material to be considered by him and his legal advisor before his interview. My intention was to serve the disclosure material on them in advance for consideration so I could use his time with us to the maximum. I then had to submit a detailed report to the prison service to justify his production and interviews. It was at this stage that the impact of his re-categorisation as a Category A prisoner hit home. He would need to be transferred to our force area with a full police escort with sirens and blue flashing lights, and we could *not* pre-warn him of his production for interview in case anyone attempted to help him escape; the fact that he had hardly received a visitor in ten years and had been moved to a lower category prison suggested this would be extremely unlikely but it was a battle that I wasn't going to win. The ruling now meant that I could not serve the advance disclosure on him until he arrived in our cells in Carmarthen and would consequently lose a significant amount of the time. His solicitor was from Nottingham and I could not inform her either until he asked for his brief to attend. I was less than impressed with HM Prison Service to say the least!

It was like planning for D-Day: the custody plan was

developed by Chief Inspector Peter Westlake and needed to factor in the following: Accreditation of Ammanford police station to hold Category A prisoners, liaison with the Police Advisory Section in London to ensure compliance with Home Office guidelines and liaison with CPS to comply with the provisions of PACE. We would also have to work closely with our legal advisor to ensure compliance with current legislation and be in contact with officers from Parc Prison in Bridgend and Long Lartin in Evesham. We would have to hire a suitable prisoner collection company to transport the inmate from prison to the police station and back. This required a blue light escort throughout the journey. Furthermore we would need to liaise with Dyfed–Powys Magistrates Court's senior clerk to consider the legal process during the periods of detention within police cells. In addition, we would need all the relevant risk assessments and custody strategies to ensure the welfare and safety of the inmate and our police officers. Finally we would need a custody detention officer around the clock, including a dedicated duty inspector based in Carmarthen for the purpose of daily reviews. The custody staff would need to be handpicked because I didn't want anyone who might engage with him or react if he became obstructive, giving him an excuse to complain and waste valuable time. It was going to be quite an undertaking.

For weeks I had discussed our approach for this interview with Lynne Harries, Glyn Johnson and Colin Clarke. I wanted Cooper to have a free, unchallenged introduction and get him speaking about his life, interests, business ventures and family life. The custody plan ensured that Cooper had nothing to complain about or distract him. Most importantly the interview team were ready and I had total faith in them. They had scrutinised the statements taken from Cooper's family during the Huntsman investigation and further interviews that had revealed a fascinating but disturbing picture. Cooper was a man who could be a loving grandfather one moment and a violent abusive father the next. We had long stared at his photographs on the incident room wall. Now the time had come to face him in the flesh and we couldn't wait.

CHAPTER 12

FACING THE MAN

The 30th of June 2008 was a day that had been circled in red on the calendar. The police escort was dispatched to HMP Long Lartin to pick up Cooper. The team had assembled at Ammanford to make last-minute preparations. In the past Cooper had used a firm of solicitors from Nottingham when he appealed against his conviction for the 1996 Sardis armed robbery, and there was every indication that he would do the same this time.

Cooper had always maintained that he was innocent of the robbery but I was of the view that this was more to do with saving face with members of his family who still believed him. His tactics were to suggest that his son might well be responsible for some of his crimes but he always stopped short of directly accusing Adrian. What we knew was that Adrian was petrified of his father and feared for his own life. Curiously Adrian had also indicated to the police that he was changing his name by deed poll to Andrew Cooper. I have never been able to work this out; I could understand if he changed his surname but why just his Christian name? In interviews he had given us a harrowing account of life at home with his father. I had asked the interview team to compare it with statements he had made during Huntsman and they were pretty consistent.

He had also provided additional information, but I put that down to the skill of the interviewer. It was also clear that although the rest of his family had little time for Adrian and questioned his account, they actually corroborated the vast majority of what he said. At different times they had all witnessed Cooper's violent behaviour towards his son, so we were happy that he was telling the truth. Adrian himself doubted our ability to prove anything against his father.

Pat Cooper wanted nothing to do with the police. She had made very damming statements against him in the Huntsman investigation, detailing a life of physical and mental abuse, but had gone back on those statements during the trial; she obviously feared her husband more than she did the police. Teresa, his daughter, was consistent throughout; she had little time for her father but had a balanced view of the investigation. If he was guilty he deserved everything that was coming to him, if not, he should go free. I have never met Teresa, but I came to respect the way she dealt with the whole matter.

The telephone rang in the Ammanford CID office. 'He's arrived!' said the voice at the other end. I suddenly had a rush of adrenaline and looked at Lynne Harries.

'Come on, Lynne, let's see him get booked in.'

The rest of the custody area was empty; it was large, cold and unwelcoming even though it was relatively new. I have been in many custody suites over the years and some of them are very daunting places to be, particularly when you have a formidable sergeant looking down from an elevated position behind the booking in desk. Ammanford was no different. We could see Cooper through the safety glass in the door leading to the custody area. This was the first time I had seen him in the flesh. He was dressed in casual clothes; his hair was short and snow white. As he walked in, he visibly tensed his body as if saying to himself, 'OK I am here now and it's time for business.' He looked fit and strong, his eyes were dark and cold as he walked up to the custody desk and stood staring at the sergeant. The officer played it by the book and was very polite and professional. Cooper took time to read the documentation before him, perching his glasses on the end of his nose. The glasses were interesting; he had made a big deal about needing them during the Huntsman interviews, clearly using them as a distraction. This time nothing had been left to chance, the Ottawa team had sourced identical glasses and although he didn't know it we had a number of spare pairs should he need them.

Just before he was placed in the cell the sergeant asked him what he wanted to eat so arrangements could be made to get food. For a second Cooper hesitated. I think he sensed that he was being treated differently to the last time he was in police custody. Cooper disappeared into the cells and contact was made with his solicitor, who was asked to come as soon as possible for interviews. After several hours on the road from Nottingham his legal representative Mrs Suzanne Jovanovic arrived at the police station and was greeted by DS Colin Clarke, who gave her a written disclosure. It contained details of the partial DNA profile from the rope used to secure Peter Dixon's hands. I wanted to ensure that we did not overstate its value and it was important that the document was accurate.

All of the interviews were subject to downstream monitoring. This meant that we could hear the interview live in a separate location where a speed typist would make briefing notes for us to consider before feeding back pertinent points for clarification to the interview team. Gareth Rees, Nigel Jones and Louise Harries were fantastic, they had a game plan and they stuck to it. Cooper performed exactly according to the psychological assessments of him, made by psychologist Dr Jenny Bunton for his parole hearings. He appeared calm, wanted to be constantly in control, and when he was made to feel comfortable he was happy to talk about himself, which was exactly what we wanted him to do. If he was asked a difficult question, however, he would lead the interviewer away from the subject, to give himself thinking time, before returning to the question to offer an overly detailed response.

I have been present in many interview rooms over the years opposite some dangerous criminals but it was a strange experience to be sitting in a room away from the action with the interview being transmitted to me. With a less qualified team I might have been tempted to demand that certain questions be asked, but this team knew exactly what they were doing, exactly what they wanted to ask and when they wanted to ask it. In the early stages they deliberately used an interviewing technique that didn't challenge Cooper. It made him more confident in the knowledge that he had a free run at saying what he wanted and painting his own picture of himself. He loved talking; the results were fascinating and as the week went on came the realisation that he was playing right into our hands.

Cooper was interviewed thirteen times over a four-day period from Wednesday the 2nd of July to Saturday the 5th of July 2008. The interview strategy consisted of eleven 'account' interviews on a number of different topics. The account interview is where a suspect gives their version of events, it's followed by a 'challenge' interview whereby inconsistencies and anomalies are highlighted, giving them an opportunity to respond. The final interview was purely on the bad character evidence that had been drawn from the previous Huntsman conviction, together with statements and interviews with his family and other witnesses.

All advanced disclosure information was given to his solicitor by means of a briefing package, including photographs. Further information was provided by means of a verbatim audio-taped disclosure. In particular I wanted to ensure that any reference to the forensic findings was accurate and admissible. On Tuesday the 1st of July 2008, Mrs Jovanovic conferred with Cooper and briefed him on the disclosure material. No interviews were carried out on that evening and Cooper was allowed to rest and consider the information provided in the briefing. The first interview commenced at 9.47 a.m. on Wednesday the 2nd of July 2008.

In the main this interview dealt with Cooper's background and personal life at the time leading up to the Scoveston Park murders in December 1985. Cooper stated that he learned of the murders of Richard and Helen Thomas from his father-in-law, Percy Thompson (now deceased). At that time he was living at 34 St Marys Park and was also developing a smallholding known as The Beeches. On 21st of October 1978, Cooper had won £94,000 and a car on Spot the Ball. This was a significant amount of money and effectively made Cooper a wealthy man at that time. The remainder of the interview concerned Cooper's financial situation including business interests at Big House Farm and buying and selling property in the area. The research carried out by the Ottawa team showed that Cooper disposed of in excess of £125,000 during this period with little or nothing to show for it. The next interview commenced at

2.51 p.m. hrs on Wednesday the 2nd of July 2008. At the start of Cooper stated, that he had given some eight or nine thousand pounds of his winnings as gifts to his family. This was the first indication that Cooper was attempting to pre-empt, or second guess, what information we had. He was attempting to explain where some of his money had gone. He was further interviewed about his business dealings, his income and buying and selling property, including vehicles. He alleged that he had been let down by solicitors on some of his financial dealings, that an estate agent had tricked him out of money over the sale a property called Valetta Villa, the bank had over-charged him on interest rates and that his son Adrian had stolen between ten and twenty thousand pounds from him over a period of time.

Cooper demonstrated that when it came to money he had a computer-like memory for the cost of certain items. For example he was able to recall that the price of air tickets to America, to see his wife's sister Lorna in 1979, was £1,250. He also recalled the profit on selling a chicken or turkey was £1–£1.50, and the cost of stabling was £10 or £15 depending on the service provided. The cost of a bale of hay was 70 pence, or 40 pence if he had to collect it from the field himself. He explained going to court with his books and his records because the tax office tried to charge him £1,200. What became clear at this point was that Cooper's memory was highly selective; something that became more apparent when discussing issues more closely related to the murders.

The second part of the interview was concerned with probing Cooper about his gambling habits, the extent of which he had consistently played down. This position was strongly disputed by witness testimony from his family and other people. Cooper maintained he was spending just three or four pounds on a Saturday, particularly in the latter years before his imprisonment, which was probably what he had told his wife and his family. What is evident from witness testimony was that when Cooper had a lot of money, he gambled a lot of money. The evidence from local bookmakers showed that it was an addiction and we believed it was the key motive for his offending.

The next interview started at 6.55 p.m. hrs on the 2nd of July. The purpose of this interview was to ask Cooper about his knowledge of Scoveston Park, Richard and Helen Thomas and the surrounding area, firearms, ammunition and ropes. Cooper suggested that a local man called Terry Valestra had given him the shotgun and ammunition, found buried under his duck run. Valestra had already given evidence at the Huntsman trial to say this was not true. In addition the ammunition under the duck run did not come from the same burglary as the shotgun. We, of course, believed that the ammunition box probably had Helen Thomas's writing on it and had been stolen by Cooper from Scoveston Park during the murders. Was Cooper trying to anticipate what evidence we had in order to explain it away? Cooper was most insistent that he had handled the gun from under his duck run, more interestingly he went to great lengths to tell the officers that in court during the Huntsman trial he had handled the sawn-off shotgun (PH/2) abandoned as the robber fled the scene of the Sardis robbery. He suggested it had been handed around the court. He was clearly thinking of DNA and the possibility that forensic science could now link it to him. In the unlikely event that he would ever be handed a gun in court, he was trying to give an innocent explanation for any DNA trace evidence belonging to him. The shotgun had been recovered from a hedgerow along with other items of property such as gloves, a fleece and the balaclava that contained Cooper's head hair. Not at any time since the gun had been found, had Cooper handled it and he had never admitted this offence; in fact during the Huntsman trial he even suggested another local man was likely to be the robber.

Cooper was further questioned about ropes and knots. He stated that in the main he always had ropes to use on his boat or for farming. He said he often picked them up on beaches and just threw them in his shed. He insisted the only knots he would tie were granny knots. The next interview took place at 10.42 a.m. on Thursday the 3rd of July 2008. Cooper was asked to clarify his comments and confirm he had handled the Sardis gun (PH/2) in court. He was vague and hedged his bets this time. 'I might have, it was being handed about,' he told the officers before going on to suggest that the prosecuting barrister and police were trying to play tricks on him to get him to handle the gun. Why was he so concerned about a gun involved in a robbery for which he had served his sentence? Cooper was shown photographs of an old single-barrel shotgun recovered from a hedge at his home address in 1998. He stated he did not recognise it.

As we know, at the time of his arrest in 1998 Cooper had five hundred keys, a large number of which were recovered from his cesspit. This was a significant find and demonstrated the extent of the searches conducted at his property. Cooper was quite agitated during this part of the interview and gave a lengthy explanation as to how he had innocently accumulated many keys over the years in what he described as his 'bucket of keys'. For me and the rest of the team, keys were obviously a significant feature in Cooper's offending. It was what we described as his 'thumb print' over the offences. Cooper clearly stole keys. Only he knew the reason why, but I felt it was a control feature, and that the keys were also mementos from his offending. Perhaps he wanted his victims to feel threatened in the knowledge that he could return to terrorise them at any time. During his Huntsman interview he suggested his pet dog had knocked his bucket of keys into the cesspit. Now he changed his story. Instead of the dog, he now suggested that it was in fact Adrian who was probably responsible for putting the keys into the cesspit. What emerged as the interviews progressed was Cooper's determination, at any opportunity, to discredit his son. It appeared that Cooper was very concerned about any testimony which Adrian might have given to police and he wanted to get his retaliation in first.

One of the keys recovered from Cooper had been forensically matched to an internal door at Norton Farm. The Thomases owned the farm and Richard had gone there on the afternoon of his murder. As a key is turned in a lock it comes into contact with the internal mechanisms and leaves unique scratches and marks. A forensic locksmith had examined these and found that the key discovered at Cooper's home had marks on it that could only have been made by the lock at Norton Farm. This was interesting, but did not mean Cooper was the murderer; the key could have been stolen some time before the murders but for me the forensic match coupled with Cooper's habit of keeping keys from his crimes, was significant.

The topic then moved on to Cooper's knowledge of the Thomases and Scoveston Park. Cooper insisted that he had only met Richard and Helen Thomas on about five or six occasions, and only in passing. He described Helen Thomas as a pushy woman, but offered little evidence to justify this observation. Two interesting issues emerged at this point; firstly Cooper suggested that he had been in contact with Richard Thomas's car. The car had been found at Scoveston after the murders with the doors open. Cooper suggested that every year Richard Thomas would visit a mutual friend called Flo Evans, who brewed her own beer and wine. Richard used to buy some of the beer from Flo and Cooper said he would help Richard load it into his car; he repeated this on more than one occasion. Cooper was trying to give us an innocent explanation for why we may have found forensic traces of him on Richard's car. Of course we didn't have this evidence but Cooper didn't know it. Cooper went to great lengths to confirm the make and colour of the Rover car; he was clearly concerned about it. Secondly, Cooper said that Flo Evans had mentioned to Richard about him renting some land at Norton Farm and that Richard had refused and driven off. He suggested that this was a typical response from Mr Thomas contradicting his supposed limited knowledge of the man.

The following exchanges from the interview are very revealing. It's important to keep in mind the fact that Cooper had been arrested for the murders in 1998 and had received a comprehensive briefing two days prior to the interviews giving him more than enough time to consider his responses:

POLICE: 'Tell me about times that you actually went to Scoveston Park.'

COOPER: 'I can't ever remember ever going to Scoveston Park. I've seen pictures of the place and I've seen in the papers and what have you. It's such a long time ago, there would be no reason for me to go there and I can't, I can't ever recall. My wife may have, to run Flo back and fore, because she used to run Flo back and fore more than I did, but not that I can recall.'

POLICE: 'You mentioned you don't think you've ever been to Scoveston Park?'

COOPER: 'No, not that I can remember.'

POLICE: 'What about the land owned by Richard Thomas?'

COOPER: 'No, the land that I farmed for Jordanston is the other side of the Gulf road, it doesn't run to it, they are separate so when you're working land like that you get to know cos different fields got different names and usages, so the farming I did was the other side of the road.'

POLICE: 'And have you ever farmed or assisted or helped Mr Thomas or worked his land?'

COOPER: 'No, no, no. You couldn't, he was a loner, one of life's loners, you just respect it like, you know.'

POLICE: 'And in relation to farming did Mike Richards or anybody else associated with you borrow any machinery or vehicles from Richard Thomas?'

COOPER: 'No, I wouldn't have thought so, no. In my opinion and in Mike Richards's opinion, no, he weren't a person that you could ask for things.'

POLICE: 'OK, we've asked you whether you've ever been there. There are different parts and we have to give you the opportunity of answering . . . have you ever been inside the house there?'

COOPER: 'I've already answered the question that I have never been to Scoveston, I can never recall going to

Scoveston so that is my answer. I can never recall going to Scoveston.'

POLICE: 'Outside then, the number of outbuildings, have you ever been to those outbuildings?'

COOPER: 'Well I'll go back to my previous answer I can never recall going to Scoveston, never.'

POLICE: 'And in relation to the fields forming part of the Scoveston estate?'

COOPER: 'No, no.'

POLICE: 'Have you ever been in those?'

COOPER: 'No, not that I can recall. I didn't do the farming up that end.'

POLICE: 'OK. Have you ever taken any vehicles there to refuel?'

COOPER: 'No.'

POLICE: 'OK. Have you ever taken any ropes to the premises?'

COOPER: 'I've never been to Scoveston Park.'

POLICE: 'OK. In your dealings with Richard and Helen Thomas did they give you anything?'

COOPER: 'Did they, no never, no. Most I ever did for them was put things in their car for them from Flo.'

POLICE: 'Did you ever give anything to them or lend anything to them?'

COOPER: 'No.'

POLICE: 'So in essence what you're telling us as far as you can recall you can never remember visiting there?'

COOPER: 'No, I can remember meeting them at Flo's, Thornhill.'

*

Cooper was clearly distancing himself from ever visiting Scoveston Park. This contradicted a number of witnesses who had put John Cooper on land at Scoveston Park and even working there. Cooper gave the impression that the murders were discussed amongst the family on a number of occasions and that they were shocked and disturbed that Richard had been involved in a gay relationship. He said that they felt this was the motive for the murders. At the end of this interview DS Rees stressed the importance of Mr Cooper recalling whether he had ever been to Scoveston Park or not.

The next interview commenced at 3.24 p.m. on Thursday the 3rd of July 2008. The first part of the interview was about Cooper's character and how he saw himself as a person. He described himself as a very kind person who would do anything to help people out. In reality people gave Cooper a wide berth. Cooper did agree that he shouted a great deal, but claimed he was not a violent man; he said the shouting was because of the behaviour of his son Adrian, who he suggested was 'out of control'. Again it was clear that he was going out of his way to discredit his son, who had already told us about a life of misery at the hands of his father. (It should be noted that nothing Adrian had told us about his father in his testimony had been put to Cooper.) Adrian had suggested his father constantly justified his own behaviour but once he had done so he would be fine. This echoed what forensic criminal psychologist Dr Adrian West had told us: 'Cooper was dangerous because he could justify everything he did.' When asked about the unprovoked assault on his former landlord Mike Richards, Cooper again deflected any blame to Richards, suggesting *he* was responsible for what happened. What we knew was that Mike Richards was so frightened of Cooper that he hadn't collected rent for over nine years, amounting to over £7,000 in lost income.

The interview then moved to the events of the 22nd of December 1985, and the murders. Cooper was questioned, and given the opportunity to comment on his whereabouts for the relevant time. He maintained he was at home, busy preparing poultry as it was just before Christmas.

POLICE: 'OK. Right, we are now going to discuss or concentrate on the events on Sunday the 22nd of December 1985. The night of the brutal murder of Helen and Richard Thomas. The way we are going to, or the questioning is going to, give you an opportunity to tell us whether you were the person responsible, OK? And by doing that for the offence of murder we have to run through the various stages of the incident, OK? And asking you at each stage whether you were the person who is responsible for each stage of the incident, OK? And also give you the opportunity to give any lines of defence, mitigation or alibi, OK? And also to give you the opportunity of explaining whether or not the sequence of events is correct, OK? So I can appreciate that some of the areas we are going to touch upon, some of the questions may be difficult but as you have seen throughout—'

COOPER: 'Sorry I don't want to interrupt. That's quite simple. I didn't kill them, so I didn't kill them, end of story.'

POLICE: 'OK. Tell me whether you were the person who approached Scoveston Park House that night?'

COOPER: 'No, I didn't kill anybody at Scoveston Park, I was feathering and preparing turkeys and delivering turkeys and doing turkeys for two weeks at least.'

POLICE: 'The crime scene assessment shows the vehicle is parked in the yard at Scoveston and that the driver's door was open.'

COOPER: 'I've seen photographs.'

POLICE: 'Tell me whether you saw that vehicle that night.'

COOPER: 'Er no.'

POLICE: 'The crime scene assessment shows that the keys to the vehicle were missing.'

COOPER: 'I see, yeah.'

POLICE: 'Tell me, were you the person responsible for taking the keys away from the scene?'

COOPER: 'No.'

POLICE: 'A crime scene assessment shows that in an outbuilding there was a deposit of blood. Were you the person responsible for attempting to conceal that item?'

COOPER: 'Er no.'

POLICE: 'From the crime scene assessment it is evident that Richard Thomas received two shotgun wounds, one was a close contact shot to the abdomen; were you the person responsible for shooting Richard Thomas to the abdomen?'

COOPER: 'No.'

POLICE: 'He also sustained a raking shot, part of which was retained in the side of his face. Tell me whether you were the person responsible for shooting Richard Thomas to the face.'

COOPER: 'No.'

POLICE: 'From the crime scene assessment and post-mortem, it is evident that Helen Thomas was shot, or received a shotgun wound to the base of her skull. Explain whether you were the person who shot Helen Thomas.'

COOPER: 'No, I was not.'

POLICE: 'Tell me whether you were the person responsible for setting fire to Scoveston Park that night?'

COOPER: 'It wasn't me, no.'

POLICE: 'Examination of the crime scene also shows, following a search of the premises, there were no shotguns present, OK. So when the police got there and the scene was searched and examined there were no shotguns present. Tell me whether you were the person responsible for removing shotguns from Scoveston Park that night?'

COOPER: 'No, it wasn't me, no.'

POLICE: 'In relation to Scoveston, just a few further points I'd like to cover. You mentioned that you may have touched the Rover car innocently whilst it was outside.'

COOPER: 'I definitely touched the Rover car over at Flo's to put stuff in the car and when the gentleman used to come in, that's right, he used to usually leave the driver's door open. You know, he'd get out of the car; he wasn't a door shutter when you went over there. Because he was never there that long. It was an in and out.'

POLICE: 'OK. In relation to Scoveston, I'm going to show you some photos now and ask you whether you've been in particular parts of this property, OK?'

COOPER: 'Sure.'

POLICE: 'I'm showing you photographs. The first one I'll be showing you is a front photo of Scoveston Park just after the fire. Can you see that photograph?'

COOPER: 'Yeah.'

POLICE: 'OK, have you ever been inside that property?'

COOPER: 'Oh no, no, no.'

POLICE: 'The next photo I'm going to show you is an outhouse at Scoveston which is photo number 2 in the same photo album. Can you see that outbuilding there?'

COOPER: 'Er, yes I can, yeah.'

POLICE: 'The next photo is of the lane leading down to Scoveston Park. Tell me whether you've been down that lane? Is there anything you feel you should tell us at the moment, then, in relation to the offence we are investigating about Scoveston?'

COOPER: 'Er, I was far too busy, far too busy. Only ten days before maybe until about a day or two after Christmas.'

POLICE: 'OK. Are there lines of enquiry or defences you think we should be investigating at this stage?'

COOPER: 'Could I speak with my solicitor please?'

POLICE: 'Yeah, we are coming to an end now anyway, so it would be an opportune time perhaps for you to have a chat with her.'

COOPER: 'OK. Just to clarify anything at this stage. May I say something before then?'

POLICE: 'Yes, certainly.'

COOPER: 'It's just to confer. Does that mean things not, not to do with me. Because I mean we are here to talk about me, at the moment, so do you mean others not concerned with me, that question?'

POLICE: 'I mean what I mean. Obviously we are investigating the offence of murder of Richard and Helen Thomas.'

COOPER: 'Yeah.'

POLICE: 'So if there's anything you feel you could assist us in our investigation with that offence, this is your opportunity to tell us about that.'

COOPER: 'Oh yeah, yeah, I want to. We spoke about this earlier on and I may have, I don't know. If it was, it was a fleeting visit to pick up machinery for Mike Richards. So Mike Richards could answer better than I. I'm really not sure.'

POLICE: 'Tell me whether you've ever been inside that outbuilding?'

COOPER: 'Oh not to my knowledge, no, I wouldn't have thought so.'

POLICE: 'The next photograph I'm going to show you is the photo from the same album of the yard area, by the outbuildings.'

COOPER: 'Yeah.'

POLICE: 'Tell me whether you've ever been to that area?'

COOPER: 'Now I'm not sure about that one. I'd have to go on Mike Richards' judgement.'

POLICE: 'We discussed blood. We found Richard Thomas's blood in the outhouse, OK? I'm showing you a photograph that is the last but one photograph in the album. Tell me whether you've ever been inside?'

COOPER: 'Not to my knowledge, no.'

The next interview was fascinating and confirmed that Cooper had watched the ITV News broadcast from the coastal path on the night of the 7th of November 2007. (The names of the actual people have been changed to protect their identity.)

POLICE: 'Thank you. As I said, you are here to be interviewed in connection with the murder of Richard and Helen Thomas. This offence occurred on the 22nd of December 1985. In previous interviews over the last couple of days we have spoken to you about numerous matters which include your knowledge of the offence, your movements on the night in question and your, your use and knowledge of ropes, guns, ammunition. At the end of the last interview you indicated you wished to speak to your solicitor, is there anything you wish to add at this stage of the interview process regarding your knowledge of the events at Scoveston?'

COOPER: 'Yes, um, you asked me a specific question after I answered to the best of my ability, ah, questions about, ah, any involvement . . .'

POLICE: 'Yes.'

COOPER: '. . . that I may have had in these murders, which I had indicated there was not. Then you asked me do I know anything else not appertaining to me about that and I indicated that I wished to speak to my solicitor.'

POLICE: 'That's correct.'

COOPER: 'I'd already had discussions with my solicitor about an item that I will reveal to you now. But because of the treatment by the police to me on previous occasions . . .'

POLICE: 'Yes.'

COOPER: '. . . I explained to my solicitor that I didn't want to ah introduce this at any early stage because I considered this um whole interview about John Cooper.'

POLICE: 'Right.'

COOPER: 'Now I have been accused of lying by the police and courts and trying to put in smoke screens about anything that I have been involved in in my life, and so this item, whether it's anything or not, it is nothing to do with me it is up to you people so I will, I will.'

POLICE: 'OK.'

COOPER: 'It's simply this, I was in Parc Prison Bridgend as you know and there was an incident in Parc Prison in November last year. It wasn't actually an incident it was something that was said to me. OK um I'll just try and give you a picture of what it was, the incident, although it may be just a throw-away and not so much me, but you have to be cautious of what it is because in prison unfortunately there are weird characters. OK so basically it is this: I do carpentry in prison and I do work for lots of guys, for inmates. I was asked by the prison to make a chair or something for the local hospital to raffle, because they know I'm pretty good and I make people things. And so I made a Windsor chair. An inmate in prison saw what I did and wanted one for his son. This inmate was called um Gareth Mills. I saw him on the landings leaning over because usually I do my writing in my cell. I went looking for him because I had finished his chair, I went to him and I said, your chair's finished its lovely blah blah, and we were leaning on the rail like this. And he said, Coop, he said, you're from Milford Haven. I said yes, he said do you know Dillon? No I don't know Dillon, I've heard of Dillon from Hakin somewhere in Milford Haven. So he said do you know Dillon? I said yes and he says – now it doesn't matter at this stage [what he said] because he either said [Dillon] was tooled up – you know what tooled up means?'

POLICE: 'Yes.'

COOPER: 'Or he said [Dillon was] drunk one night. And Dillon was supposed to have said to Mills, um he did the Milford murders. It stunned me for a while and my reaction was to say, what? He said Dillon said he did the Milford murders; I said uh have you told somebody about this? He said no, no and I said do you think you should tell somebody about this? And he said yes, yes maybe. Now Mills was going out, this was November. Now the exact date is in my diary because I thought it relevant enough to put in my diary. So all I can say is that in this moment in time, it was in November. Yes the exact date is in my diary. So Mills was getting out January this year. Now he's originally from Pembroke Dock, I actually put his prison number in there but I can't, I can't remember it offhand. He's from Pembroke Dock. He said he was going to try and get a place in Hakin or Milford Haven. Now that is the sum total of it all. Ah so I didn't want to introduce that at any stage earlier because we're here about me not about this.'

POLICE: 'Yes.'

COOPER: 'So that is what it is, nothing or whatever. So he said Dillon said to me he did the murders, and I and I said well I think you should tell somebody about it. And he says yes maybe, and that was the conversation, I walked away from him, and I sort of sat down by myself, and I entered it in my diary so it is in my diary for what it's worth.'

Cooper confirmed that the term, 'Milford Murders' related to the Scoveston Park offences. Dillon was well known to me, I had arrested him in 1995 for a robbery in Milford Haven, in which he had tied up the victim. It was big local news at the time and Cooper would have known this. He was the ideal person to throw into the frame. What Cooper didn't know was that Dillon was in prison at the time of the murders and it could not have been him. Fast-track enquiries with Gareth Mills were carried out and he denied having anything to do with Cooper, and we had no reason to doubt him. The diary was quickly recovered from his cell, and it showed an entry for the 7th of November 2007. In it Cooper indicated he has been told that Dillon committed the Milford Haven murders. That very same night I had stood on the coastal path and said that the murders were being reopened and that forensic science would have a significant say in the outcome. Even more telling was the press cuttings in the diary dated after the 7th of November, which detailed the impact of DNA evidence on high-profile cases. From the 7th of November 2007, Cooper had become very interested in DNA. He was clearly a worried man.

The next interview began at 10.46 a.m. on Friday the 4th of July 2008. Prior to the interview at 9.45 a.m, the interview advisor DS Clarke spoke to Cooper's solicitor and informed her that we needed to clarify an issue, and that we would then move on to the Dixons inquiry. Mrs Jovanovic asked DS Clarke when the results of the Scoveston Forensic issues would be known.

POLICE: 'I appreciate last night's interview was quite stressful, you had a lot to say about Adrian. Your solicitor's mentioned that you've got something you wish to bring to my attention in this interview so I'll give you the opportunity now then.'

COOPER: 'Thank you. It's just four of the points that I answered questions on yesterday and after going back to the room I remembered more details about these things so if I could just tell you more details.'

POLICE: 'Yeah.'

COOPER: 'On the point of have I been in the yard at Scoveston, I'm 95 per cent sure that I have. Do you have a photograph of the yard in Scoveston?'

POLICE: 'We don't have it in this interview; we'd be able to get one for the next.'

COOPER: 'There's something that sparked my memory and it's a clock, it's like a clock tower. Now if there's a clock tower in there, see it's a bit confusing because it's so long ago and there was lots of pictures in the paper and sometimes you think you've been to somewhere and you maybe haven't.'

POLICE: 'Yeah, I appreciate that.'

COOPER: 'But there was a distinctive clock tower, now the more I think of it, I believe I have been in that yard for Mr Mike Richards, to pick up irrigation equipment I would believe, and with me then would have been Stanley Lewis, and his sons John and Paul, Dougie Davies, Chris Thomas. It'll be a number of those, not all of them but a number of them would, those were his main workers, but it would have been for Mike Richards. And sorry, the other part is have I been in the buildings or the rooms there – the guys did nose around without a shadow of a doubt, so it's a possibility. But yes I believe I'd been in there and yes it was to pick up irrigation equipment I believe many years ago.'

POLICE: 'OK in terms of nosing around the rooms do you mean in the outbuildings or in the house itself?'

COOPER: 'Ah not in the house, no not in the house, it was in the yard, it was a full muddy yard, very impressive but very dilapidated, which for me as a builder it was not nice to see things like that, it was sad. And yeah the guys nosed round naturally but I was there to pick up irrigation equipment. But you know he, and of course he had workers to do his farms, you can't run farms, so he did have friends, acquaintances and all but for people that he didn't know, he had to really know a person first like me, and other people he didn't know, he would be one-word answers, so just to elaborate on that. And the keys, you mention, you asked me did I touch the keys of a Rover car, my answer was no, my answer is still no. But I'd like to add that that was an old Rover, I will guarantee that at least twenty keys in my famous bucket would've fitted the locks to that car, I would guarantee it. Because on older cars with worn locks, not necessarily the same make of car key would fit it, any car key would fit it if it was worn so yes, my bucket most probably had about twenty estimate, that would have opened the lock to that car, to any old car, because they were worn.'

Cooper also explained that he was part of shooting parties that would hunt on various parts of land around Scoveston Park, and that he and the men would swap cartridges. His answers revealed that he was desperate to explain any forensic trace of him that might be found in the outbuildings at Scoveston, on the Rover car and on keys and on the cartridges under his duck run. Cooper had had more than enough time and detailed disclosures to come up with these explanations. At this point I so wished we had the Rover car! Another interesting point came out of the interview. Shortly before the Dixons were murdered Cooper's landlord Mike Richards, whom he had previously assaulted, served him with notice to quit his home in Jordanston. Cooper admitted that after this he stopped going into the fields for a while so as to avoid being seen by Mr Richards. This might explain why he left his usual offending area and moved further afield to somewhere he knew well, the Pembrokeshire Coastal Path.

Cooper was then questioned about his knowledge of the Dixons and the Little Haven area. He indicated that he had seen the pictures of the couple during the investigation but did not know them. He went to great lengths to distance himself from the coastal path area, and Talbenny Church, which overlooked the murder scene.

Next, Cooper was asked about his wedding ring. He indicated that he had hardly worn it after an accident on an oil rig, and that he could not remember what it was like. He said he had taken it off and put it in a trinket box in his house. He even mocked the officers by suggesting they probably still had the ring. His voice was uncomfortable and Gareth Rees pushed him by asking him to describe it. Cooper was uneasy. Then, out of the blue, he volunteered that he had handled stolen jewellery and sold it in Pembroke. Why was he doing this? As we listened in the monitoring room it became clear: he thought we had Peter Dixon's wedding ring and that we were about to confront him with it. This was a man who had been interviewed more than forty times before and had admitted nothing, and yet here he was volunteering that he had been handling stolen property. He knew that if Gareth did produce the ring he could suggest that it had been stolen by someone else and only sold by him. Again he was trying to get his alibi and explanation in first. Little did he know how useful this tactic would prove to us. We had done our homework and officers had recovered from a jewellers shop on Main Street in Pembroke copies of the receipts given to Cooper for a wedding ring he had sold at the time of the Dixons murder.

POLICE: 'I'm going to show you some receipts now, John.'

COOPER: 'Yeah.'

POLICE: 'First receipt I'm showing you is a copy of exhibit RTS/1 which is from receipt book, and the number is 468 dated the 5th of July, 1989 with the name J. COOPER, 34 St Marys Park, Jordanston, Neyland. It says "twenty-two-carat wed" on the top and there's a signature J.W. COOPER on the bottom. Can you see that?'

COOPER: 'Yes I can see that, yeah.'

POLICE: 'Can you confirm whether or not that's your signature at the bottom?'

COOPER: 'Yes, that looks like my signature. I will add my son was very good at doing my signature as our cheque books will, my wife could confirm but, but I'm not saying that doesn't belong, I would accept that that's mine until its proved any different, OK yeah, yeah.'

POLICE: 'And the question is on the 5th of July, 1989 were you the person who sold a ring to the jewellers?'

COOPER: 'Long time ago, long time ago. I will, I've already said I used to sell to a guy in main street, Pembroke and I bought and sold all my life. Always have done.'

POLICE: 'The second item I'm going to show you is a second receipt, Police Reference number RTS which is dated the 17th of January, 1990 which is receipt number 524 and at the top is S. Gold, again with the signature at the bottom which appears to be J. COOPER. Can you see that there?'

COOPER: 'In 1990. We didn't live in the Beeches in 1990. That would be very, very suspect and do you know why, where's the "W"? Where's the "W"?'

POLICE: 'And you're pointing out you didn't live in the Beeches.'

COOPER: 'No.'

POLICE: 'And for the benefit it says J. COOPER, The Beeches, Brickhirst Road, Johnston.'

COOPER: 'Yeah, and it's a place not. It's not. It's Brickhirst Park Road.'

COOPER: 'Can I see that again?'

POLICE: 'Yes certainly. I'm handing it back to John. So what you're saying, you normally dealt with Mr Waters.'

COOPER: 'Normally. Normally.'

POLICE: 'In the same street.'

COOPER: 'Yeah. If this was me this was very odd.'

POLICE: 'Can you explain any reason why you'd go to another jeweller in the same street.'

COOPER: 'Maybe if he was shut. That would be a reason, but it would be such an isolated occasion, it's hard to remember. Yeah.'

POLICE: 'And obviously you have stated categorically that you sold your wedding ring at that time.'

COOPER: 'I can't remember. I may have sold my wedding ring. I don't know.'

POLICE: 'Can you explain or give a reason as to why you'd sell your wedding ring at that time.'

COOPER: 'I would never wear my wedding ring. I never wore my wedding ring since about '69. I can't understand why I would sell my wedding ring.'

★

The next interview commenced at 6.52 p.m. on Friday the 4th of July 2008.

POLICE: 'I understand that before we start questioning you may have some matters you'd like to bring to our attention.'

COOPER: 'Yes, yes I do. I do, a bit embarrassed but there we are, the mind goes blank, the mind goes blank. Yes in relation to two photostats that you showed me of transactions.'

POLICE: 'Yes.'

COOPER: 'Right, I'm still not sure whether I carried out those transactions, but it was not normal, I usually dealt with Mr Waters, it's not impossible that I didn't because as I explained earlier, I've been buying and selling things since I was on the site in 1979, 1980, sovereign rings and things like that, so it is a possibility. One thing I can categorically say the ring is not mine, not. I'm adamant that ring is not mine, I can't be so certain that I didn't sell it but it is definitely not mine. I had my ring for my wife's twenty-fifth anniversary because I wore it, I actually wore it. And that also coincides with my daughter's wedding, so I know; I believe I wore it for a few weeks before my daughter's wedding. Well our twenty-fifth anniversary is within days and weeks after it, so I'm pretty sure that I had my ring in 1991. Right now, I can't be so sure that I didn't sell that man that ring and that scrap gold, I can't, it's not usual and I might add that most of the stuff I was selling then was not stolen stuff, it was stuff I was buying when I was out at darts, if somebody wanted to sell that sovereign to me I would buy it and try and make a profit on it. The only stolen stuff I was selling knowingly was '92 onwards. So I still find it unusual the form of the two receipts, there's still something that's not right but I can't say it wasn't me, not my ring. My ring I had in 1991 definite. My ring – and my ring was a sunburst, you know what a sunburst is? – on the top.'

POLICE: 'Right.'

COOPER: 'It was a very distinctive, I don't know, it was a sunburst.'

Cooper had suddenly remembered details of when he had worn his ring. He knew the significance of the transaction on the 5th of July, 1989, the day the bodies were found. He knew that the jewellers shop in Pembroke was fifty yards away from the NatWest cashpoint used by the murderer twice on the 29th of June 1989. It also showed that he was comfortable committing a criminal act in Pembroke and comfortable telling us.

The interview then proceeded to the murders themselves and Cooper was given an opportunity to comment on each aspect of the murder scene and the theft of Peter Dixon's wedding ring. Cooper gave short negative responses to all questions regarding the murders but I was satisfied that the exchange over the sale of the wedding ring had hurt him; he was starting to realise that we had done our homework.

Cooper was then asked a series of questions relating to the use of Peter Dixon's cash card at the NatWest Bank in Pembroke, Carmarthen and Haverfordwest. The geography was significant. The offender, when he left the scene, had almost passed Milford Haven on his way to Pembroke but hadn't taken any cash. This was strange. Could it be that Cooper was well known in Milford Haven and stopping there would have been too risky? The sequence of withdrawals again indicated a local man because after Pembroke the offender travelled thirty miles east to Carmarthen only to return west the following day, to use the card for the last at time just after 7 a.m. in Haverfordwest. We knew from Huntsman that Cooper had been found in possession of property from a burglary in 1985. Amongst the stolen items was a National Westminster bank cash card and chequebook. A cheque was cashed at a jewellery stall at Carew Market, just outside Pembroke. Of great interest to us, was an attempt to use the card at the NatWest cashpoint in Haverfordwest at just after 7 a.m. in the morning following the burglary; the inference being this: if Cooper committed that burglary he had used the same cashpoint at a similar time in the morning to when he used Peter Dixon's card. The problem was that he had not been charged with this burglary and therefore I could not use it in his bad character interview.

POLICE: 'We now move on to the usage of the Dixons' bank card, OK, the cash card which went missing from Peter Dixon was used at 13.36 hours on the 29th of June within hours of the murders at the NatWest bank in Pembroke Dock. Explain whether you were the person responsible for using the card at that location at that time.'

COOPER: 'No it wasn't me.'

POLICE: 'Tell me you know, whether you know where NatWest bank in Pembroke is.'

COOPER: 'Not really no.'

*

Cooper went on to deny making any of the further cash withdrawals that were made with Peter Dixon's card. Cooper was then shown a photograph of exhibit JAW/106, the rope used to tie up Peter.

POLICE: 'Evidence from the crime scene has been obtained and I told you that they have been tied up, yes, and that the rope on Peter DIXON had been left on his body, OK? I'm going to show you a photograph contained in GBR/2 of the rope which is police reference JAW/106. Can you see that?'

COOPER: 'Yes I can, yeah.'

POLICE: 'Can you describe – I'm talking about the last but one picture in the album? Can you describe what you can visually see there.'

COOPER: 'Yeah well.'

POLICE: 'Can you describe the rope, to me?'

COOPER: 'Black rope, is it?'

POLICE: 'OK and also contained in that rope, can you see there's a blue, it's a dark coloured rope. Right OK and can you see in the bottom of the picture there's a distinct loop?'

COOPER: 'Yeah yeah.'

POLICE: 'Tell me whether you are the person responsible for taking that rope to the scene.'

COOPER: 'No, it wasn't me, no.'

Cooper was questioned about any bikes he had owned before being shown the artist's impression of the 'Wild Man' with a bike using the NatWest cashpoint early in the morning on the 1st of July 1989. This was the only artist's impression released by Detective Chief Superintendent

Clive Jones. I had spoken to Clive regarding this decision and his reasoning was sound and based on his vast experience. This was the only impression that he could confidently say was the offender due to the time of the sighting. Cooper was then questioned in relation to the artist's impression released in 1989 but denied it had any resemblance to him at that time. This was supported by the police officer DC Lyn Dudley who visited Cooper as part of the original investigation. He made a note on the action that Cooper did not resemble the artist's impression. At this point we had nothing to challenge this position.

The next interview commenced at 10.22 a.m. on Saturday the 5th of July 2008. The purpose was to discuss sightings of people on the coastal path at the time of the murders. Cooper had other ideas; he had had time to think and needed to explain his ownership of bicycles.

POLICE: 'OK before we start looking and asking you about various sightings of people in the area, is there anything from yesterday's interview that you'd like to bring to my attention, discuss or to clarify?'

COOPER: 'Um yes there is.'

POLICE: 'There is. OK, carry on then.'

COOPER: 'I'm sorry to do it this way but when I go back to sort of a quiet room where I can think of things . . .'

POLICE: 'Yes.'

COOPER: 'You asked me a particular question yesterday about bikes.'

POLICE: 'Yes.'

COOPER: 'And my mind was a blank, I must apologise.'

POLICE: 'Right.'

COOPER: 'I can give you information of the bikes that I owned I believe anyway.'

POLICE: 'Right, OK.'

COOPER: 'Shall I start?'

POLICE: 'Yes certainly.'

COOPER: 'Up until 1979 we didn't, we owned cars but I did have many many bikes living in Milford Haven. I used to take the kids for rides on them because I put children's seats on them so just 1979ish I had bikes in Milford Haven. After that time there's only one bike that I could remember buying.'

POLICE: 'Right.'

COOPER: 'And it was for a particular reason so that's how it come to me. I don't know the specific time but I can relate to it as when I was banned from driving on the road, so it was during that period I purchased a push bike.'

POLICE: 'Right.'

COOPER: 'It was a drop-handled sports-type bike.'

POLICE: 'Yeah.'

COOPER: 'And I purchased it from Honeyborough roundabout industrial estate and the reason was to commute between St Marys Park and the place I was building in Johnston called The Beeches.'

POLICE: 'Right.'

COOPER: 'Sometime while I was using the bike I modified it by changing the seat, because it was too uncomfortable, and the handlebars.'

POLICE: 'Right.'

COOPER: 'Put different ones on. The bike was a bit of a family joke really, they used to call it my exercise or fitness bike or words to that description and as I say I used to commute every day from St Marys Park to the Beeches to do work to save my wife on the road and she had other things to do. I'm trying to remember as much as I can about it. When I got my licence back I stopped using it and it was at The Beeches in various sheds and what have you and I believe the bike didn't come back to St Marys Park with us.'

POLICE: 'Right.'

COOPER: 'And I believe I brought it to Merlins Bridge tip with a trailer load of different sort of rubbish that I brought there. It's a council tip which you can bring your rubbish to and I made a couple of journeys to there with the tractor and trailer and I believe it went there in quite a rusty state at the time. But I used it for commuting and when I didn't have a licence.'

POLICE: 'OK thank you. Can you describe the bike to me?'

COOPER: 'I can't even think what colour it is, I think there was red in the colour, I believe, I believe there was red in the colour but it was, it was a drop-handled sports-type bike but I did put – because I found the seat a bit uncomfortable and leaning over like that, multi-speed – I put more comfortable handlebars on it. I must add I commuted daily between Milford, St Marys Park and The Beeches so I was a well known, who was well known because you have to go through Johnston to get to The Beeches from St Marys Park so everybody would have saw me, you know, everybody knew me. And they knew I was banned so I was well known in the area.'

POLICE: 'OK, can you explain to me the reason that you changed the seat and the handlebars?'

COOPER: 'They were too uncomfortable.'

POLICE: 'Right.'

COOPER: 'Yeah, much too uncomfortable.'

POLICE: 'And it what way did you find them uncomfortable?'

COOPER: 'The seat was too small on the racing bike, it was much too small and I put a large old-fashioned type seat on it.'

POLICE: 'And the handlebars.'

COOPER: 'The handlebars, there again it was too uncomfortable for me and I bought, I put on handlebars that were more upright.'

POLICE: 'Upright.'

COOPER: 'Yeah more upright, so rather than being down, I was more upright.'

POLICE: 'But a number of sightings in and around the Pembrokeshire area which were relayed on *Crimewatch*, we've spoken about the sighting and the artist's impression. There was also sighting of a male person on, sitting on a bike with upright handlebars with a younger male on a caravan site in the area not too far from Broad Haven. Can you tell me whether you were the person who was in that area during that time?'

COOPER: 'No, it was wasn't me.'

POLICE: 'Can you explain whether you cycled in the north-west Pembrokeshire area?'

COOPER: 'No.'

POLICE: 'During the summer of 1989. Can you tell me whether you cycled at all in the summer of 1989?'

COOPER: 'I would say categorically no because it was a very busy time for us house hunting.'

★

It was very clear that this interview was an attempt by Cooper to explain away any evidence or sightings of himself with a similar bike to the one in the artist's impression. At 11.05 a.m. on Saturday the 5th of July 2008 a further taped briefing concerning forensic disclosure was given to Cooper's solicitors. A very important exhibit was the rope JAW/106 used to tie Peter Dixon's wrists behind his back. The rope was still around his wrists when the body was recovered. A general swab was taken from the rope and submitted for DNA analysis. The result of that analysis showed a partial profile with a total of five components; two confirmed and three unconfirmed. All five, if they originated from one source, did not feature in Peter or Gwenda Dixon's profiles but did feature in Cooper's. This on the face of it appeared to be interesting but was far from conclusive or anywhere near being our forensic golden nugget. The frequency of this result appearing in the general public is about one in every three hundred. It needed to be put to Cooper though, and we had to be very accurate and transparent in its evidential value. Cooper was questioned at length regarding his knowledge and possession of ropes. He went to great lengths to explain how he had sailed and fished around the coast collecting and sometimes discarding ropes of all shapes and sizes. Interestingly, and in keeping with his behaviour in the rest of the interview, he suddenly remembered he had fished and launched his boat off Broad Haven and Little Haven, putting him in the vicinity of the scene. It was yet another attempt to explain away any incriminating forensic evidence we might have. Now though we had got the measure of Cooper.

CHAPTER 13

A SHOCK IN THE NIGHT

On Friday the 11th of July 2008, a week after we had interviewed Cooper, I got the management team together to discuss the interviews and to arrange a Gold Group meeting to brief the Deputy Chief Constable and Police Authority. There was a good feeling in the team; the interview process had gone very well. All the careful planning by Colin Clarke and his team had paid off. Although Cooper had not made any significant admissions, other than confessing to handling stolen jewellery, he had done the next best thing. He had talked and talked and tried to anticipate what evidence he thought we had and in doing so had given some interesting responses. We needed to dissect the interviews and understand what he was telling us.

Following the interviews at Ammanford I held a debrief with Lynne Harries, Glyn Johnson and Gareth Rees. I couldn't help thinking that after our broadcast his chosen reading in prison was all about DNA cases. It was clear to all of us that Cooper believed we had more evidence than we actually had and in responding to certain questions he had revealed where he was vulnerable. As we sat and talked it through a number of clear examples jumped out at us.

Cooper had initially indicated, that he only knew the Thomases in passing and had nothing to do with them. In reality he knew them well; he lived only a few hundred yards away and had worked on their land and bought grain from Richard Thomas. Mr Thomas had indicated to one of his farmhands that he feared Cooper and had asked him to stand nearby whenever Cooper was at Scoveston Park. Cooper had tried to buy land from Richard Thomas using Florence Evans as a 'go between'. Cooper couldn't remember visiting Scoveston Park but when it was clear that we had evidence to the contrary he remembered going there and looking in the outbuildings. Cooper remembered that Richard Thomas had an old Rover car and that he had helped to load it with beer from Flo Evans. This involved him touching the vehicle and doors. Cooper suggested he would probably have a number of keys in his famous key bucket that would fit the Rover car. Other keys found in his cesspitt fitted the locks of houses burgled in the area. Property stolen from them was found at Cooper's house and the homes of family members. Cooper said he had been given the items as gifts. I believed that he collected mementos from his crimes; items that would take him back in his mind's eye so that he could relive the control he had had over his victims. Cooper admitted visiting Norton Farm which belonging to Richard and Helen Thomas. Richard had visited the house on the day of his murder. A key to an internal door from Norton Farm was found during the search of Cooper's home. Pre-war cardboard-finished shotgun cartridges were found under the duck run at Cooper's address during the Huntsman searches; identical cartridges had been found in the larder at Scoveston Park. Then there was the cartridge box with the handwriting on it similar to that of Helen Thomas. He explained that he had attended local shooting events where the locals would swap ammunition. We now knew that Cooper had persuaded his family to tell the police that they were all at home together on the night of the Scoveston murders. This was untrue. Furthermore, around the time of the murders one of his family could remember him coming home in the dark sweating, as if he had been running, and that his hair was flat to his head as if he had been wearing some kind of a hat. He went to the bathroom to wash and told the same family member to say if asked that they had been at home together all night.

Cooper had denied any contact with the Little Haven area only to later admit he used to fish off the coast and sell mackerel from Little Haven and Broad Haven slipway. Other evidence clearly showed that he visited the area regularly with his family. Cooper had sold a man's gold wedding ring on the 5th of July 1989 in a jewellers shop in Pembroke, having initially indicated that it was his own. The jeweller was fifty yards away from the NatWest cashpoint used by the murderer on the 29th of June 2012. When shown a separate receipt detailing another transaction for a ring marked as scrap gold he admitted that the transaction on the 5th of July was not related to the sale of his own ring. Most surprisingly he admitted handling stolen jewellery, which was in total contrast to his usual protestations of innocence. Peter Dixon's twenty-two-carat gold wedding ring had been removed from his finger and we felt that Cooper believed that we had recovered it and if produced he could explain that he had only handled it and that it must have come from someone else. Unfortunately we did not have the ring but it was another telling disclosure. Cooper collected and disposed of ropes in connection with his boat. If his or anyone else's DNA was on a rope it could easily be explained. Cooper also indicated that at or about the time of the Dixons' murder he used to cycle in the Milford Haven area and that he had altered the handlebars on the cycle to make them straighter and more traditional. This would explain any evidence from locals suggesting he had a similar bicycle at the time. We knew that on the 19th of July 1989, three weeks after the murders, Cooper went to see his doctor complaining of fractured ribs. Tim Dixon was convinced that his father would have fought back during the attack. Could Cooper's injury have been inflicted during the struggle?

As we sat and talked these issues through there was one more very important disclosure that stunned us into silence, followed by a moment of realisation. Cooper was questioned about guns; in particular about the PH/2 gun abandoned following the Sardis armed robbery. The weapon was a sawn-off double-barrelled shotgun which had a short rope lanyard attached to the stock and barrel. Cooper had been convicted of this offence and was nearing the end of his sentence and yet he had gone to great lengths to suggest that he had handled the gun during the Huntsman trial. Now a decade on while he was being questioned, the interviewing officers noticed that he had written on his pad the words, 'Sardis gun, Judge Moreton destruction-order!'

Following the Huntsman trial, Judge Moreton had indeed given an order for the weapon to be destroyed but unbeknown to Cooper this had not been carried out. Why was Cooper now so concerned about a gun and a crime for which he had nearly served his sentence? It was a moment of epiphany! This had to be the murder weapon for at least one of the double killings, and probably both if it had once belonged to Richard Thomas. We knew that Cooper had previously stolen shotguns from houses and we knew that Richard Thomas possessed at least one shotgun, but none had been recovered from Scoveston Park.

While trying to be clever, Cooper was in fact telling us where to look for clues and we knew only the killer could have such knowledge. I was now absolutely convinced that Cooper had murdered four people. This was a turning point for me; if we didn't get further forensic evidence we would prepare a case based on what we had, supported by bad character and circumstantial evidence. It was therefore essential that I went through a linking process to show that the same person committed the crimes; I could then overlay his previous history of offending onto the Ottawa crimes.

I knew that the CPS at this early stage were not over-impressed with including the Milford Haven robbery and rape offence on the same indictment as four murders, but I was determined to keep it in knowing both its geographical and behavioural value to the case. The scene of the attack was within sight of Scoveston Park and contained so many elements of the Dixons' murder. We needed to persuade the CPS. Less than a week later we met Tom Atherton from the CPS to brief him on the interview and the emerging issues. As usual Tom played devil's advocate, asking probing and difficult questions with his glasses perched on the end of his nose. As time went on he was slowly coming around to our view, but still had reservations regarding the value of the Milford Haven offence. At the conclusion of the meeting it was agreed that we would submit an advice file to the CPS for consideration by both them and Gerard Elias QC. One question from Tom was important; he asked me how many other offenders we had in the system that compared with Cooper. I didn't know, but could see that potentially this would negate any bad character evidence if the defence could show there were other people like Cooper living in the local community.

The way forward was now clear: we needed to continue with the forensic review and the submissions to scientists and experts. It was also essential to identify usable evidence from Operation Huntsman and Operation Ottawa and have our forensic assessments independently reviewed by the NPIA. Cooper's interviews had to be thoroughly assessed and we needed expert opinion on the geographical and behavioural elements of the offences. It was also now our intention to strip out all of the behavioural characteristics from Ottawa before overlaying the behaviour displayed by Cooper in his Huntsman convictions. What would it tell us?

In view of Tom's comments we needed to consider all previous suspects and persons of interest for the murders and sex attack. We needed to know exactly who had not been eliminated and secure their offending history, including their up-to-date criminal offending. We also needed to know whether the crime wave had stopped once Cooper was jailed in 1998. Last but not least we needed a presentation for Gerard Elias and the CPS; there was a lot to do. This work would require additional analytical and research resources from the force. As always I had total support from the Gold Group and my senior management colleagues. We were also starting to outgrow the accommodation at Fishguard Port office and were looking for new accommodation. There was a possibility that we could use the top floor of Pembroke Dock police station but unfortunately this housed the cherished snooker table that had stood proudly in a room next to the kitchen area for as long as anyone could remember. The room would need to be cleared and HOLMES terminals fitted to make it a fully functional incident room; so for now we remained at Fishguard.

A meeting with Jonathan Smith and Des James from the National Police Improvement Agency (NPIA) was productive. After Lynne had raised some concerns I asked Des to secure some independent advice regarding the work being carried out by LGC. Jonathan agreed to review the process and was reasonably happy with the direction we were being given. At this stage I had concentrated on DNA trace evidence and steered clear of fibre evidence on the grounds of expense and advice from the scientists. We now needed to establish what human and animal hair and fibre evidence was available as well as other opportunities such as paint and soil. I was also aware that in the States the FBI was developing new techniques to analyse body fluids.

A bee in my bonnet was the profilers' position on not giving evidence. Neil Traynor and Paul Lobbe had been recommended by the NPIA and were now producing fascinating evaluations of the geography of the offences and Cooper's behaviour. I wanted them to go into the witness box, particularly Neil Traynor. I felt that geographical profiling had been around long enough for us to have nationally recognised experts who could give their opinion in court. Neil however was convinced that an analyst should give the evidence instead. In essence profilers help detectives by giving them broad parameters to work within while analysts deal in statistics; the profiler will tell you what kind of man might have committed a crime whereas the analyst will tell you the likelihood of such a man being in a particular area. We had some healthy discussions about this difference of opinion but I was not going to get my way. We had some great analysts in the force but none with sufficient experience of giving this type of evidence; it was something I needed to consider.

Work on the new accommodation at Pembroke Dock police station was under way. Lynne and Glyn and I now began the task of creating what became known as the Events Matrix. This would help me through the linking process. It was straightforward but time-consuming. Glyn created a spreadsheet which was projected onto the wall of the briefing room at Fishguard Port Office. Down the left-hand side we included categories such as: location, scene, victim(s), offender, property, violence, weapons and words used by the offender etc. We then started to populate the spreadsheet by including columns, with a short narrative which detailed the behaviour, scene and victim selection allowing us to drill down into the detail of the crimes. The double murders and Milford Haven offence were colour coded. This enabled me to see similarities as we grew the events matrix. We locked ourselves in the room for days until we had completed the work, which was then presented to the rest of the team for comment.

In creating the matrix I laid down some ground rules which reflected the ethos of the investigation: my mantra, 'We only deal in fact', created many lively and humorous moments in our deliberations. My view was that the matrix should only consist of those events that were factual and provable; this would require someone being prepared to go into the witness box and give evidence. This ensured that we did not allow opinion, assumption or legend to filter into the linking process. Glyn and Lynne were brilliant and totally different in their approach and interventions. We sat on old threadbare easy chairs in the briefing room clutching mugs of tea; mine was my beloved Everton mug. Lynne is a listener; he absorbs and then makes observations. Glyn is far more animated, if he sees something and doesn't agree, he will say so. The main areas of healthy debate revolved around the different views on what was fact and what was opinion or assumption. At one point Lynne Harries said, 'Bloody hell, boss, at this rate you will be retired before we finish this.' Eventually we concluded the matrix, it was detailed and the colour coding allowed us to see instantly areas of commonality between them. When we overlaid the behaviour, geography and victim selection displayed by Cooper in his Huntsman convictions with the Ottawa offences the results were compelling. It was like inserting a hand into a glove. As I suspected, it really highlighted the value and importance of the Milford Haven rape and robbery to the case. The SIO at the time of that attack was Aldwyn Jones, a sharp investigator and a very thorough man. His view was important to me. He believed that the attack on the children was a chance meeting with a man out in the fields, probably on his way home from planning another criminal enterprise. His route took him past Scoveston Park and by pure chance the children were playing in the field. When considering the Sardis robbery committed by Cooper the description of the attacker was identical and the use of the gun as a means of control, plus the words used to control his victims, were very similar. When we compared this with the Dixons' murder the similarities were again striking; multiple victims, robbery and sexual assault and use of a double-barrelled sawn-off shotgun. In the Milford attack the MO was identical but the number of youngsters probably explained why no one was murdered. I was also exploring the possibility of getting a mathematician to give the statistical probabilities of this kind of activity taking place in such a tight geographical location and it not be committed by the same person. In essence, how many gun-toting maniacs did we have roaming this part of North Pembrokeshire? The Milford Haven case had to be considered by Mr Elias and the CPS, alongside the double murders, I just needed to persuade them.

On the 8th of August 2008 it was agreed that an initial advice file would be submitted to the CPS to be reviewed by Gerard Elias QC, to include the usable evidence, bad character and Cooper's interviews. This would give an early assessment of the case but we were pretty certain that we would get the response, 'Nice story, but where is the forensic evidence?'

The geographical and behavioural assessments of Paul Lobbe and Neil Traynor supported my view; they clearly understood the importance of the Milford Haven offence. Having considered the events matrix and the profilers' assessments I was happy that the offences were linked and made a policy decision to formally do so, which was ratified by the Gold Group. In reality it made little difference to the conduct of the investigation as I had always been investigating them together. The linking process became more and more relevant in my discussions with Mr Elias and the CPS, and also in my responses to the media. There is a nationally accepted linking process. It involves a presentation to an examining panel including chief officers; this normally takes place when there is more than one force involved. When agreed, a lead officer is identified to oversee the operation. In our case it was simple, all offences were committed in the force area and I was already the officer in charge.

The time had come for us to assess the service we were getting from the forensic scientists. Lynne had day-to-day contact with them and he was becoming ever more concerned with the changing role of certain staff within LGC. This included the departure of Maggie Boyce to another firm, Key Forensics, while being retained by LGC as a consultant for Operation Ottawa. How much time could she really dedicate to our case? Lynne also felt that LGC could be more innovative in their decision-making or when giving direction about which examinations to carry out.

Operation Ottawa had been identified at the National Reviewers Conference as one of the most important cold case reviews in the UK and had attracted funding from Operation Stealth, which had been set up nationally, to assist forces with such high-profile cases. We were aware that members of LGC Forensics had also attended the conference and should have been fully aware of how important the case was. We needed to get around the table with LGC senior management and talk it through. On the 8th of August 2008 a meeting was held at Fishguard Port Office, Lynne, Glyn and Glan Thomas were present while LGC had sent their big guns in the form of Dr Angela Gallop. Dr Gallop was a very well-known and experienced scientist with a national and international reputation; she was director of science and innovation for LGC Forensics and was accompanied by Susie Delaney, LGC's operations head for pathology and cold case reviews. I opened the meeting by giving a situation report and outlining our concerns. I then asked Dr Gallop directly where else I could go to get the forensic services that I felt the case deserved.

Dr Gallop explained that following the DNA results obtained during the initial phases of submissions, it was felt that the areas of forensic examination should be expanded to include areas such as hairs (human and animal), and fibres. She clearly believed there were more opportunities to focus on items such as tapings and she said she that LGC felt it had been constrained to DNA examinations by the review team. This needed to be challenged and I explained that we were only acting on their suggestions as experts. It was a watershed moment, and we decided that from there on we needed a more 'innovative' phase of examination, a more flexible approach and better communications. Dr Gallop stated that she intended expanding the teams of scientists to deal with this innovative phase. Leading LGC scientists Roger Robson and April Robson would look at fibre evidence and Phil Avenell would focus on DNA.

The most interesting view put forward by LGC was the need to look at items from Cooper's home environment, not connected with the Huntsman offences, which might hold links to the Ottawa crimes. This would involve reviewing all items seized during the Huntsman searches and looking for potential links, in particular fibres and tape lifts that were retained by the FSS. Angela was a skilled negotiator and went to great lengths to reassure me that we were getting the very best service, and detailed a number of successful high-profile investigations in which LGC had played a leading role. What became clear to all of us was the total enthusiasm of Dr Gallop and this became very much her trademark. Up until this stage we had kept the scientists very much at arm's length. It was my decision because I wanted to create a clear firewall between the investigation team and the scientists. In talking with the

LGC team it appeared that they had been just as frustrated as we were. In the end we had all benefited from this face-to-face discussion. Going forward I could still retain a firewall and they could maintain their independence while we could work together to have a better a better joint understanding of each other's needs and capabilities. Without doubt this was a turning point in our relationship and would prove so in the investigation.

The Gold Group meeting of the 28th of August 2008 was a sobering one. I had now spent almost £400,000 on forensics with little to show for it. DCC Andy Edwards was very supportive and whilst we had a clear investigative strategy he knew that we could not cut corners or fall short. Superintendent Euros Lewis was looking after the impact the investigation might be having on the community and he was police representative on the multi-agency group that was monitoring Cooper's movement towards parole. 'Euros, update please,' said Andy Edwards. 'Yes, sir, Cooper will be released on the 19th of September 2008, and he is likely to spend the first three months in a hostel in Swansea before being integrated into the family home.' Those words made my blood run cold. Cooper was coming out and soon! His wife Pat had now moved to Letterston, a small village outside Haverfordwest, and it was likely that Cooper would be living with her full time by December 2008. This created another problem, because of the considerable resources that would be needed to manage and monitor Cooper in the community. This was a man who I believed had murdered at least four people, held five children at gunpoint before raping one of them and indecently assaulting another and he was about to be living in a sleepy village in Pembrokeshire.

I needed to consider tactical options such as surveillance. We already knew from intelligence that he suspected that we would bug his house for any incriminating conversations he might have with his wife. It was also difficult to imagine putting officers into fields in a rural location when we knew that Cooper liked to roam the countryside with a loaded gun, which he was prepared to use. All of these issues were flashing through my head and I was nowhere near being able to arrest and charge him; it wasn't getting any easier. On his release Cooper's control measures would be strict: there was a curfew at the hostel between 8 p.m. and 9.30 a.m. with an alcohol ban. He would have to report to the hostel every two hours, he could not visit Pat at the Letterston address and he could not contact his son Adrian. He had also been assessed by the Prison Service as high risk to the public with a medium risk of re-offending. As forecast September came and John Cooper was released to the hostel in Swansea. He had been a model prisoner during his time inside and he knew that in the early stages he had to be squeaky clean before he would be allowed to go back to Pembrokeshire.

The risk management plan was detailed and flawless. There were nine people assessed as being at serious risk, they included two police officers, Steve Matchett and Jim Morris. Both had played leading roles in his Huntsman convictions and Cooper had never forgiven them. His son Adrian Cooper was also named on the at-risk list.

The time had now come for us to meet Gerard Elias QC and off I went with Lynne and Glyn to his chambers at Park Place in Cardiff to present our skeleton case. We were taken to a top-floor room which was dominated by a large wooden table. The walls were covered in photographs of members of the Chambers at very formal functions. Mr Elias was a large strong-looking man with a good head of silver-grey hair. He looked every inch the part. I have always found top lawyers and QC's to be engaging people with a keen sense of humour, Mr Elias was no exception. He was very quietly spoken with an air of confidence, the result of being a very successful man. He was an instant hit with the team. Glyn as normal was the technical genius and operated the presentation, which I talked to for some two hours. Mr Elias said very little but listened intently. Tom Atherton represented the CPS, and at various stages interjected to support the team; he was now firmly in our camp. At the end Mr Elias looked at me and said, 'Mr Wilkins, what evidence have you actually got?' I launched into my bad character and circumstantial evidence and anything I could think of.

'No, Mr Wilkins, what usable evidence have you got that John Cooper is responsible?'

'Not a lot,' I admitted.

'No, quite,' he replied. 'Anyway, have you got time for a beer before you go?' he asked. It was now after 10 p.m. and we had a two-hour journey ahead, but I felt he wanted to speak to me. We walked to a local watering hole and stood at the bar.

'A fascinating case, Mr Wilkins. Tom is very excited about it. If I can get it before a jury I think we have a chance but the severance argument will be difficult to challenge. If you get some forensic evidence, it will be an overwhelming case and I really want to do it.'

I could see a twinkle in his eye, this was a man who had prosecuted over two hundred murder cases and was involved in the Bloody Sunday inquiry, and I could see he was up for this. The journey back to Pembrokeshire with Lynne and Glyn was filled with optimism we knew we had a class act to represent the Crown.

At this stage the bad character evidence was vital, to keep all of the offences together. If we managed to do this, then we could include all of the linking circumstantial evidence, which I believed would be compelling for any jury. Of course any competent defence lawyer would argue that the Crown had not proved that the offences were linked and that they should be heard separately thus severing the indictment and significantly weakening the case. It was vital that I worked to ensure that the cases were kept together. The bad character evidence would be subject to a separate application before the trial judge to agree what was admissible through the recognised gateways. The question of severance would also be addressed before we even got to trial and that was still far from certain. There were very many bridges to cross but I was careful not to show the team that I was concerned about our position.

Back in Pembrokeshire, I was getting the distinct impression from the Crown team that they were looking to drop the Milford Haven offence, whether or not we secured any forensic links, to concentrate on the murders. I had made my position quite clear and perhaps more importantly I had already spoken to the victims from the Milford Haven offence and reopened old wounds. They were aware that we were reviewing the offence, but at this stage not the full extent of the investigation. Many years had passed and to a certain extent some of them had tried to move on, but they all, without exception, carried the deep scars of that terrible night in 1996. None of them were in a stable relationship. It was very, very sad and I did not want to let them down again. We needed the Crown to understand that this case was not just about bringing justice for the dead but also about the living victims.

Weeks later we met Mr Elias and Tom Atherton at Haverfordwest police station and then went out to Little Haven. We parked at Howelston Caravan Park and walked the route taken by Peter and Gwenda Dixon on that fateful morning in 1989. We scrambled along the coastal path every so often catching a glimpse of Talbenny Church that stood on top of a hill overlooking the bay. We knew that the hedge line leading down from the church cut into the coastal path directly above the hidden plateau where the Dixons had been killed. On reaching this point we negotiated the steep drop to the scene. Attached to a tree was a weather-worn plaque, a tribute from a loving family to their mother and father. Gerard Elias surveyed the scene, 'This is not what I expected, this isn't some city villain who has stumbled on his victims, it's a local man, someone who knows the area and the potential for victims.' It was music to my ears. From there we went to Scoveston Park and walked up to the majestic old house. Outside it was almost the same, although inside extensive renovations had taken place. The outbuildings where Richard was attacked had been converted into a holiday let, but could still be identified from the original plans and photographs. The garage at the rear of the house that had contained Richard's Rover car was still intact. The hedges leading from Scoveston Park towards Scoveston Fort, where hoards of jewellery had been recovered, were easy to pick out. From here we went to the location of the Milford Haven attack at the rear of the Mount Estate. We walked across the field to the location where the masked gunman first confronted the children. From this spot we could see the small wooded area that hid Scoveston Park. For a few moments we stood and briefed him on the similarities between the Dixons' attack and this offence. The young victims had described the gun down to the smallest detail; double-barrelled, side-by-side and sawn off. The boys, who were into hunting, knew their guns; they detailed the lanyard and how it was connected to a metal clip attached to barrel and stock. It was like they were describing the Sardis gun, which Cooper had been so concerned about in his interviews. Gerard Elias looked at me and nodded as we walked away together and whispered, 'The jury visit will be very important to show the connectivity between the locations and the local element.' I could barely contain myself; he was miles ahead in his thinking and the attack on the children was very much part of his plan. As we travelled back to the police station, Mr Elias reinforced the need to identify any other potential suspects in the system that had a similar bad character profile; this was now my priority.

On the 2nd of September 2008 I discussed this action with Lynne and Glyn and tasked the team with identifying suspects and people of interest from both double murders and the Milford Haven attack. It was clear that there would be a considerable number of individuals who I would need to review in order to be able to give Gerard Elias the answer to his question. The Ottawa team collated the various lists and in the end there were over one thousand five hundred names. Each person was placed on a master spreadsheet which detailed their connection to the investigation and hyperlinks to their original documentation. Using strict criteria and cross-checking we were able to reduce the list dramatically. After weeks of hard work I would be left with nine men who could not be eliminated from all three offences. The linking process had given me additional elimination criteria of 'non-availability to commit all three offences'. When assessing the remaining nine there was nothing in their bad character that came close to Cooper. I could now confidently tell Tom Atherton and Gerard Elias QC that there was no one else in the system that was another John William Cooper.

Time had now come to brief Detective Chief Superintendent Dai Davies (fondly known as D.M. Davies), Detective Chief Superintendent Clive Jones and Detective Superintendent Aldwyn Jones, the men who had led the original investigations. They had all retired, but I needed them to know that Cooper was the prime suspect. I wanted to tell that I was pushing hard for the CPS to take on a bad character case as a worst-case scenario but we were still hoping for a forensic breakthrough. I also wanted to explore with them some of their decisions and gauge their gut feeling. On a bright winter's day together with Lynne Harries I visited D.M. Davies at his home in Llanelli; also present was his Deputy SIO Derek Davies and Don Evans. Don had been the Divisional Commander in Pembrokeshire at the time of both double murders and one of the first people at both scenes. I had known Don for some years, he was a gentleman and we got on well. Derek Davies was an absolute character, full of fun and a man I would love to share some old stories with over a pint. Unfortunately D.M. Davies was not in the best of health and was confined to a wheelchair, but he was as sharp as a razor, with a fantastic memory. We talked for hours about the Scoveston Park and Ottawa investigations. I was overcome with the genuine support from all three men and how excited they were that we were fully committed to detecting the crimes. It was clear that D.M. Davies was never convinced by the theory that Richard Thomas had been killed by a gay lover and he was relieved when I was able to tell him that the new forensic evidence dispelled the theory. It was fascinating to listen to the three men recalling the investigation. We could have been back in an old-fashioned, smoke-filled paper-based incident room, busy with the sound of indexers, talking about categories and interesting pieces of information, they were cops once again. It was a brilliant afternoon and we would do it again in the following months. Clive Jones had been the SIO for the Dixons murders, and was another larger than life character. We met at Police Headquarters in Carmarthen and once again it was fascinating to hear him recall the investigation. There were a number of things that struck me about the Dixons investigation. The inquiry had been hampered by a newly delivered HOLMES computer system and the 1989 investigation was not officially linked to the Scoveston Park case although both databases were being searched for possible links. Importantly for our case Clive Jones was able to confirm that he had only released one artist's impression of the man seen at the NatWest cashpoint in Haverfordwest. His rationale was sound, this was the only one he could be confident was the man using Peter Dixon's cash card due to the timing of the transaction and an eyewitness account. Again I had his total support. In each case the foresight of these detectives to retain so much material had given the Ottawa team the opportunity to apply modern-day science and investigative techniques.

Aldwyn Jones had been the SIO on the Milford Haven attack and I knew him well, he had been my detective superintendent when I was a detective inspector. He was a lovely man and a very good cop. He was now retired and enjoying a new interest as a chef and a very good one at that. Aldwyn was also a great host and when I went to see him at his house I was greeted by venison cooked in chocolate and some good red wine. The Milford attack had taken place when he was Deputy Head of CID and he was responsible for creating a great deal of the good practice and work ethic still evident in the CID today. His policy books and investigation plans were meticulous and it was easy to understand his lines of enquiry and the rationale behind them. He had also been in the force at the time of the Sardis robbery and Operation Huntsman and had clearly fancied Cooper for more serious crimes.

Early in December 2008 the forensic management group had considered the outcome of the meeting with LGC and decided to broaden submissions to include fibre evidence from the Sardis robbery, Cooper's home environment and exhibits recovered during the Ottawa investigations; it was likely to be expensive, but totally necessary. The new submissions would include all items abandoned by Cooper as he fled the Sardis robbery, clothing and items touched by the offender in the murders and Milford Haven attack as well gloves found at or near his house. Original fibre tapings and samples taken from the shed and workbench at Cooper's home had been recovered from the FSS vaults and sent to LGC, it was now up to them to scrutinise the material.

At the hostel in Swansea, Cooper was behaving impeccably; he was ready to return to Letterston and his wife. As an operational SIO I provided an on-call service to the force for major crime and other serious incidents. Over the years you become accustomed to the phone ringing at all hours of the day and night. As a rule I would keep an A4 jotting pad on the kitchen table and if the phone rang I normally asked them to ring back in five minutes, whilst I went downstairs to clear my thoughts and avoid disturbing the rest of the house.

It was 3.30 a.m. on a cold December morning in 2008 when the phone rang.

'Hello, boss, it's control room.' Before I could say, 'Give me five and phone back,' the voice continued, 'John Cooper has phoned 999, and I think he has murdered his wife.' To this day I can remember the feeling of total horror. 'You're fucking joking,' was my less than professional response. He wasn't joking, Pat Cooper was dead. Experience had taught that sometimes the information coming from the control room might not be wholly accurate because of the fast-moving nature of a live crime scene. I would usually try to calm things down and find out who was in control of the scene or situation and contact them directly to establish the facts.

In this instance Detective Inspector Roland Powell was the local senior detective at the scene. Rolly was highly experienced and had hands-on knowledge of the community management plan for Cooper. An initial discussion with Rolly confirmed that we were a long way from establishing that John Cooper had murdered his wife but it was still a highly significant situation. It has been the first day of his staggered return to the family home and the first time he had been allowed to stay overnight. The account was straightforward: Pat Cooper was lying at the side of the bed; there were no signs of violence to the body or any disturbance in the house. John Cooper had told the paramedics that they had eaten a meal and then had taken a bath together before going to bed and making love. During the night he had heard his wife gasping for breath and after a failed attempt to help her he phoned 999 for assistance. What I did not need at this stage was an overreaction just because it was Cooper. It was important now that the officers at the scene handled the situation with compassion. At the same time I wanted to ensure that any potential evidence was secured, should events take a more sinister turn. Cooper agreed to leave the house and stop with his brother. I needed a post-mortem examination and fast. Not surprisingly I had little problem in securing the services of a Home Office pathologist following a discussion with the local coroner. The pathologist was Dr Stephen Leadbeater, who I knew very well having dealt with him over the years. Stephen was an excellent pathologist, very deliberate in his manner and speech and not someone you could hurry along, although on this occasion he knew the background and was prepared to move quickly. I met him at Haverfordwest police station and briefed him on the circumstances. 'Stephen, please do not come back with "inconclusive", I need to know, has he killed her or not?' He looked at me and replied, 'Mr Wilkins, I will do my very best within the capabilities of modern-day forensic pathology, now let me get on.' Later the same day I received a call from Dr Leadbeater. We had already established that there had been a history of chronic heart disease in Pat's family, resulting in early death. Mr Leadbeater described how her heart was very swollen and contained three conditions that could have resulted in her death; and most importantly she had not died a violent death. The PM results were inconclusive about whether they had had sex in the hours before she died. My personal view, not in any medical books, is that Pat Cooper gave up and could not face living with this man again. During the Huntsman investigation she had indicated that she had suffered a life of physical and mental abuse. Following her death another member of her family told my team that my scenario was true. Pat was dreading him returning home but unfortunately she was too frightened to tell anyone.

Late in December 2008 I met Tom Atherton, Gerard Elias QC and Susanne Thomas to discuss the case; they had now considered the advice file. Mr Elias referred to other legal cases that dealt with Evidence of Bad Character. Their view was that bad character should not bolster a weak case, but they felt that this case was exceptional. They felt that the Ottawa team should develop this approach, but any decision should be delayed whilst the forensic work was going on. This would take a considerable amount of work because Mr Elias felt that the defence would quickly respond with an abuse of process argument, or 'no case to answer' following any decision to charge Cooper. The ball was back in our court, we needed to present a case to the Crown based on bad character, similar fact and circumstantial evidence while developing the forensic work. To do this I needed more staff, and as before I enjoyed complete support from DCC Andy Edwards and the Gold Group. I felt we were at a make-or-break point and the next six months would be crucial. I needed to concentrate wholly on this investigation and it was therefore agreed that I would be dedicated solely to Operation Ottawa and taken away from my other duties. When the team met in February 2009 for a briefing at Pembroke Dock little did we know the next few months would be life-changing for all those involved in the case.

CHAPTER 14

'YOU CAN'T BEAT
A BIT OF BULLY'

It was February 2009 and the team assembled at Pembroke
Dock police station. We had taken over the third floor,
and the beloved snooker table had finally gone, given to
a local club. The disclosure team was now comprised of
six officers: Temporary Detective Sergeant Barry Kelly led
the team of experienced Detectives, DC Emyr Griffiths,
DC Simon Lewis-Davies, DC Oliver James, DC Mark
Roach and DC Fred Hunter. They had the daunting
task of reviewing all of the material making up the three
Ottawa investigations, as well as Huntsman. The CPS had
now identified a lawyer to help with this process. Grenville
Barker was a very likeable man who loved Cardiff City FC.
He was easy to work with, clear about what he needed
and nothing was too much trouble for him. Our regular
discussions allowed me to give clarity of purpose to the
disclosure process and the team quietly got on with it.

The road ahead was now clear; I needed to present a
case to the CPS and Gerard Elias QC on the basis that
we would not get any forensic evidence linking Cooper to
the Ottawa offences. The forensics work would continue
to its natural conclusion now that Angela Gallop and her
team had breathed new life into it. I was impressed by

their enthusiasm and they had started to review the fibre exhibits. We knew that Cooper had been a gloved offender and his family had said that he had clothing locked away in a wardrobe in his shed which he put on before creeping out into the night. LGC now had all of the various gloves recovered from the Sardis robbery and from in and around his home. The face-to-face meetings with the scientists were working well although their view of what an examination was and mine were at times poles apart. The combination of the scientist and detective sitting at the same table discussing what they actually meant by examination was fascinating and enabled us to identify additional avenues to probe and helped understand what might have been done in the past. Together with LGC we worked through each individual exhibit and its potential for development; it was a potent combination and if this didn't work then I believed nothing would.

When it came to the linking matrix, I commissioned a review from my peers. SIOs who were not connected to the case were asked for their opinion on our processes. They were very supportive, because once the key elements of Cooper's behaviour and MO had been stripped out of the three Ottawa offences and overlaid with his convictions the similarities were startling. We had compared some 1500 suspects and persons of interest together with their offending history against the linking matrix, and none had committed serious crimes that had the same key elements that we were investigating.

One of my analysts was tasked with producing a year-by-year picture of particular types of crime that had taken place in the same geographical area as the Ottawa offences and Cooper's convictions. This was not an easy task as some records were paper-based and others computerised. Home Office rules for recording these crimes had also changed and I had to take this into account. The process would start from 1983 to the present day and provide a visual representation of how crime had changed in the area over this period. Our work on 'bad character' was very important and without forensic evidence we would stand or fall by it. The matrix gave a visual representation of what we now needed to turn into evidence.

Identification of the suspect had now raised itself as an issue, particularly in relation to the Dixons murder and I needed to discuss it with the CPS. I was satisfied that a witness had indeed seen Cooper at the NatWest cashpoint in Haverfordwest and that his was the source of the artist's impression of the 'wild man' and his bike. It was possible that other people who had seen a man of a similar description had also seen Cooper. The television appeal on the 7th of November had uncovered another witness who had a frightening confrontation with a similar man on the shoreline leading into Pembroke on the day of the murders. The rules of evidence state that if you have a suspect and he is available to take part in an identification parade, then he should be given the opportunity to participate. This was a very unusual set of circumstances though, and we were twenty years on from the crime. We had a passport photograph of Cooper from around the time of the Dixons murder, but it was of poor quality. My personal view was that an identification parade or the use of old photographs would be pointless but I needed to raise it with counsel, to ensure it was explored at an early stage. Cooper's appearance had changed significantly over the years and I could not guarantee that the photographs truly represented how he looked at the time of the sightings.

Our meticulous enquiries into Cooper's background had revealed that in 1989 he had taken part in the popular ITV game show *Bullseye*. Comedian Jim Bowen, whose catchphrase was 'You can't beat a bit of Bully', hosted the show. Contestants had to answer general knowledge questions and throw darts for prizes. Given Cooper's propensity for gambling and his enthusiasm for darts we weren't surprised that he had put his name forward for the show together with another member of the local pub darts team. What was particularly interesting was the date: 1989.

We had amassed many images of Cooper over the years in various guises and with numerous hairstyles. What we didn't have was a picture of him at the time of the Dixons' murder. If footage still existed of his appearance on *Bullseye* this could be hugely significant. I decided to call Jonathan Hill at ITV Wales and asked him for his assistance in locating the *Bullseye* show. He could hardly believe what I'd told him and set to work tracking down the programme. Jonathan knew that Central Television in Birmingham had produced *Bullseye* and it was there that he made the first enquiries. He soon discovered that much of ITV's archive was now held in vaults in Leeds and this became the focus of his search. He called the librarian in Leeds, who, without being fully aware of the significance of the enquiry, seemed rather bewildered that he was being asked to look for a single Welsh contestant amongst dozens of episodes of the much beloved show. Various searches revealed that the programme had been transmitted in the late autumn and in the run-up to Christmas. What wasn't included on the database was when the shows had actually been recorded. The librarian set to work viewing hours of footage looking for some mention of a Welsh contestant.

At the same time enquiries began to try and pinpoint the dates of these recordings. This would require considerable effort and also some good luck.

One of the senior administrators at ITV Wales, Nia Britton, had the idea of checking the financial paperwork from the series for a reference to a recording date. After twenty years it was a long shot. Incredibly, a memo from the Director of Programmes at Central TV was located, which happened to mention moving the recording dates of the show to the spring of 1989. It was exactly the time we were interested in. We were getting close. Then after deeper investigations, photocopied contracts turned up for Jim Bowen and for a make-up artist who had been booked for the recordings in May and June. Days later the librarian rang back and said that he had found an episode with two men from Milford Haven, including a certain John Cooper. Eureka! Now we knew which episode he had appeared in we were able to tie down the date of the recording. When Jonathan called me I could hardly believe what I was hearing. He said that the episode with Cooper had been recorded on the 28th of May 1989, exactly a month before the Dixons were murdered. A few minutes later Jonathan called me back saying that the librarian was about to play the episode down the line from Leeds to Cardiff. He said he would call again when he had it in his hands.

Forty-five minutes later his number flashed up on my mobile. 'It's incredible, Steve, you have to see this,' he said. It was Cooper, bold as brass, smiling and joking on national television having almost certainly murdered two people in cold blood. At the start of the show Jim Bowen chatted with Cooper and the other contestants to put them at their ease before the game started. The conversation was relaxed as the contestants talked about their lives and playing darts; Cooper was then asked about his interesting hobby.

JIM BOWEN: 'You've got an unusual hobby John, haven't you?'

COOPER: 'Oh yes, the Scuba diving.'

JIM BOWEN: 'Scuba diving and apparently it's the place to do it?'

COOPER: 'Oh we've got coastline.'

JIM BOWEN: 'Yes because is it the mountains are sort of inverted and you've got all these . . .'

COOPER: 'We've got deep water where you can swim over mountains and all sorts of things.'

You could hardly make it up. There was Cooper, just a month before the killings, revealing on national television knowledge of the area where the Dixons would be murdered.

Jonathan went on to describe how, in the quiz section of the show, Cooper's general knowledge let him down time and time again. Faster on the buzzer, with the right answers, was the female contestant next to him. Cooper forced a smile but he would have hated losing, especially to a woman. In the end Cooper and his teammate were forced into an early exit. But this wasn't quite the end of the story. As the show reached its climax the winners were given a chance to gamble the prizes they had picked along the way against the star prize hidden behind a screen. It was the great tradition of *Bullseye* to offer the star prize gamble to the runners-up if the winners refused to chance their arm. And if the runners-up then declined they would bring back the losing pair to throw darts for the star prize.

Cooper had been thrown a lifeline. Having been humiliated on national TV here was his chance to redeem himself and scoop a big money prize. Right on a cue, beaming ear to ear, Cooper walked back on to the studio floor and announced that he wanted to gamble his winnings for the star prize. It was another extraordinary chance to scrutinise the prime suspect. This time it was Cooper throwing the darts and not his partner. Yet again his misplaced confidence in his own abilities would be tested. As the drums rolled, Cooper threw his three darts and lost the lot. For a split second he looked to camera with a stare that said it all. As the credits rolled the host tried to console the pair with a friendly hug and a joke; one can only imagine what Cooper was thinking.

The *Bullseye* footage was clearly now a key piece of evidence. Here we had the prime suspect on tape just a month before the Dixons were murdered. His physique, haircut and features could all be scrutinised. The opportunity was not lost on Jonathan either. In an edit suite at ITV Wales in Cardiff he decided to view the image of the artist's impression of the suspect from the 1989 inquiry. The sketch had captured the suspect from behind his right shoulder with his face almost in profile. Watching the *Bullseye* sequence through, Jonathan then stopped the tape at the moment when Cooper adopted a similar pose. The images were then put side by side with the help of a graphic artist who pasted the still images next to one another on the screen. The result was chilling. Cooper had long bushy collar-length hair just like the artist's impression. Given that Cooper's hair is likely to have been brushed into shape by a make-up artist before the TV show, it matched closely. His features too bore a close resemblance, particularly the nose and chin.

Then there was his stocky physique just like the man in the sketch who was drawn with his shirt and shorts pulled tightly across his body. The similarity was compelling and I knew we would have to apply through the courts to get hold of the footage and the graphic images. For the first time we could see Cooper as he would have looked at the time of the Dixons' murder. In my thirty years' service I had seen many artist's impressions and photo-fit efforts, but I had never seen as close a match as this.

A critical piece of work was the research and analysis. A team of researchers was brought together and started to build up a picture of the circle of offending and criminal activity that emanated from Cooper's home with a radius as far as the coastal path. We wanted to know about certain crime pattern trends that were occurring during Cooper's offending period and post his arrest to the present day. This would include both detected and undetected offences including murder, robbery, burglary, aggravated burglary, criminal use of firearms, rape, sexual assaults, arson and attempted crimes.

The second priority was to research all Cooper's convictions together with offences that could be linked to him, in order to identify his MO. For the next few months we continued with this work from Pembroke Dock. The whole team worked tirelessly and with considerable skill and commitment. All Cooper's family had been interviewed and statements taken from them. Adrian in particular had made some chilling revelations about his father's almost nightly disappearances when he would go to his shed, change his clothing and go out into the dark across the fields. On one occasion he was able to see into the secret wardrobe that his father kept in the shed. There were photographs of people he did not recognise and items of jewellery; he also saw a shotgun, shortened at the barrel and stock. Was this the reason that Cooper went to great lengths to discredit his son? He knew that Adrian could potentially give very damning evidence against him? Again, it was all very interesting but how much could I use in a court of law?

The time had come for me and the team to lock ourselves behind closed doors and map out the evidential and bad character case as it stood. This needed to be a team effort because we all had a detailed knowledge of Huntsman, Ottawa, Cooper and what evidence was available. The team were assembled at Pembroke Dock police station and I briefed them about what I wanted. I now needed to catalogue the hard evidence, alongside the bad character case and ask the three questions I always ask in any investigation I am leading: what do we know? What do we think we know? What do we need to know? The last two questions dictate the direction of the investigation and provide answers to the first question. At this point I needed the team to put down on paper what we could put forward in a preliminary hearing or a potential court case.

The first task was to strip out the relevant parts of his Huntsman convictions. The offences were committed mainly in the early evening and in winter months. All the offences were committed within a closely defined geographical area and within a two-mile radius of Cooper's home. All the properties attacked were isolated and backed onto fields. The main item targeted was jewellery from bedrooms, although some other property, such as cash and electrical equipment, was also stolen. Of the thirty offences of burglary for which Cooper was

Helen Thomas *(top left)* and Richard Thomas *(top right)*. The fire meant there were very few good quality images of the Thomases. Richard Thomas was a private man; he probably disturbed Cooper when he returned to Scoveston Park Farm, seen here burned out in 1985.

Peter Dixon. An active man who we believed put up a fight and probably caused a rib injury to Cooper.

Gwenda Dixon. We were certain that, after blasting her to death, Cooper had stolen her spare shorts from her rucksack.

In 1989, Detective Chief Superintendent Clive Jones released the artist's impression *(right)* of the suspect who used Peter Dixon's cash card in Haverfordwest. The picture of Cooper *(left)* is a still from footage of his appearance on *Bullseye*, within months of the Dixon murders.

(Top) We believed that Cooper had buried a shotgun under the duck run and preserved it in oil to use as his next weapon of terror.

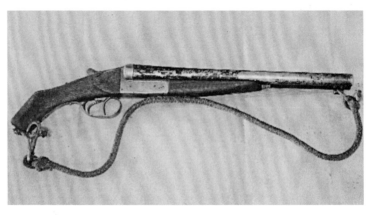

(Centre) The gun recovered on the trail from the Sardis robbery scene.

(Bottom) The day of reckoning. We had waited five years to finally arrest Cooper.

(Top) The bucket of keys found at Cooper's house.

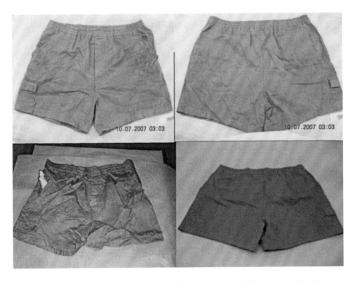

(Bottom) Four different images of the same pair of shorts, stolen from Gwenda Dixon and found at Cooper's house. The shorts provided a wealth of evidence.

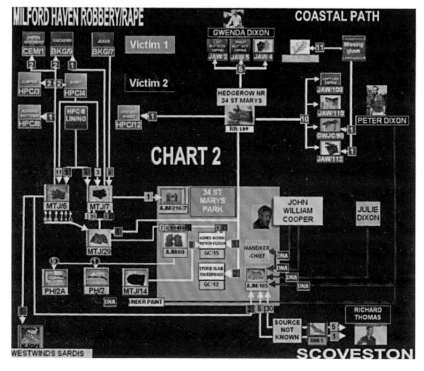

The forensic chart became so complicated that this simple web of connectivity was used to show the jury the strong links between the crimes.

The Ottawa team (and some of the evidence) in its room at court. Steve Wilkins is in the centre holding the paper.

In the months before the trial, Jonathan Hill *(right)* filmed
the team on location in preparation for his documentary. ITV had
provided the vital *Bullseye* footage of Cooper appearing on the
popular quiz show.

convicted, property from twenty-five of the victims was recovered from 34 St Marys Park or the homes of his family. (It was accepted that they had innocently received the property.) It is only when you examine the sheer number of offences that you understand why Cooper was branded 'a one-man crime wave'. We now looked at the crimes and the exhibits in more detail:

Clariston Hall – 20th April 1983

This was a night time burglary of an occupied, three-storey farmhouse surrounded by fields. Cooper entered the premises by breaking the downstairs bathroom window. Fortunately a stout internal locked door prevented him from getting past the main kitchen. Jewellery, including a gold-coloured bracelet was stolen. The bracelet was recovered in Cooper's garden fifteen years later. He answered 'no comment' in a police interview, but stated in evidence that he did not recognise the bracelet but that his wife had one similar. He stated that the grandchildren must have played with it and left it in the garden.

The Old Vicarage, Rosemarket – 25th October 1988

A night time burglary of an unoccupied, detached property, surrounded by fields. Jewellery was taken that was recovered at the Cooper's home and identified in 1998. Cooper maintained a 'no comment' interview but in evidence asserted it was his wife's or his daughter's jewellery.

13 Hazel Grove – 1st December 1989 to 31st January 1990

A burglary of an unoccupied bungalow, which backed onto fields and a bridle path from Llanstadwell towards Waterston. Entry was forced into a rear patio door. Over £2,700 worth of jewellery was taken. Some items, including a cigarette case with a built-in Ronson lighter, were found in Cooper's home. Significantly, keys were also stolen from the premises and found in the cesspit of his home. Cooper gave a 'no comment' interview, but in evidence he maintained that the cigarette case and lighter were given to him in 1984.

9 Hazel Grove – 5th November 1992

An evening burglary of an unoccupied bungalow which backed onto fields. Cooper kicked in the bottom panel of the back door and stole over £1,600 worth of jewellery, spare keys to the house and the car. The keys were found in the cesspit of his home. Muddy footprints were recovered at the scene. PC Mike Callas attended the scene with a police tracker dog, 'Bruce'. The dog picked up a scent, over the fence of the premises, onto the bridle path, down towards Hazel Hill House, across past the pumping station, and ending in Waterston fields, in the direction of Cooper's home address. He gave a 'no comment' interview but maintained in evidence he had never been down the bridle path and the keys found at his property had been given to him as some were made of brass.

Glenhill Cottage – 11th November 1993

An evening burglary of an unoccupied two-storey cottage in a country lane surrounded by fields, next door to Glenowen Cottage (scene of another burglary). The back was door forced and muddy boot prints were found on the carpet. Jewellery stolen from the property was found at Cooper's home address and at Scoveston Fort. This is important as it links Cooper to Scoveston Fort. At the time of the Scoveston Park murders jewellery from robberies in the area was also found at Scoveston Fort. 'No comment' interview but in evidence the defendant stated that Scoveston Fort was used as a 'back garden' by a number of burglars he knew and that the items recovered at his home were given to him over time. Scoveston Fort was only a few hundred yards from Scoveston Park and from Cooper's home address.

22 Hazel Grove – 29th October 1994

An evening burglary of an unoccupied property which backed onto a bridle path. Forced entry, with jewellery taken from the bedroom. Earrings and a pendant were later found at Cooper's home. In interview he stated that he had bought the earrings from a shop. In evidence, the defendant maintained that the earrings were given to him by another man and given to his daughter.

Castle Pill Crescent – 18th November 1994

An evening burglary of an unoccupied bungalow backing onto fields. Over £4,000 worth of property, including jewellery, was taken. Items were recovered at the home address of Cooper where, again, he stated in evidence that he had bought them. An internal light was on, woollen glove marks were found at the scene, a dog handler was called and a trail followed to a railway line and on to a point parallel with Scoveston Park heading in the direction of Cooper's home address.

'The Cranny' – 10th December 1994 and 14th October 1995

An evening burglary at an unoccupied bungalow surrounded by fields, this property was attacked on two separate occasions. The first burglary involved forcing a front bedroom window and attempting to break into a locked firearms cabinet. Jewellery and a 'Samsonite' bag were taken but no property was recovered. The second burglary involved forcing a back window and further attempt to get into the gun cabinet, with a packet of French-made 12-bore cartridges and two 'buck' knives being stolen. The defendant maintained that he had bought the bag and that the jewellery recovered at his daughter's house was nothing to do with him, although coins taken and recovered at his home were part of his collection. The sheath to one of the 'buck' knives was found discarded on the Sardis robbery trail in 1996.

School Cottage – 26th January 1995

An evening burglary of an unoccupied bungalow surrounded by fields, which faced a lane. Some months after the burglary, as a result of cattle straying, they found that barbed wire had been cut at the property near where a torch had been left. A car key was taken, along with a purse. In evidence, Cooper maintained that the key (which was found in the boot of his car) was one of many he kept as he often acted as a 'Good Samaritan' helping people locked out of their cars. He did not know how he came to be in possession of it, or for that matter, the purse that was found at his address.

'The Cotswolds' – 15th April 1995

Burglary of an unoccupied property backing onto fields. Over £2,000 worth of jewellery was stolen the rear patio doors had been forced with an instrument. An old, decommissioned shotgun was also stolen, along with cartridges, foreign coins and a set of darts. A security light had been snapped off. The occupant had not used the shotgun for some time, although still kept seventeen or eighteen Italian-made cartridges in a plain box in the bedroom, bought twenty years earlier. In a biscuit box recovered at the defendant's premises, eight of the occupant's Italian cartridges were recovered. Knives (of distinctive design) and coins also stolen in the burglary were recovered in Cooper's shed and car, he, again, maintained he bought these items innocently.

10 Hazel Grove – 31st July 1995

Burglary of an unoccupied house, with fields to the rear. Forced entry via rear patio doors where jewellery, cash and, significantly, tools stolen, some found at Cooper's property. He maintained that he had bought the tools and box at a market in August or September 1995.

9 Lighthouse Drive – 14th September 1995

An evening burglary of an unoccupied secluded house with the coastal path at the rear. Entry was gained by forcing the rear patio door with an instrument. Jewellery was stolen along with an air rifle and a pair of size nine boots. Jewellery was found at Cooper's home address. He maintained in evidence that he had previously bought some of the jewellery from another man, the coins were his and the remainder belonged to his wife.

Edmoor Bungalow – 18–19th September 1995

An evening burglary of an unoccupied secluded bungalow surrounded by fields, the rear boundary of the property having a hedge that backs onto fields. Wire in the hedge was cut to gain access to the property, jewellery and cash and taken. A 'Timex' watch was recovered at the property that did not belong to the occupiers and was dropped by the offender. A personal photograph recovered at Cooper's daughter's home showed John Cooper wearing an identical watch, and it was later identified as his by his wife, who subsequently retracted this assertion. Cooper denied the watch was his.

'The Gables', Sardis Cross – 18th October 1995

An evening burglary of an unoccupied dwelling house located opposite fields. The kitchen window had been forced and jewellery was stolen together with a hip flask that was found at Cooper's home address. He maintained that he had bought the property from another man.

Rushmoor Farm – 7th November 1995

An evening burglary of an unoccupied dwelling located opposite fields, next door to Westbury Hill another attacked property. Entry was gained through a forced side window. Jewellery was taken including a set of silver spoons that were recovered from Cooper's home address. Cooper maintained in evidence that they had been given to his family as a gift, contrary to his interview assertion that he had bought them.

29 St Marys Park – 21st November 1995

An evening burglary of an unoccupied dwelling located opposite fields. The property is situated near to the Cooper's own home address (number 34). Windows and a rear patio door were forced with an instrument. Jewellery and a pair of Chinese padlocks were stolen. The padlocks were recovered in the cesspit at Cooper's home. He made 'No comment' at interview.

3 Lucy Walters Close – 12th December 1995

An evening burglary at an unoccupied isolated dwelling surrounded by fields, this is the home address of Cooper's niece and goddaughter. Entry was gained by forcing a rear patio door and Christmas presents were taken. Some items were found discarded in a nearby field other presents were found at Cooper's home address. Female underwear was also stolen. Mark Jenkins, a police dog handler, tracked across fields in the direction of Cooper's home address, cut fences were found nearby giving access to the fields.

89 Honeyfields – 22nd December 1995

An evening burglary at an unoccupied dwelling surrounded by fields with a hedge at the back. Barbed wire in the rear hedge was cut giving access to the garden; the rear patio door was forced with an instrument. Jewellery, cash and keys were taken. Muddy footprints (including glove marks) found at the house. Keys recovered at Cooper's home address fitted the occupant's car. Cooper maintained that the keys had been given to him by another man. A *Nursing Times* book stolen from the house was also recovered at the Coopers' home.

43 Hazelbank – 4–6th January 1996

An evening burglary of an unoccupied property partially surrounded by fields with a hedge at the back. Front door forced, jewellery taken. Some items (e.g. earrings) recovered at Cooper's home. Cooper denied knowledge of them, but his wife maintained they belonged to her. A hole had been cut in rear hedge and a rope and wire-cutters found nearby.

9 Ardent Close – 11th February 1996

An evening burglary at an unoccupied secluded bungalow, partially surrounded by fields with a hedge at the back. The rear patio doors were forced with an instrument. Watches, documents, a wallet and a wetsuit were taken. The wetsuit was found at Cooper's home. He maintained that he had bought it from a man at Gelliswick Beach (near Milford Haven).

16 Bunkers Hill, Steynton – 23rd February 1996

Burglary of an unoccupied property which had a rear garden sloping down towards a stream and then fields. Jewellery and a pair of size nine 'Brasher' boots were taken. Property recovered from field nearby. 'No comment' interview.

23 Castle Pill Crescent – 1ˢᵗ March 1996

An evening burglary at an unoccupied detached bungalow with fields to rear. Amongst jewellery and videotapes taken was a double-barrelled Bruno shotgun and cartridges. A steel firearms cabinet had been forced open. The gun was found in a sewer pipe at the Cooper's home address, buried under the duck run in a black bin bag preserved in oil. The serial number had been ground off it, and, significantly, the stock had been sawn off. Noticeably, a replacement screw (that 'stood proud' and was not flush with the gun) had been inserted into the gun. This modification is identical to that of the gun used on the Sardis armed robbery; its function was to attach a lanyard. The occupant positively identified the shotgun as his. The videotapes later identified were found near Scoveston Fort, other items in a field nearby. Cooper blamed two local men, stating they had approached him in Coombes Drive asking whether he wanted to buy a gun for £200. He said he refused, so they threw the gun, in a bag, into the back of his car. He said that he intended to dispose of them but was 'frightened' and drove home before hiding them at his property. He then later stated that he had tried to put the gun together to shoot ducks. PC Mark Jenkins gives details of a track followed by a dog relating to this offence, leading towards Cooper's property. Items of jewellery stolen from this burglary were recovered in the same location as a single woollen glove BB/109 (this glove would later become significant).

'The Nook', Crossways – 22nd March 1996

An unoccupied property adjacent to 'The Cranny' (previously the subject of a burglary). Front window forced entry the house was ransacked. Bags, purses and a charity box taken but nothing recovered. However, green woollen fibres were recovered at the point of entry, brown polypropylene fibres by damaged patio doors and in a gap in the rear hedge where the fencing wires in the hedge had been cut. 'No comment' interview. These fibres would be matched to points of entry at other burglaries in the series in which property was recovered from Cooper, therefore linking the offender to the offences.

5 Roebuck Close – 4–8th April 1996

An evening burglary at an unoccupied dwelling house surrounded by fields. Jewellery and a 'Head' rucksack were taken. The rucksack was found on the trail left by Cooper as he fled the scene of the Sardis robbery. Cooper gave a 'No comment' interview. Brown polypropylene fibres found at the point of entry matched fibres recovered from the points of entry of other burglaries in the series.

Westbury Hill – 4–9th April 1996

An evening burglary at an unoccupied detached, modernised farmhouse surrounded with fields. Rear forced window entry, with a farm gate used as a ladder to facilitate access.

Jewellery along with other items, including videocassettes, were taken and recovered at Cooper's property. There was also evidence of cut fences nearby. Cooper stated in evidence that he did not know where these items came from.

3 Penry Point – 2ⁿᵈ October 1996

An evening burglary at an unoccupied detached house with fields to the rear. The rear patio doors had been forced with an instrument. Jewellery and a portable television set taken. Items of jewellery were found in a field near to Cooper's home address. He maintained in evidence that some of the items he had bought himself and others belonged to family members.

Glenowen Cottage – 23–27ᵗʰ October 1996

A dwelling situated on a lane backing onto fields, entry was being gained through a kitchen window at the front of the house. A video recorder, personal stereo and television set (amongst other items) were taken. The video and personal stereo was recovered from Cooper's home, the television set from another family member, given to them by Cooper. Cooper stated that he had bought the television and stereo from two local men.

9 Bunkers Hill – 31ˢᵗ October 1996

This count should be seen in conjunction with the next burglary at 28 Castle Pill Road, as both properties are located close together and were burgled on the same night. This was an evening burglary of an unoccupied bungalow backing onto fields on Halloween night. A police dog trail ultimately led officers from the burgled premises to a gate directly opposite the defendant's home address. Quantities of jewellery were stolen. Some of the items were recovered at Cooper's home address. Cooper again, maintained that they were his belongings, having bought them at some point before the burglaries.

28 Castle Pill Road, Steynton – 31st October 1996

Burglary with intent to steal of an occupied bungalow, where, at approximately 7 p.m., the lone female occupant noticed one of her bedroom doors open. On investigation, she saw that the bedroom window blind had been damaged and the window forced open. There was evidence that someone had forced open the rear garden gate, the inference being someone had rushed out over the garden and into fields behind to escape. As stated above, police being called, a police dog with handler PC Mark Jenkins followed a trail from the premises, over fields and to a gate directly opposite the defendant's home address. A map demonstrated the route of the dog trail and a cut fence in a hedge to facilitate a more direct escape route. The route took the dog across fields and across the access lane of Scoveston Park Farm. In fact the dog handler spoke to Cooper, whom he knew. Cooper denied knowing anything about the burglaries and said his own dog had been disturbed.

'Westwinds', Sardis – 22nd November 1996

This offence concerns an armed, shotgun robbery inside the occupant's home. The property, a detached bungalow, is situated at the end of a row of bungalows, is flanked by a field to the south. This offence has significant similarities to elements of the attack on the children at Milford Haven and the Scoveston Park murders, if accepted that this probably started as a robbery on a lone female (Helen Thomas). The robbery occurred at about 7.50 p.m., the occupant was in her living room awaiting the arrival of her husband, and the front door was unlocked. She was alone when a male entered the living room, wearing an army camouflage-type jacket, a balaclava and brandishing a sawn-off shotgun. He had white trainers on covered in mud. He shouted to her, words to the effect of *'get down'*, *'are you on your own?'*, *'don't look at me'*, *'where's the jewellery?'* and *'I want money'*, before physically attacking her by striking her to the face and body with the firearm. (Gwenda Dixon and the male victims of Milford Haven robbery/rape were struck about the head with a firearm or blunt instrument.) He confronted her in the living room and then dragged her into the bedroom and covered her head with a pair of jeans. (A shirt was found around the neck of Helen Thomas, and the victim of the Milford Haven rape was made to cover her head with her clothing.) The defendant then tied up Mrs Clark (hands behind her back) before causing her injury. The defendant then searched the premises for money and jewellery. A quantity of jewellery and a handbag were taken. As the defendant fled the premises, the victim pressed a panic button that sounded the alarm. The defendant departed through the front door and over a bank where wire had been cut in the fence to the property. Wires in the fields to the rear of the bungalow had also been cut during the week before the robbery. A witness saw the offender, Cooper, still wearing a balaclava fleeing the scene and chased him before being confronted with the firearm, enabling him to escape. The route taken by Cooper from the scene was followed by PC Mark Jenkins and his dog. The route passed through thorn hedges that would have potentially caused injury to the offender as he fled the scene. On the Monday after the robbery, Cooper had scratches and facial injuries, witnessed by a neighbour. Along that route, in a hedgerow, a number of items were recovered. And can be summarised as follows:

Shotgun (exhibit PH2)

The stock was sawn off in an identical manner to the gun recovered buried under Cooper's duck run and stolen from 23 Castle Pill, Milford Haven. A new screw had been inserted through the trigger guard and stock of PH2 and secured to the top tang. The screw also stood 'proud', as per the repair and modification to the gun from Castle Pill. A screw, the tip of which was broken, was recovered from Cooper's garden shed. That screw, in the opinion of the firearms expert, Ian Johnson, *almost certainly originated from the gun*' at the position where the new screw had been inserted. It had the same semi–circular pattern on the head and thread as the other screws and fitted snugly into the recess. A short length of cord attaching the rope-sling to the end of the stock was similar to a length recovered from Cooper's home. It was made of the same nylon, had the same weave, the same thickness and was put together in the same way. There was black paint on the gun similar to black paint found on Puma trainers that were found in Cooper's shed.

Two cartridges (MDS 1 and JR19)

Both were live shotgun cartridges. They were 'Maionchi' cartridges similar to some of the cartridges recovered buried in Cooper's duck run.

Threaded tool – a home-made jemmy (MTJ10)

There was black tape securing the rope to the tool and the Allen key head. It was identical to the black tape recovered on the plastic box with the cartridges buried under the duck run and a roll of tape recovered from Cooper's home. A black tape mark was also found at the point of entry in the burglary at Glenowen Cottage in October 2006, and there was black tape on the torch abandoned at the scene of the Sardis robbery. Beneath black tape on the tool were brown polypropylene fibres identical to those found at the scenes of seven of the burglaries. This again provided a scene-to-scene link. The Allen key was identical to two other Allen keys recovered from Cooper's garden shed. There is no doubt that this tool was the instrument used to force the patio doors.

Length of cord (MTJ6)

This was also the same nylon as that attached to the gun PH2 and cord found at Cooper's home address.

'Head' rucksack (MTJ8)

Positively identified as stolen in the burglary at 5 Roebuck Close Milford Haven in April 1986. Brown polypropylene fibres found at this point of entry matched other scenes.

Duracell batteries (X2) (MDS4), torch casing (MAR1) and light section (BJJ2)

There was black tape on the torch casing which matched tape recovered from Cooper's home. White cloth inside the casing matched white cloth inside the buried box containing cartridges and a separate piece of cloth found in Cooper's summerhouse. The weave was observed as being relatively uncommon.

Balaclava (MTJ14)

Found discarded on the Sardis robbery trail. Hairs recovered from the inside and outside of the balaclava were subjected to Mitochondrial DNA testing and compared with head hair samples from Cooper. Crucially, there was a match between Cooper's sequencing and the sequencing of the hairs from the balaclava. Cooper's Mitochondrial DNA sequence was relatively uncommon. Furthermore, green fibres were adhered to the balaclava that were identical to a green fibre on tapings from the conservatory window at the rear of 'Westwinds', the Sardis robbery, a green fibre taping at the point of entry to 'The Nook', Crossways, Milford Haven and green fibres adhering to a green/purple fleece jacket (MTJ29).

Green/purple fleece jacket (MTJ29)

This jacket was found on the robber's trail between the balaclava and a black handbag positively identified by the victim of the Sardis robbery. The jacket had green fibres adhering to it identical to the green fibres on the balaclava; the inference being that Cooper had abandoned it as he fled the scene. Cooper's wife, in witness statements, stated that the jacket was identical to the one she brought back from America for her husband. In evidence during the Huntsman trial, however, she changed her mind. Cooper, in police interviews, told the officers that he had tracksuits in 1995 that his wife had brought back from the US. He added that they had subsequently been stolen from him. However, in evidence during the Huntsman trial, he maintained that those tracksuits had been burned on a bonfire. He denied the jacket belonged to him.

Puma trainers (MTJ28 and DGG1) – size 9

Footmarks on the trail from 'Westwinds', Sardis, were similar to the soles of those Puma trainers abandoned on the

Sardis robbery trail. Footmarks in the field opposite 'The Nook', Crossways, Milford Haven were also of a similar size and pattern to the Puma trainers, but limited in their value as there was no fine detail. Cooper maintained in evidence that he wore size eight shoes. The 'Brasher' boots worn by Cooper to commit some of the burglaries were size nine. A pair of size nine Wellington boots was recovered from Cooper's house. From the point where the Puma trainers were found, it was a short distance downhill to a disused railway line, now a public footpath, and Cooper's home address. This was the route he took as he fled the scene of the Sardis robbery. The laces on the Puma trainers had been cut, it is likely as he fled the scene he pulled the knife from the 'buck' knife holder which was then discarded, cut the laces on the trainers, which were again discarded. The knife was never found; having dumped his sawn-off shotgun, the knife would have probably been his weapon to use against any pursuer.

We had now detailed the connecting evidence and behaviour from his Huntsman convictions and already there were some startling similarities with the Ottawa offences so we needed to continue the exercise. We turned our attention to Scoveston Park.

Scoveston Park

Richard Thomas was born in 1927 and was fifty-eight years old at the time of his murder. Helen Thomas was born in 1929 and was fifty-six years old when she died. Neither of them had married and they lived together at Scoveston Park. Both Scoveston Park and Cooper's home address are at the geographical centre of a two-mile radius, which includes all the burglaries, and the Sardis armed robbery. After the fire, the post-mortem evidence revealed that Richard Thomas would have died instantly from a gunshot wound to the lower abdomen. He had also sustained glancing gunshot wounds to the head. There was no evidence of smoke inhalation, indicating that death had already occurred before the fire took hold. Owing to the damage caused by the fire, Helen Thomas's body had fallen through from the bedroom above. Under her clothing were items of bed linen, a piece of foam mattress, together with a length of knotted rope probably used to tie her up. Similarly, there was no evidence of smoke inhalation. Forensic scientists discovered a blanket on the half landing where Richard Thomas's body had been discovered. The conclusion was that the blanket bore all the hallmarks of having been dragged through mud and vegetation bearing a heavy object. Blood belonging to Richard Thomas was found splattered on offcuts of plasterboard in an outbuilding. Further examination revealed the presence of two lead cartridge pellets in the plasterboard and one embedded in the blood-splattered plaster on the wall. The conclusion is that Richard Thomas was killed in the outhouse and his body dragged on the blanket into the main house. The hypothesis is that this was a robbery that escalated into murder. The perpetrator had gone to Scoveston Park intending to commit burglary in the knowledge that Helen Thomas was alone in the house. He was disturbed, possibly by the late and unexpected arrival of Richard Thomas, and events spiralled into murder. Evidence demonstrates that Richard Thomas was the owner of at least one shotgun, yet no weapons were recovered at the house, leading to the conclusion that the perpetrator stole his gun or guns. No spent cartridges were found at the scene.

Furthermore, a cartridge box (AJM/216/6 and 7) recovered at Cooper's home address had handwriting on it, which could have belonged to Helen Thomas, though this was not conclusive. The cartridge box was found with other items of stolen property, including a shotgun, buried under the duck run at Cooper's home. Also recovered from the same location was ammunition identical to cartridges recovered from Scoveston Park. Shotgun wadding found on the Dixons' bodies was similar to wadding contained in other cartridges recovered from his home address.

Cooper's alibi was now dubious; he had told his family to tell the police that they were all in the house together on the night of the murders, when in fact this was not true. His daughter Teresa now cast doubt on his alibi and related an instance when her father came home with his hair flat to his head and sweating. He quickly went upstairs and washed and then told her to say they had been in all night if asked. Teresa could not remember if this was the night of the Scoveston Park murders and its value was limited but I had no doubt that it *was* the very night in question.

The Dixons

At the time of their murders, Peter Dixon was fifty-one years old and his wife fifty-two. They lived in Oxfordshire and regularly spent time in the summer at Howelston Farm caravan site in Little Haven. They arrived at the caravan site on the 19th of June 1989. They were last seen alive by fellow campers at about 9.30 a.m. on the 29th of June 1989, approximately an hour before they were murdered, walking out of the caravan site in the direction of the coastal path. At around 10.30 a.m. a number of witnesses heard gunshots in the vicinity of the coastal path. In all five shots were heard, comprising two sets of two followed by one final shot. The evidence of the Home Office pathologist Bernard Knight confirmed that Peter Dixon was shot three times and Gwenda Dixon twice in an execution-style killing. The three wounds to Peter Dixon and the two wounds to Gwenda Dixon were inflicted by a double-barrelled 12-bore sawn-off shotgun fired at close range. On the 5th of July 1989 at about 3 p.m. their bodies were found by police officers approximately 600 yards from the caravan site. The bodies were situated in a clearing, in thick vegetation between the coastal path and the edge of the cliff. Their bodies had been hidden by branches and uprooted plants from the nearby area. Peter Dixon's NatWest cash card and wedding ring were missing. No spent cartridges were found at the scene. Gwenda Dixon's body was naked from the waist down. Blue acrylic fibres were recovered from the belt, shorts and body of Peter Dixon and the sweatshirt and body of Gwenda Dixon. Fibres were also recovered from the branches used to conceal their bodies. Peter Dixon's hands were tied together behind his back.

Enquiries at NatWest revealed that Mr Dixon's cash card was used on four occasions after his death. The new video evidence of John Cooper on *Bullseye*, filmed less than a month before the murders, had an uncanny resemblance to the artist's impression and suspect seen at the cashpoint. We know that on the 5th of July 1989, Cooper sold a man's gold wedding ring to a jeweller on Main Street in

Pembroke. This location is less than fifty yards from the NatWest cashpoint used by the murderer on the 29th of June 1989. We also knew that Cooper frequented Pembroke to sell stolen jewellery. In the 2008 interview it can be shown that he told lies about this ring. Furthermore Adrian Cooper related an instance when he took his father's car to drive up to Little Haven at the time of the murders to see what was happening. Cooper found out and went berserk at him, suggesting that the car had a bald tyre. Adrian felt his reaction was disproportionate. Cooper had known that Adrian was out in the car but only reacted when he was made aware that his son had been to Little Haven.

Milford Haven attack

At approximately 7 p.m. on Wednesday the 6th of March 1996 three teenage girls and two boys from the Mount Estate walked towards woodland and across a field via a stile, which was situated near a school. Having entered the field, they walked into the woods, through a barbed wire fence, stopping to play on a rope swing. They then planned to cross the river through an area called 'Black Bridge' before heading up to North Road in Milford Haven. When they got to the river it was high tide and too deep to cross so they turned back and retraced their steps. As they re-entered the field, they saw someone with a light or torch coming towards them. As the man approached them, he pulled out a gun and ordered them back down the field telling them to lay on their stomachs the floor and to put their faces on the grass. He then struck Steven on the head with the gun. The man then grabbed Jayne by her hair and dragged her a few feet away from the others, warning them not to look. The man then took out a knife, told her to stop crying, before lifting up her top and groping her breasts. He then undid her trousers, told her to take one leg out and to be quiet. It was at this point that the man raped Jayne. She was then told to get dressed, and they were all told not to tell anyone what had happened because he knew where they lived. Before he left, the man asked the teenagers for money then approached Susan, who was still lying on the ground, and indecently assaulted her by pushing up her bra and groping her breasts and between her legs. He repeated his threat that if they told anyone, he would kill them. He then fired the gun as he left. No spent cartridge was recovered. The man was confident in controlling multiple victims in an isolated rural location. The offence involved robbery and had strong sexual element and he used a double-barrelled sawn-off shotgun. He didn't commit murder, but the circumstances were very similar to the Dixons' attack. Perhaps on this occasion the offender would have found it too difficult to shoot all his victims. The youngsters though were left in no doubt he would have used the gun. The words and threats used were very similar to those used by Cooper during the Sardis robbery. The two male victims at Milford Haven were into field sports and described the weapon as a side-by-side shotgun which had a lanyard clipped to the barrel and butt. Their description bears a very strong resemblance to the Sardis gun PH/2. All the youngsters involved in this attack later took part in a voice-recognition identification procedure. Three of the five young victims selected the voice of the defendant, John Cooper, as the person who had been the assailant.

At this point the Ottawa case was based on these connections, allowing us to make the following conclusions.

In relation to the three Ottawa offences, our position was that Cooper carried out the attacks using a shotgun. There was clear evidence that the weapon used in both the coastal path murders and the Milford Haven attempted robberies and sexual assault was a double-barrelled sawn-off shotgun. There was evidence from Cooper's previous offending to link him with shotguns generally. There were clear similarities in the way the shotgun was used in the Sardis armed robbery and some of the Ottawa offences. On the 15th of April 1995, Cooper burgled a house, 'The Cotswolds' in Sardis. A shotgun and cartridges were among the property stolen. The cartridges were found in a biscuit box during a search of Cooper's home buried under his duck run. On the 1st of March 1996, five days before the Milford attack Cooper burgled a house at 23 Castle Pill Crescent in Steynton. A double-barrelled Bruno shotgun and cartridges were stolen. This shotgun was recovered at Cooper's address, preserved in oil, wrapped in cloth and buried in a pipe. The stock had been modified in an identical manner to the Sardis shotgun PH/2. It was clear this gun had been preserved so that it could be recovered at a later date. Castle Pill backed onto a field near to where the attempted robberies and sexual assaults took place. Adrian Cooper indicated that his father possessed various shotguns during the period covered by the offences. He once saw the sawn-off barrels of a side-by-side shotgun in a room normally kept locked by Cooper. He stated that Cooper also had a single-barrelled shotgun and an over-and-under double-barrelled shotgun. He stated that Cooper shortened the single-barrelled shotgun by sawing the barrel and shaving the stock before fashioning a strap, which he attached to the gun. This is very similar to the appearance of the gun (PH/2) used by Cooper in the Sardis robbery.

On the 22nd of November 1996, Cooper robbed Sheila Clark at gunpoint in her home in Sardis. The shotgun (PH/2) was recovered after being discarded in a hedgerow. The shotgun bears an uncanny resemblance to the gun described by the two male victims of the Milford Haven attack. Cooper burgled a house called 'The Cranny' on two occasions. On the first occasion he attempted to break into a locked gun cabinet, and on the second occasion he stole a packet of 12-bore shotgun cartridges.

It was clear that Cooper stole keys from his victims. It was our position that at the time of the Scoveston Park murders, Cooper stole Richard Thomas's car keys. Mr Thomas's keys were missing. A key, found amongst many other recovered on the ground near a shed at Cooper's home address, fitted Norton Farm (AJM/445) Why was he in possession of a key to a property owned and visited by Richard Thomas on the day of his murder? On the 5th of November 1992, Cooper burgled 9 Hazel Grove, Llanstadwell. House and car keys were stolen; they were recovered in his cesspit. On the 26th of January 1995, Cooper burgled School Cottage in Waterston. He stole a car key that was later found in the boot of his own car. On the 21st of November 1995, Cooper burgled 29 St Marys Park in Jordanston. He stole a pair of Chinese-made padlocks that were later found in his cesspit. On the 22nd of December 1995 Cooper burgled 89 Honeyfields in Neyland. He stole car keys that were later found in the boot of his car.

We believed that Cooper had taken ropes to the scenes of both the coastal path and Scoveston Park murders. Peter Dixon's wrists were tied together behind his back. A length of knotted rope, which may have been used to tie Helen Thomas, was recovered underneath her charred body. There was clear evidence that Cooper had used ropes in the offences for which he had already been convicted. During the course of the Sardis robbery Cooper tied the victim's hands behind her back in a similar manner to Peter Dixon, with rope that he had brought with him. Adrian Cooper confirmed that his father always had lengths of rope in his shed. Sixty lengths of rope were found at his property, some with loops tied in them, similar to the ones recovered from Peter Dixon and the victim at Sardis. When Cooper burgled 43 Hazelbank in Llanstadwell, he cut a hole in a hedge at the rear of the property and rope and wire-cutters were found nearby.

It was clear that Cooper targeted lone females and Glyn Johnson was of the view that he might have been a 'peeping Tom', a view I increasingly shared. At Scoveston he deliberately entered the house at a time when he believed that Helen Thomas was alone. There was evidence from his previous offending to show that he targeted lone females in their homes. When Cooper committed the robbery at Sardis on Sheila Clarke, he did so when her husband was away and she was alone. On the 31st of October 1996 Cooper burgled a house at 28 Castle Pill Road, Steynton. At the time of the burglary, the female occupant of the house was present and alone.

Initially it was thought that a man's shirt, found around the neck of Helen Thomas, was a gag, but I think this unlikely because Scoveston was so far away from a road that any screams for help would not have been heard. It is far more likely that it was used to cover her head to prevent her from recognising her attacker; Cooper was a man she knew well. During the rape of Jayne, the attacker covered her face with her top. During the gunpoint robbery at Sardis Cooper placed a pair of jeans over the victim's head.

The fact that fibres were recovered from body tapings of all victims suggests that Cooper wore woollen or knitted gloves at the time of the coastal path murders and the Milford Haven attack. It was clear that during the Huntsman offences Cooper wore woollen gloves. On the 18th of November 1994, Cooper burgled a house at 19 Castle Pill Crescent. He left woollen glove marks at the scene. On the 22nd of December 1995, Cooper burgled a house at 89 Honey Fields. He left woollen glove marks at the point of entry and inside the house. During the investigation of the robbery at Sardis, the police discovered black/blue fibres and woollen glove marks at the point of entry. Fibres were also found at the point of entry at a number of burglary scenes that matched; therefore linking the offences.

The local area had been plagued with cut fences over a number of years. What I didn't want to do was to suggest that he was responsible for all of them. Fences on farmland can of course be cut and damaged by machinery. Farmers are probably the best people to recognise the difference between accidental and a deliberate act. I only wanted to include those cut fences that could be linked to a specific offence with reliable evidence. What was clear was that the person responsible had an excellent knowledge of the area and knew his way about the fields and hedgerows. The cut fences served two purposes: easy access and escape routes. Some were cut in such a way that they would frustrate or injure a person in pursuit. In a three-wire fence, the two lower strands would be cut leaving the top one intact. His escape routes on occasions would cross Scoveston land and go past the scene of the Milford Haven attack. (That was another reason I wanted the Milford kept attack together with the murders.) There was evidence that Cooper cut fences near to nine of the burglary and robbery scenes. On two occasions dog handlers had tracked across fields to Cooper's house, and on one occasion PC Mark Jenkins tracked him to the lane outside his house and actually spoke to Cooper. Significantly, if we took these offences as the outside of a wheel all the tracks and cut fences were like spokes leading to Cooper's house at the centre. It was a geographical profiler's dream.

Another interesting point for the statisticians was that there were only eight unsolved double murders in the UK where a shotgun had been the weapon; we had two within a few miles of each other in Pembrokeshire. The Dixons' murder was the only offence outside the tight geographical wheel, but Cooper had served us up with the reason for this, recalling that at the time he was keeping a low profile in the area around his home because his landlord had served him with a notice to quit.

We believed it was a compelling account and the initial crime pattern analysis was also showing some interesting data. From his arrest and remand in custody for the Huntsman offences, similar offending in the area had gone down by a staggering 90 per cent. There had been no other armed robberies where a shotgun had been used and certainly no double shotgun murders. It was an interesting story, but its strength was in keeping all of the offences together and I had grave doubts that we would be able to do this as we moved towards any trial. The forensic work continued on the fibres and we all knew this was our best and last chance. I needed that 'golden nugget' of forensic evidence to place in the middle of the story to make it an overwhelming case; surely after all the hard knocks we were due a break?

CHAPTER 15

THE GOLDEN NUGGET

It was April 2009 and I had booked Lynne Harries, Glyn Johnson and myself on the Major Crime Review course at South Wales Police Headquarters. Martin Lloyd-Evans and Paul Bethell led the session. Both were retired senior detectives with probably eighty years' service between them; they were always very knowledgeable and good fun. I had spoken to Martin on quite a few occasions and he had given me excellent support and encouragement. We listened for days about how cold cases had been detected after twenty and thirty years, all as a result of a forensic approach. It confirmed to me that we were doing everything right and in many ways we were ahead in our approach. I can remember sitting in the classroom thinking, 'Why not us, surely we deserve a break?' The course ended on the 23rd of April 2009, and I stood in the car park with Lynne and Glyn.

'I can't believe we have not had a break in the forensic evidence,' pondered Lynne. We chewed it over for ten minutes before getting into our cars and driving back to Carmarthen. As I headed out of Bridgend towards the M4 the hands-free phone rang in the car.

'Hi, Steve, it's Angela,' I instantly recognised the well-groomed tones of Dr Angela Gallop from LGC Forensics. 'Are you driving, Steve?' she said.

'Yes, but no problem I am on hands-free,' I replied.

'No, Steve, I think you had better pull over because that golden nugget you were after, we've got it.'

The hairs on the back of my neck stood on end and I went completely cold. Luckily I was near a lay-by and I was able to steer off the busy main road.

'Angela, I love you,' were the first words I could think of; she laughed.

'The shorts AJM/165 recovered from Cooper's bedroom, we taped them for fibres and noticed a faint stain on the tape lift. We were able to go back to the exact spot on the shorts and remove a tiny flake of blood. It's Peter Dixon's blood!' The words stunned me into silence, I had waited for this call and I could feel the emotions welling up inside me. 'Steve, are you still there?' she asked.

I managed to pull myself together and replied, 'Angela, thank you so much, you have made me a very happy man, I can't begin to tell you what this means.'

Angela then went on to tell me the discriminating value: 'It's the strongest Steve, one in a billion.' In simple terms this meant that the likelihood of it coming from any person other than Peter Dixon was one in one billion. It was a stunning result.

All I could think was, 'Got you!'

We had waited for almost three years and now the meticulous hard work and planning had paid off. I knew this evidence now made our case a forensic one supported by some fantastic bad character and circumstantial evidence. Other motorists passing the lay-by must have thought that I was having a bad bout of road rage. I was banging my hands on the steering wheel while at the same time screaming, 'Yes, yes, yes, yes!' I must have repeated it twenty times.

Then I thought, crikey, is Angela still on the line and had to check that I had in fact ended the call. I cannot begin to describe the feeling of total elation. As a detective you always want to work on the 'big one', and this was as big as it gets. Now we had tangible evidence and a very strong case. The next two phone calls were to Lynne and Glyn who had worked tirelessly. Both were over the moon and the calls between us were quite emotional. I decided not to tell the rest of team by phone and just sent a message asking them all to be at Pembroke Dock police station the following morning for a briefing.

The next day I had them all together and Glyn had prepared a short PowerPoint. As planned, I started to recap on the evidence so far. By now I had spoken to Dr Gallop again and she had explained fully the process, which had recovered the blood. I asked why it had not been found before on the initial work looking for blood and trace DNA. Her explanation was simple, and one I was now repeating to the team. The test for blood is a bit like playing the game Battleships; the scientist tests certain areas of the garment, but not the full one, based on experience and the circumstances of the case; in essence they are trying to hit a target area. The tape process is very different because the scientist tapes all of the exposed area, and then seals the tape in a bag so it cannot be contaminated, before examining it with powerful microscopes. Having done this it's easy to return to the garment and know exactly where a certain tape lift has come from. I could see the team looking puzzled. Glyn then displayed the photograph of the green shorts AJM/165, and I continued: 'LGC have carried out tests on the green shorts recovered from Cooper's bedroom.' I saw one of the team look at me and I knew she had twigged about where this was going. Glyn then flicked to the next slide; it was the same shorts only this time written in large red letters were the words 'Got the bastard!' As the picture came up I told them the result. Their initial response was far more controlled than mine had been on receiving the news, but as it sank in, the room echoed with the sound of happiness. It was a fantastic scene, hugs and handshakes and again one or two tears from people genuinely delighted that all of the hard work and commitment had given us the first breakthrough. It was now my job to refocus the team and bring us back down to earth.

'This is fantastic news team and I am delighted for you all, but this is only the start and we have got a long way to go. We now need to establish the integrity and continuity of this evidence and prepare a case. I will be speaking to the CPS this morning to inform them and arrange an urgent meeting.'

The following few days were a whirlwind. The team were bouncing and the buzz and in the incident room was tangible. As I was about to contact Tom Atherton on the telephone I could hear Lynne Harries in the room opposite on the phone to the fibre expert Roger Robson. It sounded like an interesting call. I walked into Lynne's office and he had a huge grin on his face.

'Come on, Harries, boy, spit it out,' I said.

'That was Roger, he has compared some fibres from the glove BB/109 found in the hedgerow near Cooper's house and they are identical to fibres taken off the belt on Peter Dixon's shorts and the branches used to cover the bodies of Peter and Gwenda Dixon,' replied Lynne, 'and that's not all, boss, fibres from the gloves MTJ/5 and MTJ/7, the ones worn by Cooper on the Sardis robbery, have been found on the clothing of the rape victim from the Milford Haven job.'

This was unbelievable, we had waited for years to get a breakthrough and now I had direct evidence to connect him with two of the Ottawa offences in just forty-eight hours. It was clear, that like gold mining, LGC had hit a rich evidential vein. Experience told me that they would find more as they had now found his vulnerability. Cooper was clearly forensically aware. He knew about fingerprints and DNA and was therefore a gloved offender. He chose to wear woollen gloves and that was now becoming a significant weakness and potentially fertile area for us. In Roger and April Robson, we had two fantastic experts who filled me with optimism because of their sheer enthusiasm and commitment. It was clear too that they felt confident that they were at the start of a trail of evidence that would link Cooper to more of the Ottawa offences.

As I expected, Tom Atherton was delighted and I could hear the excitement in his voice. He would brief Gerard Elias QC and we agreed to meet on the 29th of April 2009. The meeting was businesslike and focused; there were important issues to discuss and decisions to be made. The first issue was the impact of the evidence on the investigation, and the potential arrest of Cooper. The evidence we now had linked him directly to the murders of Peter and Gwenda Dixon and the attack on the five children at Milford haven but not the murders of Richard and Helen Thomas. It was my view however that we were now in a position to arrest him for all three offences and that the question of the Milford Haven case being dropped was redundant. Tom clearly agreed though he still had concerns that the trial judge would question the value of keeping the Milford Haven attack on any indictment. I was determined that this would not happen. Tom Atherton and a colleague listened as I outlined the evidence on which his arrest would be based.

We now had a powerful DNA link between Peter Dixon and shorts recovered from Cooper. There were fibre links between a glove, BB/109, recovered from a hedgerow less than one hundred yards from Cooper's home address, and Peter Dixon's belt. The glove was found amongst jewellery stolen from a burglary at 23 Castle Pill Crescent Milford Haven on the 1st of March 1996, just five days before the Milford attack. In the same burglary a Bruno shotgun and cartridges were stolen. The gun was later found buried under his duck run and Cooper was convicted of this burglary. Peter Dixon's gold wedding ring was stolen from his finger during the murder. Cooper had sold a man's gold wedding ring on the 5th of July 1989 in Pembroke. He admitted in interview in 2008 that he had lied about this ring and its origin. The jewellers was fifty yards away from the NatWest cashpoint, used by the murderer. Cooper was filmed for the popular television quiz show *Bullseye* three weeks before the murder of Peter and Gwenda Dixon. Cooper had a remarkable resemblance to the artist impression of the man using Peter Dixon's cash card in Haverfordwest on the 1st of July 1989. A partial DNA profile on rope used to secure Peter Dixon's hands contained elements common to Cooper. There was a fibre link between the rape and indecent assault victims and the gloves MTJ/5 and MTJ/7; the gloves were discarded by Cooper following the Sardis armed robbery and he of course had been convicted of this attack. Cooper's voice had been identified by some of the victims of the Milford

Haven attack. A key found on Cooper's property was from Norton Farm, a property owned by Richard Thomas and visited by him on the day he was murdered. A large bunch of keys were missing from Scoveston Park and we had evidence that Cooper stole keys from his victims. There were also significant similarities between Cooper's bad character and the behaviour displayed in the three Ottawa offences.

Tom Atherton was well aware of the ongoing work in relation to bad character, geographical and behavioural profiling and crime pattern analysis and we quickly agreed that, together with the forensic evidence, we had now reached the threshold to arrest Cooper for all three offences. I was delighted, but for me there was a competing demand going on in the background. On one hand I now had enough evidence to arrest him with a realistic prospect of a successful outcome; on the other hand I knew I was going to get more forensic evidence. The problem was, Cooper was out in the community and we had information that he was gambling again on the horses. The warning words of Dr Adrian West were still ringing in my ears. Cooper's wife had died and he wasn't working other than doing odd jobs for his elderly neighbours. How long would it be before he started to offend again? Taking everything into consideration I could not afford to wait for the forensic work to be completed. The interviews would need to cover all bases so we would not need to go back to him at a later stage, especially if his defence was going to be, 'It wasn't me, I wasn't there.'

At the same meeting I confirmed with Tom that there would be no requirement to go through a visual identification procedure due to the time elapsed. I also informed him that there would be a substantial 'hearsay application' as a number of our potential witnesses had passed away. The shorts were clearly vital to the case and we needed to do more work on this item to try and secure the wearer's DNA. This involved the scientist looking in places like the waistband and pockets to find DNA from the person. If we could find traces of Cooper it would negate any attempt by him to distance himself from the shorts.

I left the meeting with Lynne and Glyn with the green light to arrest Cooper for the murders of Richard and Helen Thomas, the murders of Peter and Gwenda Dixon, five attempted armed robberies, a rape and indecent assault. To say we were happy is an understatement. There were new problems exercising my mind though; if, following his arrest and interview, we were in a position to charge Cooper we would only have eight weeks to submit an initial file to the CPS. (An extension of up to a maximum of twelve weeks was the most likely outcome.) It was pleasing to know that decisions I had made on disclosure and securing statements would put us ahead of the game, but it would still be tight. The Gold Group meeting two days later was uplifting, and an opportunity to break the news to the senior team. It also helped me avoid any awkward questions regarding forensic costs, which were now over £800,000 and likely to double before we were finished. I needed additional staff, in particular experienced detective sergeants to put the files together. I was told that Gareth Rees would remain with me after the arrest and interview, and that DS Paul Jones would join him. Paul had worked with me on the murder of a retired police officer and I had been very impressed with his skills. He was a jolly, round faced ex-Royal Navy man with many an exciting story of close escapes in exotic locations and he would prove to be a fantastic addition to the team.

Accommodation was again becoming an issue because the force had earmarked the top floor at Pembroke Dock police station for a customer service unit. Ottawa was clearly in for the long haul and it would not have been right for us to move now because I wanted the team to concentrate on preparing for his arrest and interview.

Over the years I had spent many hours with Tim Dixon, his sister Julie and Peter's brother Keith, all of us hoping that this day would come. They were obviously stunned by the news. Richard and Helen Thomas did not have any real close family members but again their relatives were briefed. My discussions with them and their response will remain private between us. At this stage I chose not to tell the victims of the Milford Haven attack, but made a decision to inform them the night before the arrest. My concern was not that they would disclose the planned arrest, but some of them had large families and I could not be sure that someone would not unwittingly let the cat out of the bag. However I did tell them that I was leading a review on their case, giving me an opportunity to introduce family liaison officers prior to the arrest. These were very important roles and were performed by DC Donna Thomas and Sergeant Helen Coles. They would have a very difficult job because of the emotional demands made on them by the victims.

The date was set, John William Cooper was to be arrested on the 13th of May 2009 and interviewed at Haverfordwest police station. It sounded simple but there was much to be done to prepare. Time was precious as we had less than two weeks to plan for the arrest and I needed to ensure the team were match fit for the big day and beyond. There were a number of pieces of work that I needed to assign and Gareth Rees, Louise Harries and the interview team had to be brought back together. To be honest, they had prepared so well that it was just a matter of refreshing and developing their interview strategy.

The arrest and custody plans were pretty straightforward. Cooper collected his paper from the local shop in Letterston every morning at 8 a.m. He would be arrested on the street and quickly taken away. This meant we wouldn't need a firearms team to arrest him at his house and this would buy us some more time before the press became aware. Head of Corporate Communications, Rhian Davies-Moore had prepared a number of press releases and considered the top twenty questions we might be asked at any conference. It was agreed that Detective Chief Superintendent Steve Mears and Deputy Chief Constable Andy Edwards would face the media on the day of arrest allowing me to concentrate on directing proceedings. A number of searches would need to be carried out at Cooper's address and in his car. The community fall-out would be picked up local officers. The Ottawa offences had been significant events in local history and many people had suffered as a result of Cooper's actions. We needed to have contingency plans in place to protect his home and family. Members of the Dixon family lived in the Thames Valley and Hampshire force areas and they too were visited and given support. Following the arrest a number of people and organisations would need to be contacted and briefed and trigger plans were developed to this end.

On the 12th of May 2009 Lynne Harries and I visited all of the victims of the Milford Haven attack and informed them that Cooper was to be arrested the next day. It was more difficult than I had anticipated; the prospect of them going to court had a significant impact and they were caught between two emotions, one of relief that he had been identified and one of total horror at the thought of facing him in a courtroom. I knew that there would have to be significant support provided to them after he was arrested. That night I sat at home going over the plans and wondering what the next day would bring. I then sent the following message to all of the Ottawa team, one that I had on my office wall, one that I believed in very deeply. 'There is no greater responsibility or duty placed on a human being than to investigate the circumstances of the death of another human being. That responsibility has been placed on us and in discharging it to the very best of our ability, we will do so without fear or favour in pursuit of justice.'

At 7 a.m. on the 13th of May 2009, I briefed the arrest team at Haverfordwest police station. I had decided that Lynne Harries and Glyn Johnson would arrest him; it was only right that it fell to them following three years of extraordinary hard work. Ready for action, they left quickly with their back-up team and made their way to Letterston. At 8 a.m. I briefed the search team who would comb his home and car for evidence. I was particularly interested in documentation relevant to the investigation and any evidence of his continuing gambling habit or use of pornography. Glan Thomas briefed the forensic teams in line with our agreed strategy. It was now a waiting game. A control room was set up in the police station which involved a link to the HOLMES computer system and speed typists to make a contemporaneous record of any interviews with

Cooper. Detailed briefings had been prepared for Cooper's legal team and we sat in the control room with DS Gareth (Rambo) Rees and Detective Constable Louise Harries and went over our plans. They were clear and focused, and I had total confidence in them. I could sense their desire to get Cooper into the interview room.

The radio crackled and it was clear that Cooper had left his house on foot, making his way to the local paper shop. This was the signal for Lynne and Glyn to position themselves so as to intercept him as he reached the shop. The radio went quiet, then suddenly burst into life, 'Arrest team with subject now . . . he's kicked off.' Cooper emerged at the side of the local paper shop where he was confronted by Lynne and Glyn, they informed him that he was under arrest and took hold of an arm each. Cooper was clearly not impressed and dragged them both off towards his house, Lynne and Glyn dangling from each arm. It showed us all that Cooper was a very fit, strong man, even though he was in his sixties. In his prime he must have been a real handful. Fortunately support was close at hand and officers came from all directions and finally, shouting and struggling, Cooper was placed under arrest. While all of this was going on a man walked up to the paper shop, tied his dog to a post and went in and bought his daily paper. The same man then walked out of the shop, untied his dog and nonchalantly walked off past all the commotion without giving it a second glance.

Cooper was now under arrest and he was taken before the custody officer at Haverfordwest police station, booked in and placed in a cell. He chose to use the same firm of solicitors from Nottingham but while we waited for his brief to arrive the custody clock was ticking. We had an initial twenty-four hours to interview him; this could be extended by a further twelve hours by a superintendent before we would need to take him before a magistrate for a warrant of further detention which could give us another thirty-six hours. Cooper had intimated to the custody sergeant that his lawyer intended to travel down overnight ready to begin the next morning. In certain circumstances the police can object, and get alternative legal advice for a prisoner if it will cause an unnecessary delay to proceedings, but I wanted to avoid this at all cost. It was important that Cooper had the legal representation of his choice otherwise this could give him an excuse to play up. With this in mind I spoke to his solicitor and pointed out the gravity of the situation and the need to attend without delay.

Thankfully she understood and hotfooted it to Pembrokeshire. I then received news which chilled me to the bone. Whilst searching his car the team had found a length of rope, a pair of woollen gloves, records of his betting and they discovered that he had ordered an Ordnance Survey map of South Pembrokeshire. To me it seemed it would have been just a matter of time before he returned to his murderous ways.

CHAPTER 16

'CHARGE HIM WITH THE LOT'

The stage was now set for the interview team to confront Cooper with the forensic evidence. At the end of the questioning and after final challenge interview I would be seeking agreement from the CPS to charge Cooper with a number of the Ottawa offences if not all of them.

The interviews were to be videotaped and streamed to a monitoring room where a speed typist and I would record the key points. I would also be able to ask for further research, on any issues arising so that the interviewers had, at fingertips, all the information they needed. They had planned and rehearsed for this moment many times over they were without doubt the most prepared interviewing team I have ever known in my long service. The operations room was a tense place. The press were already onto the fact that a significant police incident was unfolding in Letterston and their interest was gaining momentum. The danger is to say nothing and risk the media running off in all directions looking for the story or a new angle. My view is that it's better to work with them and give them what they want, within the rules of engagement, and let them know when they can have an update. By now journalists were calling on Cooper's neighbours and asking them about him. It came as no surprise that he was seen as a quiet and polite man who even asked some elderly residents if he could do some gardening work for them. If they had taken him up on the offer, I could not begin to think of the possible outcome.

I sat with the interview team and went over the interview plans, it was clear that the strategy was ambitious and I was not sure we would have the time to get it all in. It was unlikely that I would get a warrant of further detention because we had previously interviewed him at length, and it would be difficult to put a case to a magistrate that we needed more time. We adapted our strategy accordingly and a detailed disclosure document was prepared for Cooper's solicitor laying out the forensic evidence. Gareth Rees and Louise Harries were now in the driving seat and at last the interviews were about to begin. On the 13th of May 2009 at 8.09 p.m., Cooper was interviewed about gloves, including the single glove BB/109 found in a hedgerow near to his house and a pair of gloves AJM/60 found in his kitchen. This is a short extract from that interview:

POLICE: 'In 1998 a number of gloves were recovered from your home address OK. For example we recovered a black wool glove, AJM/267; a pair of navy coloured woollen quilted gloves, AJM/268; a blue woollen glove, AJM/270; a damaged dark coloured glove with only the cuff remaining, AJM/378; another glove AJM/383, one blue material glove with fingers torn off; JAL/48 a right-handed workman's glove; BB/109 which is the one in the field; and I've also a pair of navy coloured gloves which are woollen or cloth material which are insulated, AJM/60.'

COOPER: 'The gloves wearer in our family was my son Adrian for his motorbikes.'

POLICE: 'OK and what about the workman gloves then?'

COOPER: 'I've already said I very rarely used gloves at work, they get in my way.'

POLICE: 'You say that Adrian used to own gloves for the motorbike. What type of gloves would Adrian . . . ?'

COOPER: 'He used to wear all sorts, wool ones, leather ones.'

POLICE: 'Right OK and in relation to his gloves, would you on occasions use his gloves?'

COOPER: 'I very rarely used gloves, I find them cumbersome but they were all round the place, in the caravan, in the bedrooms, everywhere.'

POLICE: 'And I have to ask you, John, in relation to previous matters where you were charged with burglaries and other offences, did you used to take gloves with you?'

COOPER: 'I didn't do those burglaries, whether you believe it or not, or a robbery.'

POLICE: 'You can see I've got to ask you the questions.'

COOPER: 'Yeah, you keep asking them.'

POLICE: 'In relation to gloves and the issue of the fibres have you any further questions?'

COOPER: 'I have not, no.'

POLICE: 'At this stage I've no further questions in relation to what we've discussed so far, yeah? What we'll do tomorrow, John, is we'll go through some clothing recovered at your home address, particularly the ones pertinent to the artist impression.'

COOPER: 'Artist's impression.'

POLICE: 'The artist's impression, I said at the start of the interview.'

COOPER: 'Oh yes I understand, yeah.'

POLICE: 'And again we've got to ask you questions in relation to that OK? So at this stage I have no further questions, is there anything you'd like to say at this stage?'

COOPER: 'Yes, as I said before I wasn't the only liver in 34 St Marys Park, I wasn't the only one staying there, look at the history of St Marys Park, and especially Adrian Cooper.'

Cooper denied using gloves and again introduced his son Adrian without directly implicating him. The interview resumed the following morning at 09.05 a.m. Cooper was shown an album of photographs, which contained a picture of the shorts AJM/165. They were then compared with the shorts in the artist's impression:

POLICE: 'Um, we did discuss briefly shorts in your previous interview I think we touched upon it, and we asked you if you owned a pair of khaki shorts and I think you replied no and you said that you owned possibly dark shorts.'

COOPER: 'My wife bought shorts and they're usually dark or more sober colours.'

POLICE: 'What would you say is a more sober colour then?'

COOPER: 'Well your blacks or navys.'

POLICE: 'Right OK. Um, would you know where she got those shorts from?'

COOPER: 'Your normal shops or markets.'

POLICE: 'Right OK.'

COOPER: 'May I . . . ?'

POLICE: 'Of course yeah.'

COOPER: 'Usually if I was wearing shorts I would be wearing sandals.'

POLICE: 'Not shorts and boots is what your . . .'

COOPER: 'There, I can't remember ever, I don't know but usually, shorts, sandals, always, and no socks.'

POLICE: 'I think in the last interview you said that you wore shorts but not often, so what, where would you wear shorts?'

COOPER: 'Well summer weather, summer weather, yeah.'

POLICE: 'OK. Do you know how many pairs of shorts you had?'

COOPER: 'Oh . . .'

POLICE: 'Will talk specifically again later . . .'

COOPER: 'I would say maximum two or three pairs.'

POLICE: 'OK, what about in 1998 then, how many shorts?'

COOPER: 'I've never owned more than I think about two or three pair of shorts at any time.'

POLICE: 'OK. Obviously clothing was recovered from your home address.'

COOPER: 'Certainly.'

POLICE: 'I'm showing John a photo album, can you see there's a pair of shorts AJM/165?'

COOPER: 'Yeah.'

POLICE: 'OK were they, are they your shorts?'

COOPER: 'Um, if they were in the house, most probably yes.'

POLICE: 'OK and do you know where those shorts are from?'

COOPER: 'Oh my wife usually bought those sort of things.'

POLICE: 'OK. In relation to those shorts, you pointed out earlier that the shorts in the artist's impression . . .'

COOPER: 'Yeah.'

POLICE: 'Yeah, would you accept that those shorts resemble the shorts in the artist's impression?'

COOPER: 'No not a bit no.'

POLICE: 'OK, have you ever seen the shorts in this photograph TWB/1 before?'

COOPER: 'I believe those are my bathers actually.'

POLICE: 'OK. And just to confirm, during the search of your home address . . . Two pairs of shorts were recovered, a black pair of shorts and those shorts, they're the only shorts.'

COOPER: 'That's virtually what I said.'

POLICE: 'OK. So do you accept that those short are yours?'

COOPER: 'Yes those might have been my bathers.'

POLICE: 'Your bathers, right. And where would you wear those.'

COOPER: 'On the beach.'

POLICE: 'Are there any other shorts or anything you wish to add or change in relation to shorts then?'

COOPER: 'Only to point out that those, those are long-legged shorts.'

POLICE: 'OK you're pointing to the difference, then, you say they're not similar and that they're longer on the artist's impression.'

COOPER: 'Well those are short-legged shorts, that's long-legged shorts.'

POLICE: 'Just to explain for people who obviously who can't see what's taken place. You're pointing at the photograph I've put back in the box.'

COOPER: 'Yes, I'll clear it . . .'

POLICE: 'Saying they are short.'

COOPER: 'The photograph is showing long, what I would call long-legged shorts.'

POLICE: 'And by the photograph you're pointing at the artist's impression.'

COOPER: 'Yes.'

POLICE: 'So you're, is it correct, John, you're saying the artist's impression has got long-legged shorts.'

COOPER: 'I would call them long-legged shorts.'

POLICE: 'Yeah and that the photograph you saw on shorts, seized from your home address are short-legged shorts.'

COOPER: 'Yeah bathing-type shorts.'

POLICE: 'And you're saying that those are your bathers.'

COOPER: 'I would imagine so yes.'

POLICE: 'Can you just tell me these were recovered from your home address in 1998, and as I explained earlier during the course of searches, officers give them reference numbers OK, the reference number these shorts are AJM/165 which were again recovered from your home address from your bedroom in 1998, OK. Can you tell me how long would you have owned those shorts?'

COOPER: 'Two or three years.'

POLICE: 'Two or three years. OK. And it's quite important, do you remember where you got them from.'

COOPER: 'As I said before, my wife most probably bought them for me.'

POLICE: 'OK, so would you have owned those shorts in 1989 the year of the murders of Peter and Gwenda Dixon?'

COOPER: 'I would doubt it very much.'

POLICE: 'OK, we're talking now then, nine years before the date of recovery.'

COOPER: 'They wouldn't have lasted that long.'
POLICE: 'OK thank you.'

In the interview Cooper accepted that the shorts were his, and confidently told the officers that they were shorter than those in the artist's impression. His efforts to distance himself from certain exhibits were telling us exactly where to look. In the next interview the forensic evidence connecting him to the murders of Peter and Gwenda Dixon was put to him:

POLICE: 'OK John. I've interviewed you in 2008 and interviews here today, and the interview will be carried out in the same manner. OK?'
COOPER: 'Yeah.'
POLICE: 'Before I start the interview, you've had a meeting or briefing with your solicitor in relation to the forensic disclosures being made.'
COOPER: 'Yes, yes.'
POLICE: 'OK. Can we just clarify then, the previous interview you were shown a photograph of a pair of shorts.'
COOPER: 'Yes.'
POLICE: 'Which you identified as being your bathers.'
COOPER: 'Yes.'
POLICE: 'And we established they were recovered from your home address.'
COOPER: 'Yes.'
POLICE: 'And you said if they were recovered from your home address they're probably yours.'
COOPER: 'Yes.'
POLICE: 'Is that still the case?'
COOPER: 'That's still the case.'

POLICE: 'OK. You've been interviewed by us in July 2008 in relation to the murders of Peter and Gwenda Dixon. Since that time further enquiries and forensic examinations have continued, and we need to discuss those results with you and give you an opportunity to give any explanation or comment you wish. A solicitor has been provided with the interim forensic results for the examination of a pair of shorts AJM/165 and you've confirmed that you've had the opportunity of discussing that matter with your solicitor?'

COOPER: 'Yes.'

POLICE: 'I must stress to you the forensic examinations of submitted items connected with this investigation are continuing. In light of the forensic result, is there anything now you wish to change or clarify from your previous interviews in respect of these offences?'

COOPER: 'Only I'm vague about the length of time I've owned any shorts. I do not know.'

POLICE: 'OK.'

COOPER: 'I said two to three years, I don't know how long I've had them. I would be surprised if they were nine years old.'

POLICE: 'You would be?'

COOPER: 'Very surprised.'

POLICE: 'Right, OK. We are carrying out enquiries to establish the origin of those shorts.'

COOPER: 'Yes.'

POLICE: 'For example, which country they were manufactured and which areas of the world they've been distributed in, yeah. And those enquiries are ongoing with us. Can you confirm that you went to visit Lorna in America in 1979?'

COOPER: 'Um, I can confirm I went to visit her; I'm vague about the years.'

POLICE: 'Right, OK. So what period of time would you have been out to visit her?'

COOPER: 'I know we went in the 70s. I know we went in the early 70s, 79 yeah. And I know we went after.'

POLICE: 'OK. During those visits did you or Pat purchase any shorts in America?'

COOPER: 'Not that I can recollect.'

POLICE: 'You're saying they were your bathers.'

COOPER: 'That's right, yes.'

POLICE: 'OK, what size are you John?'

COOPER: 'Medium am I?'

POLICE: 'OK. And when you're saying they're bathers, would you have worn them on holiday in America? Has any other person worn those shorts?'

COOPER: 'Probably.'

POLICE: 'Right and who would that other person be?'

COOPER: 'My son.'

POLICE: 'If we have a look at the forensic results which we've received. Whilst examining the fibre tapings taken from the shorts AJM/165, which were recovered from your home address, they were looking for fibres similar to those from the Dixons scene. And they identified some small fragments of blood on one area of the tape, a full DNA profile matching Peter Dixon was obtained from one of those fragments. They've estimated the probability of obtaining that profile, the blood had come from someone other than, and unrelated to Peter Dixon, is less than 1 in 1 billion, OK. And do you appreciate the significance of that?'

COOPER: 'Certainly, certainly.'

POLICE: 'In light of that they carried out a highly detailed microscopic examination of the shorts and this revealed the presence of a tiny two millimetre square bloodstain in the relevant area of the garment itself. They profiled the stain and it produced a weak partial DNA profile, the components of which matched those of Peter Dixon. They've been able to prove on that result and they can confirm that there's an incomplete profile which was obtained, which matched that of Peter Dixon. They've estimated the probability of obtaining that profile if the DNA had come from someone unrelated to Peter Dixon is less than 1 in 480 million. Do you understand the significance of that?'

COOPER: 'Yes, yeah.'

POLICE: 'Can you explain to me why forensic results have indicated that there's blood matching the DNA of Peter Dixon on your shorts?'

COOPER: 'Can I explain it? Well I can't explain it. As I said before my wife sourced most of my clothes, 90-odd per cent of my clothes. Where she got the shorts from I do not know, how long I had the shorts I do not know. I would wear second-hand clothes. Right I'm just trying to make sense of all this right, now, I've already told you that Percy Thompson, my father-in-law, he used to come out to us five or six times a week, he worked for the animal rescue. He used to bring costume jewellery for the kids, toys for the kids, and sometimes if he brought things for me I would make a donation and larger items like tools, and I remember a weights bench for my son and things like that. I would make a donation. He would bring me out, he was, he had a number of jobs; he did the animal rescue, collecting items and helping to sell them on a market stall. He worked on Milford Docks and for Frank Newin and he went to the TA's. He was a sergeant in the TA's. Later on he worked at Doughty's and he worked with Tom Newin first then Frank Newin and the TA's. He would bring me ex-army boots for work, right. Overalls that was donated, OK. I would wear those things. I used to wear and still do wear trousers more than jeans, but I would wear jeans, but my shirts were bought, I didn't wear second-hand shirts, but I would wear second-hand clothes. And sometimes, my wife would produce clothes that could have come from Percy Thompson. He got embarrassed when he was interviewed about that and of course he, he was an old man, I understand it, it doesn't matter. He did it.'

POLICE: 'So are you trying to say those shorts may have been . . .'

COOPER: 'May have been.'

POLICE: 'May have been?'

COOPER: 'They were produced by my wife or sourced by my wife. They may have come from a second-hand source. At the moment I have one second-hand item in my wardrobe, which is an overcoat that I wore to my wife's funeral, and that was bought for my cousin's funeral in '98.'

POLICE: 'But we've established that on your shorts, the forensic examination has revealed a DNA profile matching that of Peter Dixon's.'

COOPER: 'Yes.'

POLICE: 'To 1 in a billion and also blood on the shorts itself, sorry 1 in a billion was the tapings and 1 in 480 million on the shorts, OK.'

COOPER: 'Yes.'

POLICE: 'In relation to the blood on your shorts, yeah, have you any explanation to give as to how that blood could have innocently appeared on the shorts?'

COOPER: 'I really do not know. As I said my wife sourced the shorts, maybe from Percy, maybe from a shop, I don't know whatever she sourced. More worryingly is my son used to take my clothes, whenever he wanted and that would be more of a worry for a father, but I don't know.'

POLICE: 'Have you any reason to suspect that he'd borrow your bathers?'

COOPER: 'He would take whatever he wanted, whatever he needed.'

POLICE: 'I have to ask you, John, was that bloodstain deposited on those shorts at the time that Peter Dixon was killed?'

COOPER: 'I never killed anybody in my life.'

POLICE: 'Have you ever visited the scene of the murders after Peter Dixon was killed?'

COOPER: 'No.'

POLICE: 'During the period the 29th of June 1989 and the 5th of July 1989, do you recall your movements on those days? We've established on the 5th of July you sold a ring in a jewellers in Pembroke . . . have you any other information or have you got any other alibi to offer us for that period of time?'

COOPER: 'No, but I would like, I'm glad you brought that up – the ring, the ring. At the last interview you intimated that only one, two, a number of rings were sold about that time. Does it say it's a man's ring or a lady's ring? I'm not sure.'

POLICE: 'A man's wedding ring was stolen from Peter Dixon.'

COOPER: 'Yeah, on the receipt, does it say a man's wedding ring or a female wedding ring?'

POLICE: 'It doesn't say female or male.'

COOPER: 'Right. Shall I add something most of the jewellery or what have you that I used to sell like that, scrap usually, was to Mr Waters, as I've already told you. Now, you can go round the jewellers and find out when you sold scrap gold to jewellers, if the ring was not resaleable, right, it would go in as scrap gold. Now for you to say that only so many rings were sold is total nonsense, because if you go round them jewellers they will tell you that if the ring was not resalable it would go down as scrap gold, so to say there was just that couple of rings sold is nonsense.'

POLICE: 'You mentioned just now that you don't believe the blood on the shorts is from Mr Dixon, is that what you're saying?'

COOPER: 'I don't believe it is no. How can it be if they're my shorts? I didn't kill him.'

POLICE: 'OK, no further questions. Is there anything you would like to bring up? The time now is 11.55 hours.'

Cooper appeared desperate in his attempts to divert his ownership of the shorts, it was clear he knew the significance of the shorts, again he offered his son as a possible user of them. The interview then moved to the Milford Haven attack.

POLICE: 'On the 6th of March 1996 at approximately 7 p.m., three females and two males were walking in the field to the rear of the Mount Estate in Milford Haven when they were approached by a male person wearing a balaclava and carrying a gun and a torch. One of the females was raped and another was indecently assaulted, OK? Were you the person responsible for the offences committed on the 6th of March in a field behind the Mount Estate?'

COOPER: 'No I was not.'

POLICE: 'Now I appreciate with the passage of time as we've spoken about previously this may be a difficult question to answer, but however bearing in mind you chose not to answer questions in the last interviews regarding these offences, I'm giving you the opportunity now. Are you able to tell me where you were on the 6th of March 1996?'

COOPER: 'I've no idea honestly.'

POLICE: 'With regard then to the area of the offence, um it occurred in a field behind the Mount Estate in Milford Haven and we've had some discussion in previous interviews about the area and you've described in the last interviews with us in July last year with regards to you mentioned a place called Black Bridge and Spinksy's house and I think you mentioned a little boat that you used to keep in the area. So we've got a photograph now that I'll come to shortly. If I say first of all then what area or what parts of that area would you visit specifically?'

COOPER: 'Well we used to live in Milton Crescent, we used to live in up until 1977.'

POLICE: 'Until 1977.'

COOPER: ''77.'

POLICE: 'And when you lived in that area would you frequent the fields in the area?'

COOPER: 'Oh the Pill, I had a boat in the Pill.'

POLICE: 'Right OK, which I understand is close to the Mount Estate but on the other side of the road somewhere.'

COOPER: 'Uh yeah, yes, not too far away. 19 . . . sorry 1978, we were down there 'til 1978.'

POLICE: 'I have a photograph of the area because obviously in the last interviews you discussed the area; I think it's important if we put a photograph in front of you. We can be specific isn't it and say this is what we're talking about so it avoids any confusion.'

COOPER: 'OK.'

POLICE: 'I'm now going to show John, in interview formally, an aerial photograph of the area of the offence which was Black Bridge and the Mount Estate and this photograph was recovered from the enquiry documents to do with the Milford Haven Rape OK and the Exhibit for this is GDR/30, um which was produced by myself on the 8th of May of this year from the Incident Room at Pembroke Dock, OK? If I turn towards you now it's an aerial photo going from the top third of the photograph there are obviously housing estates in the central section or band and the lower right-hand band there are a number of agricultural fields bordered by hedges and trees and then at the bottom left-hand corner there's a waterway and at the bottom there appears to be a farm. OK? Can you see that map there and that would have been as it was in 1996.'

POLICE: 'Does that make sense to you? This is your Black Bridge is it?'

COOPER: 'Yeah.'

POLICE: 'The offence of that we're talking about has occurred in this field here.'

COOPER: 'Well that's Mount here.'

POLICE: 'Yeah which is of the three sort of upper fields in the picture, it's the central one then. If I ask you have you ever been into that field?'

COOPER: 'Oh no.'

POLICE: 'Have you ever walked through that field?'

COOPER: 'Not in, not in living memory no, no.'

POLICE: 'Right OK. Were you in that area on the 6th of March 1996?'

COOPER: 'No, most certainly not.'

POLICE: 'The victims then in the offences that we're talking about in '96 were video interviewed and described the male who committed the offences against them OK? The victims described a male with a balaclava, there's also . . . um they talk about a jacket worn by the offender which one victim describes as a wax jacket. The offender was wearing boots described by one as black combat boots. The offender was wearing jeans. The offender was also wearing gloves OK, and I'm now going to ask you questions in regards to the clothing and what clothing you may have had during the period of 1996 OK? Did you own a wax jacket during that time?'

COOPER: 'No.'

POLICE: 'Have you ever owned a wax jacket or anything that could be resembling a wax jacket?'

COOPER: 'Plastic jackets.'

POLICE: 'Plastic jackets.'

POLICE: 'OK, did you own a jacket which you'd say was similar to a wax jacket?'

COOPER: 'No, I'd wear softer jackets.'

POLICE: 'OK, what about balaclavas in 1996, would you have been in possession?'

COOPER: 'I had a balaclava on my boat.'

POLICE: 'Right OK and what use would you have for wearing balaclavas?'

COOPER: 'Fishing.'

POLICE: 'Fishing?'

COOPER: 'Yeah.'

POLICE: 'Is that the only time you'd wear balaclavas?'

COOPER: 'Fishing.'

POLICE: 'OK and obviously in the last interview with us you spoke about . . . well not the last but one of the interviews today you spoke about working boots. Would you have worn walking boots or working boots in 1996?'

COOPER: 'To work yes, yes. Tough black, tough cheap boots.'

POLICE: 'And we've discussed in previous interviews your use and your possession of gloves and you've stated that you wouldn't often wear gloves but there would have been gloves around your house over the years.'

COOPER: 'Yes.'

POLICE: 'In relation to clothing, have you ever owned an army or combat type jacket, camouflage?'

COOPER: 'Possibly, Percy used to bring stuff like that and I'd use stuff like that for working.'

POLICE: 'Right.'

COOPER: 'Possibly, but more like bottle green or something like that.'

POLICE: 'Bottle green.'

COOPER: 'Yeah.'

POLICE: 'OK and you've said that you they were Army Surplus or . . .'

COOPER: 'Possibly yeah.'

POLICE: 'OK thank you.'

COOPER: 'OK, I've mentioned that the offender was in possession of a shotgun OK. Did you own any guns in 1996?'

COOPER: 'Uh no.'

POLICE: 'Did you have possession of any guns?'

COOPER: 'Oh no, no, no, my licence, I give up my licence long before then.'

POLICE: 'OK.'

COOPER: 'No.'

POLICE: 'The gun used in this offence has been described by the victim to officers as a sawn-off, double-barrelled side-by-side shotgun and having a strap which was connected with pins and clips, OK?'

POLICE: 'OK and obviously in the last interviews we discussed in July now last year the offence of the Sardis robbery and you mentioned that the gun was handed round court and you believed that you may have handled it at that time OK? So apart from potentially handling the gun at that time, have you ever had in your possession or held any gun matching that description?'

COOPER: 'Years before yes, I used to have a shotgun licence, yeah years before.'

POLICE: 'We're talking about a sawn-off . . .'

COOPER: 'A sawn-off . . .'

POLICE: 'Double-barrelled . . .'

COOPER: 'No, no.'

POLICE: 'On the 22nd of November 1996 a robbery occurred at a premises Westwinds in Sardis alright and following that robbery searches of nearby fields resulted in the recovery of a number of items which included a sawn-off, double-barrelled shotgun and that gun has been linked to yourself OK and I have a photograph of the gun recovered following the Sardis Robbery. I'm now going to show John Cooper a photograph contained in an album of in relation to the Sardis offence with two photos in the album. The second photo is of a sawn-off shotgun with a lanyard connected by clips that were contained in a brown evidence sack. OK and obviously John you can see the photograph of the gun . . .'

COOPER: 'Yeah.'

POLICE: 'My colleague has just shown you and in my opinion then the description given by the victims to these offences of the gun that was used is very similar to that gun. It's a sawn-off, double-barrelled shotgun and it specifically has a strap or lanyard which is connected to both ends by clips.'

COOPER: 'You say so yeah.'

POLICE: 'Would you say so?'

COOPER: 'Don't know.'

POLICE: 'Haven't I . . . if I said to.'

COOPER: 'Well it's a sawn-off shotgun yes and it's got a strap connected each side.'

COOPER: 'That's the gun they had in one of these rooms in here, yeah.'

POLICE: Yeah? Down from the trigger mechanism and the stock area, the clip is similar to one, like a dog lead clip.'

COOPER: 'A snap-on clip yeah yeah . . .'

POLICE: 'Yeah?'

COOPER: 'Yeah.'

POLICE: 'OK and obviously the gun in my opinion is very similar to the gun as described by the victims of the attempted robbery and rape. Is that the gun used in the rape and attempted robbery, the same gun as was recovered by police?'

COOPER: 'I don't know that . . .'

POLICE: '. . . following the Sardis robbery.'

COOPER: 'I've no idea.'

POLICE: 'OK. Obviously you have been linked to the offence of robbery to the gun from the offence of the Sardis Robbery that has led to your conviction OK. Were you the person who pointed the gun at five youngsters in a field in Milford Haven and searched the victims for money?'

COOPER: 'No.'

POLICE: 'Were you the person who subjected one of the young females to rape?'

COOPER: 'No.'

POLICE: 'Were you the person who indecently assaulted another of the females?'

COOPER: 'No.'

POLICE: 'OK. Have you any explanation, alibi or defence to offer in respect of the investigation of the attempted armed robbery, rape and indecent assault which occurred in Milford Haven on the 6ᵗʰ of March?'

COOPER: 'Have I?'

POLICE: 'Have you any explanation, any innocent explanation, alibi or defence to offer?'

COOPER: 'I know nothing about it sorry, I know nothing about it.'

POLICE: 'Exhibit, and we've spoken about what exhibits are, MTJ/7 is a glove OK? This glove was recovered from a hedgerow on the 23ʳᵈ of November 1996 following the Sardis Robbery that we've discussed. Tell me what you know about that glove.'

COOPER: 'I have no recollection about the glove at all.'

POLICE: 'OK. Was it your glove?'

COOPER: 'Oh it wasn't my glove, no.'

POLICE: 'OK. Unfortunately I don't have a photo of the Exhibit MTJ/7 but it's I know we talked about gloves earlier and Gareth showed you a glove which linked to the Dixons, it is a separate glove to that, OK, so we're talking about a completely different exhibit.'

COOPER: 'Oh I see OK.'

POLICE: 'This is MTJ/7, so it's a different exhibit OK. An examination of the knickers of the female who was raped on the 6th of March 1996, which is Exhibit BKG/9, has led to the recovery of a fibre and that fibre is described as undistinguishable from the fibres of the glove MTJ/7, which was obviously recovered following the Sardis Robbery. Have you any explanation for that?'

COOPER: 'None at all.'

POLICE: 'Were you the person who wore gloves in the commission of the offence of rape on that date?'

COOPER: 'No I was not.'

POLICE: 'OK, that glove then is linked to yourself as it was recovered from a hedgerow, along with other items which have been linked to the offence of robbery in Sardis for which you've been convicted.'

COOPER: 'Falsely convicted.'

POLICE: 'OK we're talking about an offence, a very serious offence of a rape, a sexual assault and attempted robbery of five youngsters in a field on the outskirts of Milford Haven. Can you tell me whether you were the person who pointed a gun at those children?'

COOPER: 'I was not that person.'

POLICE: 'OK. Can you tell me whether you've been in that locality for any reason in possession of a shotgun?'

COOPER: 'No.'

POLICE: 'Can you tell me whether you used to visit fields in the areas to shoot rabbits or other prey?'

COOPER: 'No.'

POLICE: 'OK. Can you tell me whether or not you had in your possession a large lamping light?'

COOPER: 'Large lamping light? I had rechargeable lights that I know of, yeah.'

POLICE: 'OK and what did you use those for?'

COOPER: 'Well working outside, we lived in the country; we always had to have torches, always.'

POLICE: 'Have you any alibi, I know the officer's asked you, for that evening?'

COOPER: 'I don't know what I was doing on that day.'

POLICE: 'OK. When did you first hear about the incident?'

COOPER: 'Local, local uh news. Maybe Percy, Percy used to bring most of the news from town out to us.'

POLICE: 'Can you see the significance and the reason why we're questioning you about this offence in that a fibre from gloves from the incident at Sardis has been linked to a fibre from inside the underwear of the rape victim?'

COOPER: 'I can see the significance of everything that happens, no matter what, shoplifting down in Milford Haven and whatever is tenuous line trying to put it back to John Cooper. Well you people must stop this.'

POLICE: 'And the way that we investigate offences is to look at evidence, to look at suspects and to question them.'

COOPER: 'Yes.'

POLICE: 'I've no further questions in relation to the Milford Haven rape. If we move on now to another matter which you've already been interviewed on in

2008 by myself, Louise and also DC Nigel Jones. In connection with the murders of Richard and Helen Thomas at Scoveston on the 22nd of December 1985. I'm not going to cover all the detail of the previous interview, OK, but what I'm going to do is to ask you to comment, 'cause I think it's only fair, on some fresh information that we've received, OK? To sum up, add you initially stated in the previous interviews that you hadn't been on the grounds of Scoveston Park and then you later recalled an incident where you may have been in there to retrieve some irrigation equipment and then you asked us whether there was a clock tower there. We went to check and there was. Is there anything else you wish to add with regards to occasions you've visited Scoveston?'

COOPER: 'I've only ever been down to Scoveston about two or three times that I can recollect.'

POLICE: 'OK.'

COOPER: 'And one of the occasions would have been with Flo and my wife in the car. With Flo Evans, sorry, right. Are you aware who Flo Evans is?'

POLICE: 'Yes.'

COOPER: 'She was their nanny.'

POLICE: 'Yeah we discussed it in previous interviews, OK. You were also questioned in relation to knowledge and contact with Richard Thomas. You said you'd only met on a few occasions and those meetings had been at Flo Evans' house.'

COOPER: 'Oh yeah mostly.'

POLICE: 'And you mentioned, if my memory serves me correct, that you helped put some items in the car and may have touched all the doors of Richard Thomas's Rover.'

COOPER: 'Yeah, yeah, yeah.'

POLICE: 'Yeah? OK. We asked you in the previous interviews whether or not you'd been to the property to purchase any feed or hay and you said you hadn't.'

COOPER: 'Yes.'

POLICE: 'OK, is that still the case?'

COOPER: 'What would I buy off him? Let me explain, right. I was only a smallholder right, small . . . I used to rear calves up. Somebody like Mr Thomas would be buying not what I finished, what somebody had finished after me. He had older stock, right. Why would I buy hay, straw or barley off Mr Thomas? I don't know whether he did sell it or not, but why would I? Mike Richards used to sell me all I wanted as part of my wages. And we went through that and explained it.'

COOPER: 'Yes.'

POLICE: 'Do you remember the previous interview I detailed you a statement from a Christopher Davies who said that you'd visited there to purchase feedstuff and you said you hadn't, OK?'

COOPER: 'Yes.'

POLICE: 'Have you ever argued with Richard Thomas regarding the price of hay?'

COOPER: 'I've never bought a thing off Mr . . . Mr Thomas. I had no need to. I bought it off Mike Richards, ask him.'

POLICE: 'From your initial comments and, obviously the contents of statements, it suggests to you playing down your knowledge and relationship with Mr Thomas. What have you got to say to that?'

COOPER: 'He wasn't a man I could socialise or many

other people could socialise. It was difficult to get a good day out of the man down at Flo's. I met mostly down Flo's.'

POLICE: 'OK so we've talked about the cut fences at that . . . were you the person responsible cutting fences in, on or around Scoveston Farm fields?'

COOPER: 'You wouldn't go near the place because the man didn't tolerate things like that.'

POLICE: 'And what about afterwards?'

COOPER: 'After?'

POLICE: 'After 1985. Have you ever cut any fences in or around Scoveston?'

COOPER: 'I haven't been across the land there.'

POLICE: 'OK. In your last interviews we spoke about Mr Raymond, who you call the son of Davey Raymond.'

COOPER: 'Yeah.'

POLICE: 'Yeah? In fact it's Davey Raymond's younger brother OK? You seem surprised.'

COOPER: 'I didn't know that.'

POLICE: 'And he's the victim of the burglary at 23 Castle Pill on the 1st of March 1996, OK? We've been through in previous interviews today about recording the fact that he didn't have any ammunition or shotguns, sorry any ammunition stolen at the time of your shotgun, OK? In previous interview you said to us, "Go and speak to him about it" and in fact to confirm, as we did earlier, we have. He has denied that the cartridges recovered from your duck run were from his address, OK? So obviously then I've explained earlier the significance we find . . . do you remember I showed you photographs in the previous interviews of a box with Maxim 5 written on, on the Baikal box?'

COOPER: 'Oh yeah.'

POLICE: 'Yeah?'

COOPER: 'Yeah.'

POLICE: 'And that's been examined by a handwriting expert who said that those details on that box were not written by yourself, were not written by Richard Thomas but may have been written by Helen Thomas OK and the ammunition, the cartridges in there are the same type as those used in the murders of Richard and Helen Thomas. I've got to ask you that as a result of that and other evidence were you the person responsible for murdering Richard and Helen Thomas?'

COOPER: 'No I was not.'

POLICE: 'OK. By telling us or trying to link the shotgun ammunition with the shotgun, were you trying to distance yourself from the shotgun, from the Scoveston incident and to lead our investigation in another direction?'

COOPER: 'I've already explained how they came into my possession.'

POLICE: 'So again I'll ask you, were you the person responsible for the murder of Richard and Helen Thomas?'

COOPER: 'No I was not.'

The interviews had been fascinating and the potent combination of male and female officers had worked a treat; Cooper did not like it. Much of his violent offending had been directed against women and, when challenged by Louise, the real John Cooper had come to the surface. At one stage he had almost said something insulting to her, but had just about managed to hold onto his tongue. I think he was going to make a derogatory comment about her being female. 'Young lady, I won't say it,' said Cooper. What was it he was going to say? At the conclusion of the challenge interview I was happy we had put the relevant issues to him. There is a temptation to keep hammering on, but for me this would have been pointless and unnecessary. I sat with Lynne Harries and Glyn Johnson and reviewed our position and we were happy. 'OK, team, let's speak to the CPS and get a decision,' I said, sensing the anticipation in the room. As the day had gone on I had spoken to the CPS on a number of occasions and they were fully across events. I didn't have to wait long for their response: 'Charge him with the lot!'

There are not many times in a career that you get the chance to charge a serial killer. It was important that I chose people from the original team who had been in for the long haul. The honour fell to DC Nigel John and DC Steve Rowe, both had made significant contributions to the investigation doing some of the less glamorous but no less important work. When I asked them to charge Cooper they had a look of disbelief, quickly followed by a look of satisfaction and determination to be professional to the end. At 7.02 p.m. on the 14th of May 2009, John William Cooper was charged with the following offences:

- The murder of Richard Thomas at Scoveston Park on the 22nd of December 1985.
- The murder of Helen Thomas at Scoveston Park on the 22nd of December 1985.
- The murder of Peter Dixon at Little Haven on the 29th of June 1989.
- The murder of Gwenda Dixon at Little Haven on the 29th of June 1989.
- Attempted robbery on XXX at Milford Haven on

the 6th of March 1996.

- Attempted robbery on XXX at Milford Haven on the 6th of March 1996.
- Attempted robbery on XXX at Milford Haven on the 6th of March 1996.
- Attempted robbery on XXX at Milford Haven on the 6th of March 1996.
- Attempted robbery on XXX at Milford Haven on the 6th of March 1996.
- The rape of a 16-year-old female at Milford Haven on the 6th of March 1996.
- Indecent assault of a 15-year-old female at Milford Haven on the 6th of March 1996.

Cooper made 'no comment' to all charges. The only emotion he showed was when he was charged with the sex offences on the children. For me this was nothing more than concern for himself, not for the victims. Cooper had spent over ten years in prison and he knew how other inmates treated child sex offenders and how this could possibly impact on him. Nigel John and Steve Rowe came back into the control room. 'Done, boss.' There were no cheers or backslapping, just a collective sense of satisfaction that the hard yards had been rewarded. I knew that we would face many challenges before he would be standing in the dock, but I also knew I had the right team to get him there. I spoke with DCC Andy Edwards and Chief Superintendent Steve Mears who had been preparing for a news conference to make the announcement that Cooper had been charged. The media interest was huge and an indication of things to come. As we took stock of the extraordinary events we knew it would be almost two years before we saw Cooper in the flesh again. Then he would be standing in the dock of a courtroom.

CHAPTER 17

PREPARING FOR THE BIG HOUSE

The last few weeks had been a whirlwind with little time to draw breath; Cooper had now been remanded into custody. Speculation had started in the press suggesting Cooper was responsible for other murders and everyone wanted to get my views on this theory. *My* focus was on providing the best case for the Crown and nothing else. Two days after charging Cooper I pulled the management team together. We agreed that Gareth Rees and Paul Jones would act as Officers In the Case (OIC) and be responsible for the file preparation which was split into four sections, Scoveston Park murders, Dixons murders, Milford Haven robbery/ rape and Evidence of Bad Character. Lynne Harries and Glyn Johnson were identified as the team leaders and would co-ordinate the activity of the rest of the Ottawa team that had now grown to eighteen staff.

Like the rest of my management team I believed that other forensic 'golden nuggets' would inevitably come our way. The disclosure team needed to be aware of any possible angles for the defence whilst reviewing the vast amount of material. It was clear that they had an excellent working relationship with Grenville Barker from the CPS who had provided considerable advice and guidance on the process. I insisted that I wanted to be as transparent as possible with the defence in relation to disclosure and would work with them in discharging this responsibility. Failure to get a proper hold of the disclosure process had been the graveyard of many high-profile investigations and I was determined this would not happen to Ottawa; we had come too far only to fall at the final hurdle.

The main challenge in the file preparation work was identifying where there might be gaps in our evidence. Many of the expert and scientists contributions were in the form of reports and not evidential statements and a significant number of the police officers involved in the investigations had either retired or passed away; there were also holes in some of the continuity evidence about how exhibits and material were moved from A to B and so on; the records of continuity existed, but statements had not been taken from those responsible for individual movements. Gareth and Paul needed to pull together a skeleton file and find the evidence where possible to fill the gaps. It was clear that the Forensic Science Service had vast amounts of documentation and case notes connected to Ottawa and they needed to be recovered and transferred to LGC Forensics. The documents would help them assess the integrity of any potential fibre or DNA evidence and this could be vital to the court case.

The role of the family liaison officers was now crucial, particularly for the Milford Haven victims. Three officers were identified to provide this support. They were Fred Hunter, Helen Coles and Donna Thomas. I had an excellent relationship with Tim and Keith Dixon and Julie Pratley (née Dixon) so would continue to deal with them directly. It was important that the family liaison officers were clear about their role. They would provide support to the victims and be their link with the investigation. They would not discuss the evidence, identification issues or the location and identity of Cooper's family.

Facebook was a new social phenomenon and comments about the case were already appearing. There had also been daubing on walls in Milford Haven, some supportive of Cooper, some not. I knew that the Milford victims had access to Facebook and it was important that they did not engage in local gossip. I was also concerned that this would negatively impact on Cooper's family, who had behaved impeccably during the process. I did not want them to be affected and I took comfort in knowing that Dean Richards, the local commander, had dedicated resources to manage the community impact. The victims themselves were at the forefront of my mind. They had suffered long-term effects from that night; Maria, in particular, had suffered significant health problems, directly attributable to that terrible attack. Steven and David had never gone out into the fields again and it had also changed their lives. They had become withdrawn, nervous and personal relationships had been affected. Susan and Jayne had suffered the most harrowing effects and they would need considerable support over the coming months. I needed them to give evidence and stand in court with the man who had terrorised them. At this stage I was not convinced that I could get them to do this, so the work of the family liaison officers would be essential.

The time scale for the initial submission of a file would be tight, but achievable and again I was determined that we would not be found wanting, give the defence the opportunity to criticise us. Discussions had already taken place regarding a possible venue for a trial, likely to take place in the summer of 2010 in Cardiff or Chester. Tom

Atherton from the CPS had a view that the Presiding Judge for the West Wales area would not accept the trial being moved from his jurisdiction and would want it heard in Swansea. This presented hidden problems; the first was the selection of a jury not tainted by the reporting of the case. The second was the location of Cooper. He was now a Category A prisoner and in a maximum-security jail. Neither Swansea nor Cardiff prisons are Category A security locations and so would be unable to hold Cooper; this would mean him being escorted from Long Lartin in West Mercia on a daily basis. Clearly this would be impractical and something would need to be sorted out. Thankfully this was not my problem, but Tom was still of the view that Swansea would probably be the venue.

Another pressing issue was the current location of the team. We had now outgrown Pembroke Dock and needed to move. A possible location had been identified at Pier House in Pembroke Dock. It was a large three-storey building owned by the Port Authority and its top floor consisted of a series of offices. The location was ideal; it had been recently re-decorated and had one very large room that could act as the incident room and one large enough to store the files and documents. Following negotiations it was secured and with great assistance from our IT Department and with a significant security upgrade, we were able to move in. The office was in a fantastic location with views down the Milford Haven waterway. I of course checked the window ledge for binoculars, Fred Hunter was not going to catch me for a second time!

The media interest in the case meant we would need a robust strategy and Rhian Davies-Moore and her team started to think about how we would handle the trial. The BBC

Crimewatch programme had indicated that they intended to broadcast an update to both murder investigations on the 2nd of June 2009. The press were also aware that the Dixon family made an annual pilgrimage to Little Haven on the anniversary of murders to lay a wreath at the scene. It was important to me that Tim and Julie and their family did not suffer the same unacceptable intrusion and treatment they had received from the press in 1989. I leaned on Rhian to call in some favours from the press to avoid this; thankfully the media were very sympathetic and behaved impeccably.

It was also my plan to carry out a reconstruction of the Dixons' murder at Little Haven on the anniversary. The news broadcast back in 2007 had already shown us that there were still witnesses out there and the reconstruction would generate a great deal of interest; it would also be an opportunity for the local officers to provide some reassurance to the local community. We would need the assistance of the National Park in closing off parts of the coastal path ensuring privacy for Tim and Julie. The National Park and local council would become excellent partners in supporting us up to and through the trial process. Closing the path would give me an opportunity to reconstruct the scene and compare it with how it looked back in 1985. It had changed significantly. Young saplings were now fully developed trees, and the old stile below Talbenny Church had long gone. The closed-off areas allowed us to secure evidential photographs and put ourselves back in the mind of Cooper to try and understand why he had selected that location. It was clear that the elevated view from Talbenny Church enabled him to see potential victims walking the coast path and at the same time gave him enough time to walk down the slope and climb over the stile to intercept them. The reconstruction was an important part of the case preparation and went like clockwork. It was now time for my senior team to visit LGC. We had now identified some critical exhibits recovered during the searches of Cooper's home and from the Sardis robbery trail:

- A pair of gloves recovered from the kitchen of 34 St Marys Park, exhibit number AJM/60.
- Fibres found in sweepings taken from Cooper's workbench at 34 St Marys Park, exhibit number GC/15.
- Fibres found in sweepings from the floor of the work shed at 34 St Marys Park, exhibit number GC/12.
- Shorts recovered from 34 St Marys Park, exhibit number AJM/165.
- A single glove found in a hedge near to 34 St Marys Park, exhibit number BB/109.
- Pair of gloves abandoned by Cooper on the Sardis trail, exhibit numbers MTJ/5 and MTJ/7.
- Double-barrelled sawn-off shotgun abandoned by Cooper on the Sardis trail, exhibit number PH/2 and the lanyard attached to the same gun PH/2A.
- Balaclava abandoned by Cooper on the Sardis trail, exhibit number MTJ/14.
- Fleece abandoned by Cooper on the Sardis trail, exhibit number MTJ/29.

The LGC team had now received the case papers and fibre lifts from the Forensic Science Service and had started to compare them with the exhibits recovered from Cooper's offending and his home environment. The FSS samples had been recovered from the victims with tape lifts:

- Tapings from the body of Gwenda Dixon, exhibit reference JAW/2, JAW/4 and JAW/5.
- Tapings from the clothing and body of Peter Dixon, exhibit reference JAW/100, JAW/110, GWJC/90 and GWJC/112.
- Forensic paper pants belonging to Milford Haven rape victim, exhibit reference CEM/1. (provided to capture shedding fibres).
- Pants belonging to Milford Haven rape victim, exhibit reference BKG/9.
- Jeans belonging to Milford Haven rape victim BKG/7.
- Jumper belonging to Milford Haven indecent assault victim, exhibit reference HPC/3.
- Shirt taken from Milford Haven indecent assault victim, exhibit reference HPC/4.
- External tapings jogging bottoms taken from Milford Haven indecent assault victim, exhibit reference HPC/8.
- Internal tapings from the linings of jogging bottoms exhibit reference HPC/8. Dr Phil Avenell from LGC Forensics had now raised wearer's DNA from the shorts and from a handkerchief in the pocket. The DNA profile *was* that of John Cooper. During interview he had accepted the shorts belonged to him suggesting they were his swimming shorts. He had been at pains to point out that his shorts were shorter than those in the artist's impression.

As we travelled to Oxford to meet with the scientists, Lynne and Glyn had obviously been talking about the Sardis gun, PH/2. We all believed this was the murder weapon but did not have the evidence to support this view.

Scientists had identified that the barrels of the gun had been hand-coated with Hammerite and identical paint had been recovered from Cooper's shed. Lynne and Glyn were aware of a previous case where paint had been removed from a skirting board to reveal the blood of the killer and felt that this avenue needed to be explored with LGC. I also expressed my suspicions regarding the shorts, why had he gone to such lengths to tell us they were shorter than the artist's impression.

The meeting was a happy one and it was the first time I had seen the LGC team since they had discovered the blood of Peter Dixon on the shorts. They could see my obvious delight. Angela Gallop chaired the meeting with Phil Avenell, Roger Robson and April Robson also present; straight away there was good news. Fibres recovered from the clothing of the Milford Haven rape victim were identical to fibres from the gloves MTJ/5 and MTJ/7. Bingo! I now had evidence to connect Cooper to the Milford Haven attack. Any lingering concerns that this case might fall by the wayside had now gone and I could have kissed Roger Robson there and then. He and April had been recovering and grouping fibres from the various items and tape lifts and were of the firm view that on initial viewing there were some interesting and encouraging similarities: they were clearly on to something.

Our relationship had developed into one of total respect for one another. It meant that we could now ask some more probing questions regarding the examinations. Following the discussion with Lynne and Glyn there were two items I needed to explore; I wanted to know exactly down to the finest detail how they had examined the gun. Phil Avenell went into great detail on how it was taken to pieces and every nook and cranny was swabbed for trace DNA. Tape lifts had been taken from the lanyard but the paint had not been removed from the barrels. I then asked Phil if he could forensically sterilise the outer surface of the gun and then remove the paint to see what was underneath it. The thinking was that any evidence found underneath the Hammerite coating must have been left there by the person who had painted the gun. The same paint of course had been found in Cooper's shed. The conversation then went onto the shorts. Roger described them in fine detail and how they had recovered the bloodstain but his next disclosure was interesting. He informed us that the hem on the shorts had been re-stitched using a home sewing machine. They had been shortened after leaving the manufacturer. We knew that Pat Cooper made a living from making curtains on her own sewing machine and more than likely had been responsible for any alterations. I then asked Roger if he had unpicked the hem to see what had been sealed inside during the stitching process. He hadn't but agreed to do so. Without doubt the process of bringing the scientists and detectives together was paying dividends. It allowed us to bring our knowledge of the scene and sequence of events to the table. On the way home we all agreed that there was a great deal more to come from LGC. They were an excellent team and clearly very interested in our investigation. It was important than ever that the forensic work carried on to a natural conclusion, but it had to be managed in line with the trial date.

Justice John Griffith Williams had been identified as the trial judge and he would need to be satisfied, at case management hearings, that all work was being carried out expeditiously. The general consensus of opinion was that the defence would need a considerable amount of time to consider the material and would probably not object too much to any delays.

Because of the forensic breakthrough our initial case was starting to change. I had now got strong forensic evidence linking Cooper to the Dixons murders and the Milford Haven attack. Lacking was a forensic link to Scoveston Park. The proximity of Scoveston to Cooper's home and the fact that the Norton Farm key belonging to Richard Thomas had been found on Cooper's land presented a strong circumstantial argument that he was responsible for the murders. The temptation with bad character evidence is to throw everything into the pot and it can become more of an attack on the individual rather than clear evidence that a person behaves in a certain way.

Whatever the complexities of the case, we worked with junior counsel Mike Jones and prepared a Bad Character Application to go before Justice Griffith Williams. There was a considerable amount of evidence to show that Cooper was a violent man who physically abused his son Adrian. There was also evidence that he had displayed significant cruelty to animals, but following discussion with Gerard Elias QC I felt that it added little to the case and could be seen as a character assassination exercise. We decided not to use it.

The next few weeks had the feeling of being Christmas Day, every day. LGC was on a roll but the news I received on the 14th of August 2009 was beyond anything I could have hoped for. The paint had been removed from the barrels of the sawn-off shotgun PH/2, the firearm used by Cooper during the Sardis armed robbery, and blood had been found near the end of the barrel and at the breach of the gun: it was the blood of Peter Dixon. We now had the murder weapon and Lynne and Glyn's hunch had been spot on. No wonder Cooper had continued to protest his innocence over the Huntsman investigation and convictions; he knew that gun directly connected him to the Dixons' murder.

This evidence and disclosure to the defence would have a significant impact on the case. Cooper now lodged an appeal against the 1998 Huntsman convictions and appeared to be more focused on this than fighting the Ottawa charges. The reason was now very clear. Cooper knew what potential traps lay for him in the exhibits abandoned on the Sardis robbery trail. He had to try and distance himself from the gun because he knew its value to the police. If he could successfully appeal his Huntsman convictions he would remove a significant plank of evidence but he faced a major problem. In order for his appeal to be granted, Cooper would need to show that there was new evidence to support his position. His protestations of innocence were not regarded as new evidence and his application duly failed. Another problem for him was that the Huntsman exhibits were now inextricably linked to the Ottawa charges and I had tasked LGC Forensics with carrying out work on them that would if anything strengthen the original Huntsman conviction. Over many hours, mugs of tea and the occasional pint, I sat with Lynne, Glyn and the rest of the team hypothesising over his likely defence. The usual approach would be for his defence team to attack the integrity and continuity of the key exhibits and evidence. 'It wasn't me and I wasn't there' had been his response in interview, but now faced with the forensic evidence this position would be seriously undermined to say the least.

We believed he would continue to claim his innocence over the Huntsman convictions as a major part of his defence. This would make for a messy trial and I hoped we could avoid this happening. The other option he might go with was to offer up his son, Adrian. He had during his interviews made suggestions regarding Adrian but never gone as far as to directly accuse him. A big problem for him was that at the time of the Dixons' murder Adrian was living in Birmingham and he also had an alibi for the Scoveston Park murders. Blaming others would not be a new concept for John Cooper; during his Huntsman trial he had implicated a local man for the Sardis robbery. Again there was no evidence to justify this; in fact this man was captured on CCTV at a local garage at the time of the robbery filling his car with petrol. In the fullness of time it would become clear that Cooper was to rely on a combination of all options available to him, as was his right to do so.

The forensic evidence was still continuing to build up and as anticipated provided additional evidence to strengthen the Huntsman conviction:

- Fibres from the Sardis balaclava MTJ/14 were recovered in the sweepings taken from Cooper's workbench GC/15.
- Fibres from the gloves AJM/60 (found in Cooper's house) were recovered on the Sardis shotgun PH/2 and its lanyard PH/2A.
- Fibres from the Sardis glove MTJ/5 were found on the Sardis fleece MTJ/29.
- Fibres from the Sardis fleece MTJ/29 were found on the Sardis glove MTJ/5.

- Fibres from the fleece MTJ/29 were found on Cooper's workbench GC/15.
- Fibres from the Sardis fleece MTJ/29 were found on the Sardis glove MTY/7.
- Fibres from the Sardis glove MTJ/5 were recovered at the point of entry at 'Westwinds' the scene of the Sardis robbery.
- Fibres from the Sardis glove MTJ/5 were found on the cartridge box AJM/216 (which was buried by Cooper under his duck run together with a stolen shotgun).

Without any doubt this evidence connected the items he had abandoned as he made his escape after the robbery with his home. The fibre links to his workbench and floor sweepings from his shed were interesting. This was Cooper's secret place, a location that his family avoided because it was his domain. This is where he would go to change before disappearing into the night; this is where he kept his secret wardrobe, which he probably destroyed just prior to his arrest in 1996. He must have feared the net was closing.

We were now up and running at Pier House in Pembroke Dock. Gareth Rees and Paul Jones were impressive in their approach to pulling the files together and securing the necessary evidence. I had now tasked Lynne to oversee this work and had asked Glyn to concentrate on the continuity and integrity of the key exhibits. Glyn was the master of the spreadsheet and I tasked him with producing a timeline for each exhibit detailing its movements and he then compared this with other key exhibits. Anticipating an attack on integrity of evidence, I wanted to identify any

PREPARING FOR THE BIG HOUSE

opportunities for contamination. If I could show that there was no opportunity for fibre exhibits to come together or for blood to contaminate clothing, I could go a long way to closing off this defence.

For various reasons proposed trial dates came and went. The defence did not object too loudly as they were experiencing their own problems. But as time went on more forensic 'golden nuggets' were being revealed. It had already been established that fibres from the gloves MTJ/5 and MTJ/7 had been found on the clothing and underwear of the Milford Haven rape victim and indecent assault victim. The location of these fibres was also consistent with the sequence of events described by the victims during their attack. Just as interesting was what we call a two-way transfer, which provides very strong evidence that two items have come into direct contact. Fibres from both victim's clothes and underwear were found on the gloves MTJ/5 and MTJ/7, gloves directly linked to Cooper.

There were also some interesting results from the glove BB/109, found in a hedgerow near to Cooper's house. Fibres from this glove had already been recovered from the bodies of Peter and Gwenda Dixon and the branches covering their bodies. A fibre from this glove was now found on the ground sheet given to the Milford Haven indecent assault victim. (When assault victims provide their clothes to the police, they do so whilst standing on a forensic ground sheet. This ensures that any fibres shed by the victim are captured on the ground sheet and preserved.) We were satisfied that Cooper was wearing the gloves MTJ/5 and MTJ/7 when he attacked the children. The presence of this single fibre from BB/109 suggests that all three gloves have come into contact with each other at some time, probably in the wardrobe in Cooper's shed. This was an important find. It again provided a direct link between the Dixons murder and the Milford Haven offence.

The forensic evidence for these two particular offences was very strong and, if taken into account along with the evidence of his bad character, I felt it would be overwhelming. I was firmly of the view that any jury who accepted that Cooper was responsible for the costal path murders and the Milford Haven attack would have no problem in accepting he had murdered the Thomases who lived only yards away from the scene. Unfortunately, the man who mattered, Gerard Elias QC was not entirely convinced by my view that ordinary people on the jury would see this connection.

The next set of forensic results made any difference in our views totally redundant. The shorts had not finished giving up their secrets. After unpicking the hem, sealed inside, the scientist had recovered fibres which were from the gloves MTJ/5. They had also recovered two balls of fibre in the pockets of the same shorts; these fibres had been compared with fibres recovered from the sock BM/1. The sock came from the badly burnt body of Richard Thomas and was remarkably intact. The fibres were the same, we did not have the source garment from which the fibres were shed, but its meaning and value were clear. The likely scenario being this: the woollen gloves used by Cooper when he dragged a lifeless Richard Thomas back into the burning building had been at some stage in the pockets of the shorts. The source garment had probably long gone, but its value in connecting Cooper to the murders of Richard and Helen Thomas had not. When I heard this news could hardly believe my ears. I now had a pair of shorts recovered in

Cooper's bedroom which had revealed forensic evidence connecting him to four murders, one armed robbery, five attempted armed robberies, a rape and an indecent assault. Cooper's own DNA was on the shorts and he had accepted ownership of them. In my wildest dreams I could never have expected that after almost three years of nothing, I would now be in this position with such a wealth of strong forensic links to the Ottawa offences. The mood in the office was quite strange. We had now become so used to receiving good forensic news that this development passed with little comment. The challenge we now faced was presenting the evidence in a format that the jury would understand. The scientists would need to begin their evidence by explaining their scientific processes and what their terminology actually meant and not get lost in the technical language that might alienate the jury.

Modern courtrooms contain televisions and computers, and visual presentations of evidence and the use of CCTV is an everyday occurrence. To meet this demand a number of private companies have sprung up nationally offering the production of such presentations to the police and CPS; such a service does not come cheaply and my experience told me that all too often they can become style over substance leading to a challenge in court. All too often this can overshadow the impact of the evidence. I wanted to keep control of ours because it was clear that Mr Elias intended to open the case using such a presentation. The cost of outsourcing it would be enormous. The answer was at hand. We would do it in house and for the cost of £500 worth of software. Glyn Johnson was confident he could do just as good a job and from what I had seen I believed him. As our new 'graphics wizard', Glyn set about creating a detailed presentation that would be used to open the case and every day thereafter.

Just when I thought we had used up all of our luck, along came another piece of forensic evidence that had us all scratching our heads. When Phil Avenell had examined the unpicked hem of the shorts he found blood and believed it was a mixture of DNA from Peter and Gwenda Dixon. That would have been extremely useful, but on further examination Phil eliminated that conclusion. The true origin of the DNA was totally unexpected. It was the DNA of their daughter Julie Dixon. We thought this must be impossible because Julie was in Cyprus at the time of the murders and Phil ruled out a secondary transfer. There could only be one explanation and it was in keeping with Cooper as an offender who kept mementos: the shorts must have belonged to the Dixons. The more we discussed this possibility the more likely it became. The shorts had an elasticated waist and the rear pocket was high on the hip and there was no zip or button fly. One of the female officers, Debbie Chodecka, made quite a telling observation. 'Those hips are roomy, boss, and they are female shorts.' Looking at photographs of Peter, he always wore shorts that were appropriate for the task in hand; his running shorts were an athletics type and his walking shorts always had a clip fastener, zip fly and a leather belt to hold them up. We did not have a clear photograph of Gwenda in shorts, but what we did have suggested that they were the type of shorts she might have worn. I then spoke to Tim and Julie, and was surprised to learn that they did not know that their mother was wearing long trousers at the time she was murdered. Without any prompting Tim added that if his mother were wearing long trousers she would always put a pair of shorts in her holdall to change into if it became hot. The answer was there and made perfect sense in the circumstances.

In the process of moving bodies around in the scene it is highly likely Cooper would have become bloodstained, particularly on the front of his legs or trousers. If he were to go into Pembroke Main Street in the middle of summer, he might have been seen covered in blood. The clean shorts belonging to Gwenda Dixon provided him with a change of clothing. He had kept them after the murders and again this fitted with a man hellbent on control. Every time he wore them it took him back to that time and place on the coastal path. Now I am not a man who believes in the supernatural or anything of that nature, but I did ask myself, for a moment, if Peter and Gwenda weren't having the last say from their resting place and providing me with all of the evidence I needed.

That was to be the final piece in what was now a very complicated jigsaw. It was head down now for our day in court and I was very happy with our case. Cooper's position was becoming clearer. He had employed a number of experts to review the forensic evidence, ballistics, fibres, DNA and a locksmith to look at the Norton Farm key. They were also exploring a theory that the blood on the shorts was as a result of the rehydration of dry blood. In essence they were suggesting that a dry flake of Peter Dixon's blood had found its way into the open bag, containing the shorts and been rehydrated with water. I was now very pleased that we had taken the decision to document the recovery of all exhibits and to record what other material was next to them. In doing so we could show that no blood exhibits had been anywhere near the shorts. Phil Avenell was also confident he could respond to such a suggestion in court. I was happy that we could negate any challenge to the forensic evidence; the continuity and integrity schedules had been reviewed by LGC Forensics and had described our handling of material as meticulous.

What was more concerning to me was that the Huntsman trial appeared to be the real focus of the defence. They were concentrating on this conviction in an effort to distance Cooper from the Gun PH/2. It appeared that the new and additional forensic evidence strengthening that conviction had completely escaped them and their focus was on the identification evidence from the victim of the Sardis robbery, Sheila Clarke. She had given a description of the man who attacked her in her home. She described him as agile and young. It has to be remembered that she based this on a masked man who moved quickly and was nimble on his feet. She would not have been able to tell how old he was and it was simply an impression based on what she saw.

The identification issue was not the real concern; Mr Elias feared that the defence were going to try and re-run the Huntsman trial by calling witnesses from that case, thirteen years after the conviction. We would be in the ridiculous situation of having to effectively reconvict him of those crimes before moving onto the Ottawa offences. The provisions of Bad Character Evidence allow the Crown to show a jury that a career criminal or repeat offender is more likely to be guilty of an offence because in essence they always display a particular behaviour when they offend. In order to allow this evidence the Crown must satisfy the trial judge that the Bad Character Evidence is relevant and admissible. This happens at a separate hearing before a judge where the prosecution and the defence put their case forward; I cannot believe that the Law Lords who drafted this law intended it to allow career criminals to re-run previous convictions and re-call witnesses and worse than that, the victims of their crimes. My fear is that rape victims could be called on again and again by a serial offender in contested cases, sometimes years after they have moved on from their ordeal. This is an issue I would later take up with the Director of Public Prosecutions, Kier Starmer.

This issue was heard before Justice Griffith Williams, the trial judge, and in a twenty-seven-page ruling he found in favour of the Crown. We all thought this was a sensible decision. Not long after though Cooper and his legal team successfully appealed the judgement and he was now able to call witnesses from the Huntsman trial, including the Sardis robbery victim Sheila Clarke. On reflection this was probably the safest decision the Appeal Court could make. Not allowing it would probably give grounds for Cooper to appeal should we gain a conviction. The ruling did not make our job any easier; we would now be trying a case with four murders, five robberies, a rape, an indecent assault and thirty house burglaries. On occasions I had to remind myself which case I was actually heading up.

The months passed, as did some potential trial dates. The main delays were now down to the defence. It was clear that their experts were having difficulty in finding problems with the key forensic evidence. All of the case papers and documents for disclosure were set out at Pier House and the team had a detailed floor plan and register of what was where. I had invited the defence to bring a team and go through disclosure and I would make my team available to assist and also to facilitate scene visits. The defence put four days aside for the disclosure process but they gave up after just two days. They came expecting to find gaps and holes in our evidence when in fact they found the opposite. They were faced with a highly professional and slick team who could put their hands on any requested documents in just seconds; disclosure would never raise its head again.

The trial was now set for spring 2011, and this would not be changed. Glyn was doing a fantastic job preparing the Court presentation and opening with Gerard Elias QC. It was superb in its simplicity; all of the relevant experts had agreed its content and best of all the defence were also happy with it. In fact Mr Mark Evans QC, Counsel for the Defence, would himself use it as part of his case. I have no doubt that if I had outsourced this work it would have cost in excess of £150,000.

The jury visit would take place over two days in Pembrokeshire and Carmarthenshire and would cause considerable disruption to traffic and the local community. The planning needed to be meticulous and local officers, Inspector Gareth Thomas and Sergeant Martin Vaughan, developed an excellent and detailed plan, which again would showcase the professionalism of our staff. This was supported by an equally detailed press strategy developed by Rhian Davies-Moore and her team. The press issues were significant; they wanted as much access to the jury visit and locations as possible, within the rules of engagement. They also wanted pre-trial briefings and press packs and continued access to material during the trial process. The response was comprehensive and included a password access to Dyfed-Powys Police web site that allowed them to download photographs during the trial process. As an SIO, it was very comforting to know that once plans were agreed I had people who would deliver them to a very high standard.

One of the issues we needed to address was the ability of witnesses to refresh their memory regarding statements and documents some of them had made some twenty-five years previously. The defence agreed to the process and a procession of retired officers and other witnesses did so under controlled conditions. All police witnesses were reminded of court etiquette in a written note. This included their mode of dress and the fact that they should travel to and from court alone and under no circumstances discuss the case or their evidence with other officers. I wanted to ensure that the jury and defence saw a highly professional outfit and could make their own judgement. This was difficult when it came to the retired officers as the court resembled a reunion on occasion, with officers seeing each other again for the first time in years and we had to sometimes remind them of where they were.

Weeks before the trial came the saddest of news. Maria, one of our victims from Milford Haven, had passed away. It devastated the team. Of all of the victims, Maria appeared to have been affected the most and had been constantly in bad health since that night. It was a travesty that she would never see her tormentor standing in the dock. Maria's death had the opposite effect on Jayne and Susan: they appeared to strengthen in their resolve to face Cooper and achieve justice for them all; I was immensely impressed by their courage.

The Ottawa team were now involved in the final preparations and working closely with the legal team. The incident room was full of large maps and boxes of jury photographs and files. Mark Roach and Olly James had hand-made large orange markers, which resembled twenty-foot lollipops. These would then be placed in the hedgerows to mark the location of key exhibits for the jury who would be bussed to various locations at which they could see the geography of Cooper's offending. They were simple and highly effective. In fact, so much so, that I was concerned that they might disrupt shipping in the Milford Haven waterway! As the trial date loomed the incident room was moved to a small police room in Swansea Crown Court and set out in the cramped conditions. It was the 21st of March 2011, the day before the trial and the team were remarkably composed and ready. That night I sat at home and events of the last five years flashed through my mind; the team coming together at Fishguard, the hours of discussion about 'what might have happened' and the years of frustration. As I did, a smile came over my face and I knew I could not have asked for a better team. In the end we had spent close to £1.5 million on forensics but we could justify every single penny. That night I slept well.

CHAPTER 18

DAY OF RECKONING

It was the first day of the trial. Five years of detailed planning, investigation, inspirational forensic work and plenty of optimism had gone into building the case against John William Cooper. It was now up to a jury to determine his guilt or innocence by due process of law at the Crown Court of Swansea. The adversarial trial of case number T20097163 of four murders, a rape, indecent assault and five attempted robberies would reverberate around the wood-panelled walls of Courtroom One for ten weeks. A pool of more than a hundred potential jurors had been slimmed down to fifty-one; a larger number was needed because of the estimated length of the case and its complexity. On the 22nd of March 2011 the jury of twelve were sworn in as the bespectacled Cooper looked on from the dock whilst holding onto his folder of papers, something that would become a feature of his daily routine.

The arena was now set for the battle to take place between two equal parties, the prosecution that attempts to prove its case beyond all reasonable doubt, and the defence that seeks to undermine the prosecution's case and to *create* reasonable doubt. In essence it is a definition that has always troubled me: the task of the defence is not to prove the innocence of the defendant but to prevent the prosecution from proving guilt.

Our 'champion' was leading criminal barrister Gerard Elias QC. He had vast experience and gravitas; a Roman virtue that would soon be evident to all who saw him in action. He was a real gentleman who shared my love of cricket; seeing him in court in his robes was like watching a sporting icon walking into a room of adoring fans. Collaborating with him was his son David Elias and senior Crown advocate Mike Jones: they were a formidable team. Their combatant, defence counsel Mr Mark Evans QC was a recorder on the Wales and Chester circuit. Mr Alistair Munt, a tall and very pleasant man who was a specialist criminal and military defence barrister, supported him.

The trial judge, Justice John Griffith Williams, was a Justice of the High Court and a remarkable character. He took his place at the head of the court on a raised platform where he was able to cast his eye over the proceedings. A cry from the usher, 'Court rise,' would see everyone rush to their feet as he entered bedecked in his red coloured robes. Woe betide you if you failed to show your subjection to the court by not standing for the judge; his knowing look would cut you to the quick.

Witness protocol would unfortunately deny me access to the courtroom whilst the prosecution case was being heard. It was standard practice but I made sure the team gave me a full briefing afterwards. Mr Elias QC poignantly delivered the prosecution opening, accentuated by Glyn Johnson's superb presentation. This also afforded Glyn the opportunity to sit at the front of the court for the entire ten weeks, sandwiched between counsel and the judge; it must have been a daunting prospect as he operated the presentation for both the prosecution and defence. At times he would have to anticipate where they were going next to allow the technology to catch up.

I know that he and counsel had worked tirelessly to ensure that as Mr Elias QC chronicled the horrific circumstances of the case all the key points were illustrated on the fifteen screens in the courtroom. I had total faith in Glyn but I often considered what might happen if the computer broke down or the screens went blank. I did get some reassurance from his response, 'Don't worry, boss, I've got it all backed up.' Whatever that meant.

The opening went like clockwork in front of a packed court and press box. The IT worked and it was clear that Mr Elias had performed to the best of his ability. This was to be his last case and it could not have been a better one to go out on. We had got past the first hurdle. Glyn came back into the police room at the end of the opening statement and I shook his hand. 'Well done, mate, a fantastic piece of work, thank you,' I said. The defence opened their case, telling the jury that they would hear evidence that they would be able to cast doubt on. The battle lines were set and one by one the witnesses started to filter into the box. All appeared to be going well, until we were informed that the judge had halted the trial after a note had been passed to him by a member of the jury.

After a few nail-biting hours sitting in our drab little side room we discovered that a member of the jury was former Scenes of Crime Officer with another police force. 'How can this be?' echoed around the corridors of the court. 'Surely this would have been disclosed prior to the selection process . . . heads will roll!' I am glad to say the fault lay in the internal court process of the court, not with us. The jury were discharged and the process of reselection started again. Glyn at this point had the look on his face of a rabbit just before a ferret grabs it; he was getting reassurance and counselling from Mr Elias. 'Don't worry, Mr Johnson, I once had to do an opening four times.' Needless to say the second opening in front of a new jury went like clockwork having benefited from the unexpected rehearsal. We went home that night to review the fruits of our labour as the information hit the national news. 'A sixty-six-year-old grandfather used cold and calculating violence to carry out two of the most infamous double murders in Welsh history, a jury was told today,' was the headline. 'This was not a man fleeing to Cardiff or the big smoke of London,' was the quote used from Mr Elias. 'These two double killings amounted to merciless executions for pitifully small gain,' reported the television news.

The following day our drab little room was stacked top to bottom with files which represented a mere fraction of the two million documents that formed the case. Two small tables housed Lynne and Glyn together with the kettle and the cake and biscuits, which cost me a fortune over the ten weeks. I found a little shop near to the court, owned by a very pleasant and jolly gentleman. After three weeks, he would greet me with, 'Hello, Mr Wilkins, good day in court? I have your usual ready to go'.

As the trial played out in chronological order the events at Scoveston Park became the focus and former DC Frederick Henry Hunter was invited to the intimidating 4'x 4' witness box; I would describe Fred as a younger version of the late Eric Morecambe and equally as funny except today his humour went out of the window as he was asked to relive his memories of twenty-six years ago when he assisted the undertaker in removing the remains of Richard Thomas from the ruins of Scoveston Park.

'Mr Hunter, did you sit in the front or back of the hearse?' Mr Evans, the defence barrister, asked.

'In the front, M'Lord, the coffin was in the back,' replied Fred.

'Yes, yes I'm aware of that,' replied Mr Evans abruptly. 'So you were in the front, was there a glass partition between you and the coffin?'

'I believe so, M'Lord, as I banged my head on it when I got in,' described Fred.

Our assumption from Mr Evans' obscure line of questioning was that, as expected, he was attempting to explore the avenue of forensic contamination. In other words, could Fred's contact with the deceased in 1985 have facilitated the movement of fibres? Fred was released from the box but would have to return later in the trial because his thirty years of service meant he had worked on other parts of the case.

At the time of the first murders Don Evans was a superintendent and sub divisional commander of Preseli Division, as it was then called. He was next to give evidence and was a softly spoken gentleman, who had been the first senior officer to attend the Scoveston Park scene. His account took the jury to the heart of the crime and as he described the finding of Richard's body, pictures of the burnt remains were displayed on the screens. It was a sobering moment for the jury.

Later that afternoon one of the exhibits officers from Scoveston, ex-Constable David Morgan, caused our very own exhibits officer Neville Evans to have a panic attack as the wrong map of the scene was unfolded. It was Neville's mission every day to ensure that the relevant exhibits were present in court. You would see him in the morning like a squirrel gathering nuts; only today one of his nuts was missing. After a number of these occasions he affectionately became known as 'Swinging Doors Evans', as this would be the last thing you heard as he scampered from the court to recover the necessary exhibits.

The second week brought an increased pressure on the team as the facts of the coastal path murders were disclosed in the presence of the Dixon family. It is harrowing enough for a court to listen to the appalling details but to know that the family of the victims were also listening was tough. I had spent many hours with them talking them through what they were likely to face. I didn't want them hearing something in court for the first time. The evidence began with the account of ex-police constable Mike Calas, a dog handler for most of his career. He described the moment he discovered the Dixons' bodies on the coastal path on the 4th of July 1989.

'I was led to the bodies by the smell of death,' Mr Callas explained. He went onto to say that he and a colleague entered the wood on the Little Haven side of the stile through ferns onto what appeared to be a defined path. Mike explained how he had stepped down off the coastal path onto a lower level and how ferns had been pulled down to hide the access. He described how he had made his way into the undergrowth past two fox or badger holes and how he then walked straight down towards the cliffs via a path possibly made by an animal. About twenty yards down this path he cut across to his left, through the undergrowth, where he came upon an open area of leaf mould and bluebell leaves. To his right he could see some blue-coloured articles on the ground and now the smell became more pungent. He moved forward and saw, through the leaves and undergrowth, what appeared to be a leg. He called to his colleague because he thought that he had found the Dixons. He moved more branches to discover the bodies of Peter and Gwenda Dixon. Gwenda was lying face down in the direction of the sea. Peter's fully clothed body was also face down. Gwenda was partially covered with fern debris. A whole fern had been uprooted by her right thigh. He concluded by explaining that they then left the bodies and returned to the coastal path and had walked past a leather boot as they did so. They headed back towards Little Haven and conferred with Chief Superintendent Don Evans in the lay-by below the junction at Talbenny. There was an eerie silence in the courtroom as the judge adjourned for lunch. Not that anyone in the room had much of an appetite after hearing such horrific details.

It was going to be a long ten weeks listening to such devastating evidence and witnessing the effect this experience had had on people's lives. However back in our room I could always rely on 'Rambo' DS Gareth Rees to lighten the mood. Mr Gerard Elias had inadvertently left his barrister's wig unattended. Without a second thought Gareth tried it on and surprised us all with his performance as a QC. He didn't wear it for long before hastily returning it for fear he would be caught by the real Queen's Counsel.

That afternoon, the former Home Office Pathologist Professor Bernard Knight gave evidence. This distinguished gentleman had the unfortunate task of conducting the post-mortem examination of both Peter and Gwenda. His evidence was to the point and went uncontested as he explained the wounds, marks and bruises discovered on both bodies. Again sitting at the front of the court were Tim and Julie and the rest of the Dixon family. Professor Knight's evidence concluded what had been a long day before the judge dismissed the court. The following morning the jury visits would begin bringing a huge logistical challenge for Dyfed-Powys Police. Fortunately the team had spent many hours preparing. Glyn would accompany the jury with an agreed script at each designated point. Inspector Gareth Thomas and Sergeant Martin Vaughan had managed the police resources and logistics for this visit which covered an area the size of Cheshire. This would be an opportunity for the jury to review the professionalism, efficiency and accuracy of the service; it had to be right.

The first day would see the police escort leave Swansea Crown Court with the judge, jury and court ushers, followed in hot pursuit by defence counsel, prosecuting counsel and crown prosecutors. Those who didn't form part of the main entourage at times struggled to keep up with the police motorcyclists. One poor prosecutor in particular had to drive flat out in his very small Ford Fiesta. Fortunately everyone arrived safely at the Ocean Café Bar and Restaurant in Broad Haven where they were well looked after, for which we will be eternally grateful, as we did not want to get off on the wrong foot with the judge. After a short break the escort left for Little Haven and the coastal path. They were shown the location where the Dixons' tent had been pitched in 1989 and then after a short drive the group left the coach to walk to the coastal path. Sea mist was hanging over the area, which made their route even more precarious. As Glyn led the party, the judge commented on how close to the edge the path was. Glyn replied, 'Don't worry, M'Lord, if you should slip, I've been instructed to jump before you to soften your fall.' I had indeed told Glyn that in the case of a disaster save the one with the wig and the red robe! Fortunately for Glyn this amused His Honour and all came back safe and well. The route from the coastal path down to the scene had been equipped with temporary wooden steps by the National Park which allowed the jury safe passage to the exact area where Gwenda and Peter had been discovered. They stood in absolute silence with their heads down almost like they were paying their respects. A map had been mounted on a board to show the jury the location of the bodies and clothing. They again stood quietly studying the map and the scene, trying to piece it all together. After a few questions they had seen enough and made their way back to the coach.

It had been a very sobering experience in such a beautiful place. The afternoon provided a tour of the cash machines used to take money from the Dixons' account in Pembroke, Haverfordwest and Carmarthen. The jury were also shown the close proximity of the jewellers in Pembroke to the cash machine where Peter Dixon's card had been used. We all retired that evening extremely satisfied that we had portrayed Dyfed-Powys Police in a professional manner and done both the families and victims proud.

The second day started with the same dash across West Wales. The coach drove past the location of a number of Cooper's burglaries before arriving at Scoveston Park. There the jury wandered around the outer yard and were shown the location where Richard Thomas's blood had been found in the outbuildings and where his Rover car had been abandoned. As they walked down the long driveway Glyn gave a running commentary identifying the key locations.

The front door was opened to reveal a very grand hallway and large staircase; this had also been altered during the restoration. The jury were asked to remove their footwear as they examined the premises. Two at a time they climbed the staircase to inspect the half landing where Richard's body had been discovered. This now beautifully restored mansion was in stark contrast to what had been discovered on that cold December night. Again a very subdued jury left the house and got back into the coach ready for the visit to 34 St Marys Park, the property that had held so many secrets about Cooper's life. This again had been renovated and was now a far cry from the eerie grey house that was once Cooper's home. The house, grounds and hedgerows were shown to the jury and a huge poster-size map of the area and plans of the original site assisted them.

By now they must have had a feeling for the area and from here they were taken to the Sardis robbery location and Cooper's escape route, highlighted with the orange fluorescent markers. These markers showed the location where, following the Sardis robbery, items like the sawn-off shotgun, gloves and balaclava were discovered. Again the jury went on foot to walk the route taken by Cooper as he made the short journey to his house. That evening I had suggested to the team that we meet for a quick beer at the local Cleddau Bridge Hotel, situated on the other side of the river some two miles from the scene. As I turned into the elevated car park of the hotel I looked across the river towards the village of Neyland and Sardis. I burst out laughing. I could see quite clearly a bright orange florescent marker, still glowing in the distance in the middle of a hedgerow.

After two days of chaperoning the jury around Pembrokeshire we were back in the courtroom.

Dyfed-Powys Police was congratulated that morning for the professional manner in which the two-day visit had been conducted; Glyn also received a personal thank you for his expertise as a tour guide. Later that day the courtroom was to echo the sounds of the hit TV show *Bullseye*, as the jury watched the footage recorded in 1989 of Cooper participating in the television quiz show. It was played in order to show the jury how closely Cooper resembled the man in the artist's impression. It clearly demonstrated what Cooper looked like less than a month before he executed the Dixons. The matching images had been compiled with the assistance of ITV graphic designer Tina Williams. The defence clearly misunderstood what Tina had actually be asked to do and while she was giving evidence started to question her about what he described as the highly technical facial mapping equipment he assumed she must have used to match Cooper's profile. A very confused-looking Tina responded that she had simply jogged the pictures along frame by frame until she found the best match in much the same way that you might freeze-frame a DVD. She told the court, 'I have no facial mapping equipment.' It wasn't long after this that the bemused Mr Evans sat back down in his seat realising his error. The *Bullseye* footage was an extremely significant piece of evidence that made a huge impact.

In the afternoon a local woman by the name of Jennifer Phillips gave evidence. She stated that whilst working on the potato harvest, she met a man called John Cooper who lived in Jordanston. She believed that it was in 1983 and that Cooper had been a casual worker at Jordanston Farm. She had described Cooper as a man who bragged about what he had done with the money he had won from gambling. When she first met him he was living in a caravan at Johnston and later moved to the house owned by Mike Richards. She went on to say there would be general conversation between everyone but on one particular occasion she distinctly remembered Cooper talking about Richard and Helen Thomas of Scoveston Park. She knew Richard and Helen, and she made some sort of comment to Cooper about how good they were to her. John had replied with words similar to, 'Richard's a nice old boy, he lets me go down to Scoveston and get logs.' This was evidence that Cooper had a clear knowledge of Scoveston and the Thomases; something he had always denied.

The day was concluded with the evidence of a woman by the name of Jane Mather who described the afternoon of Thursday the 29th of June 1989 whilst she was working in Main Street in Pembroke. She said, 'I noticed a strange, odd-looking man standing outside Lloyds bank. He had a bike with him. He looked as if he'd just got off it and was standing very close to it. The bike was facing in the direction of Lamphey. I would describe the bike as looking old, well-worn with straight handlebars. I would describe the man as follows: He was about 5'10" tall and medium build; he looked to be about middle to late thirties; his hair was straight, collar-length and going grey; his face looked long but not drawn; it was red looking either from cycling or from the sun; he looked a bit unshaven scruffy looking. He was wearing a dark coloured short-sleeved tee shirt with I think a collar and some buttons at the collar. He was wearing shorts or 'cut-off' trousers that were about four inches above the knee. I think they were blue. I am not sure what he was wearing on his feet. In his hand he had what looked to be a Kwik Save plastic carrier bag; it was red and white in colour. He had the top of the bag twisted around his hand; the bag looked to be just under half full.' The jury listened to Mrs Mather, while giving Cooper the occasional glance, almost as though they were comparing him now to her description of twenty-three years ago.

We were finished for the weekend. Two weeks had passed by so quickly but on our return on the Monday it would be the turn of Timothy and Julie Dixon to give evidence. It is always distressing when a family are expected to give evidence in such tragic circumstances but all agreed that both Timothy and Julie would have made their parents extremely proud in the way that they presented themselves; Timothy reliving the moments when he realised his parents were missing and Julie describing how she holidayed in Cyprus at the time. Their spell in the witness box was short and both the prosecuting and defence counsels respected their loss.

It was a short session that day after the judge adjourned, giving counsel time to prepare for the start of the Milford Haven witnesses the following day. Video statements of complainants involving serious sexual offences taken by the police are admissible as evidence at a trial. This video evidence recorded as far back as 1996 was played to the jury. Everyone in the courtroom was captivated, listening to these children as they described the events of that March evening. These were living victims providing evidence of Cooper's monstrous behaviour.

In the afternoon the defence required the two female victims who were subjected to the sexual assaults to present themselves in the witness box so they could be cross-examined. Screens were put in place, as is normal in such circumstances, to protect their identities and the press were asked to leave the courtroom. Both Jayne and Susan had shown tremendous courage in attending court and had been fantastically supported by Helen Coles and Donna Thomas, but even so, the modern-day court is still in the Dark Ages when it comes to facilities for such witnesses. They had to sit in a side office with few home comforts. The screens used to provide anonymity from the court were broken so they had to be leant against the witness box making them feel like caged animals.

Both girls cried throughout the questioning as they were asked to recount the horrific events. The defence repeatedly asked the rape victim if in fact she had been raped; a question that we felt seemed a little strange considering Cooper denied ever being there; why was it so important to try and cast doubt on her ordeal if the attacker was somebody else? The courage of these victims was also recognised by the Dixon family and Mr and Mrs James, cousins of Richard and Helen Thomas. They were visibly moved by the account and the dignity of Jayne and Susan, as indeed we all were.

Thursday the 14th of April 2001, and Cooper's son Adrian was called to Swansea Crown Court, and was allowed special measures because he felt so intimidated and threatened by his father. Adrian gave his evidence via video link from a separate room outside the courtroom. He provided stark revelations about how he had seen his father leaving the house with the saw-off shotgun slung across his chest under his jacket. Cooper grunted at the back of the court, calling Adrian a liar as his son gave his evidence. Adrian continued to disclose how he had seen items like jewellery, shotgun cartridges and other items in his father's shed and larder. There was no love lost between

Cooper and his son, and Adrian painted a picture of a life of fear and violence at the hands of his father. He also recognised the clip used to fasten the lanyard PH/2A onto the murder weapon, the sawn-off double-barrelled shotgun PH/2, as a clip fastener for a dog lead, previously owned by Cooper. It was significant that his own son felt it was necessary to give an insight into life with his father and clearly this was the reason that Cooper felt it necessary to try and discredit his son at every opportunity. He knew that Adrian could provide significant evidence about his habits and link him to certain firearms. After all he was one of the few people who had seen him disappearing into the night. Under pressure, it was suggested by Mark Evans QC that Adrian was a liar, 'No! Do you really think that I want to be here today?' he snapped.

In the afternoon Sergeant Teleri Bowen, a former scenes of crime officer, nervously stood in the witness box and awaited the questions from Mr Evans. Teleri, during the exhibit review stage, had re-bagged the shorts which had proved such a wealth of damning evidence. She told Mr Evans, 'I removed the handkerchief from the right side pocket and examined it. During the examination an apparent hair strand was recovered and separately placed in a sterile pot. There appeared to be brown-coloured staining on the handkerchief. The handkerchief and fluff were placed and sealed in a separate paper bag. The shorts were then returned to the original bag and sealed. The hair and handkerchief, which had both been placed into separate packages, were placed in a separate paper bag with the original shorts and packaging.'

Mr Evans seized the moment and spent several minutes questioning Sergeant Bowen about the fluff, to the bewilderment of the prosecuting team. Mr Evans insisted that the fluff had been lost during this repackaging stage and the re-opening of the bag at LGC's laboratory. He laboured the point so much that the judge decided to adjourn for an hour to give both parties an opportunity to agree on the whereabouts of the fluff. We retreated to our rooms and examined the photographs provided by LGC and Teleri. Comparing the two it was quite easy to see that the fluff had not in fact disappeared but merely changed position. Back in the courtroom, the 'bit of fluff' saga was brought to an end with both parties now agreeing on its whereabouts.

Someone who will always be remembered for having played a major part in the capture of John Cooper, although reluctant himself to take such credit, is ex-PC Mark Jenkins, the dog handler. He established a web of routes from Scoveston, Sardis and a number of the burglaries scenes back to 34 St Marys Park. To say that he was extremely nervous in giving this evidence would be an understatement and in his thirty years' service he had managed to avoid such an experience. However, now retired, he stood in the witness box wearing his suit, and gave an excellent account of the evidence that ultimately lead to the arrest of Cooper in 1998.

Scenes of crimes officer Kenneth John Greenish, better known as KJG and whose initials appeared on almost all crime reports written in Pembrokeshire finished the day in the witness box. As one of the leading scenes of crime officers John had a great deal of experience and expertise. Like Dr Watson from Sherlock Holmes he would gladly attend a scene and within seconds give you a full synopsis of the circumstances surrounding the death. He was here to give evidence explaining which exhibits he had repackaged due to their condition. There followed another attempt by the defence to challenge the condition of the exhibits and to advance the potential cross-contamination theory.

Our fourth week in court facilitated the experts Ian Johnson and Thomas Warlow (who were the prosecutions firearms experts) and Andrew Sweeting, a forensic scientist. All these witnesses were from the Forensic Science Service (which closed in March 2012). In addition the jury heard from Graham Morris, the retired Managing Director of Eley Hawk shotgun cartridges.

Dr Philip Avenell, our DNA expert from LGC, became involved in a challenge from the defence by their expert Mr Hodge about blood found on the shorts. Mr Hodge suggested that the blood had been rehydrated and transferred onto the shorts from another exhibit, which had housed the wet blood of Peter Dixon. Mr Hodge described how he had conducted such an experiment in the window of his bathroom and had observed such a transfer. Dr Avenell quickly demolished his home experiment and explained to the jury that the rehydration theory could be largely discounted by the continuity work we had done. At no stage had any blood exhibits been stored with the shorts and therefore at no stage could such circumstances exist. Dr Avenell had conducted the same experiments under proper scientific conditions and rehydration could only occur in certain, highly unlikely circumstances and only within a short window of opportunity. We were slowly dismissing their possible defences one by one and in a very measured and professional way. Dr Avenell was also able to compliment the team on the way they had handled exhibits which in turn gave him confidence in the integrity of the material.

Even a courtroom stops for bank holidays. The break meant that over the next four days everyone would get a rest, or at least that's what we thought. Back in our little room pondering over a nice cup of tea we were asked by Mike Jones to see AJM/60 the gloves recovered from Cooper's house in 1998. The gloves had been recovered from Cooper's kitchen and linked by fibres to the murder weapon, placing the gun in his hands. 'Yes, not a problem, Mr Jones,' Nev confidently replied. We all sat around and watched the colour slowly disappear from Nev's face as he frantically opened the bag but did not produce AJM/60. 'Don't worry,' Mike said, 'I'll come back in a minute.' Nev's face went from a lighter shade of pale to a glowing red as he alerted us all in the office that he couldn't find AJM/60. Just like Corporal Jones in *Dad's Army* the instruction, 'Don't panic!' was given as we all set about searching the room. After ten minutes and still no sign of the exhibit, panic did set in. I had total faith in Neville, but by this stage I was starting to feel very uncomfortable. Earlier that day the fire alarm had gone off in the building resulting in us all evacuating to a grassy verge opposite the court. As we did so, we had to grab the exhibits from the courtroom and carry them with us. At this stage I chose not to alarm Mr Elias as I was confident the matter would be resolved. I was wrong. We searched high and low without any joy. The exhibits are all marked up and bagged but for ease of movement they were placed in larger carrier bags and black bin liners, very similar to the ones in which we placed our rubbish every night ready to go in the skip. As was his way Lynne Harries suited and booted volunteered to search the said skip on what was a very warm, late spring day. 'Stig of the Dump', as we nicknamed him, could be seen, up to his knees in bin bags, opening them one by one. The sight of him rummaging through discarded food and nappies will remain with me forever, but the glove was nowhere to be seen.

What if someone had taken the exhibit and left the building with it? What if the cleaner had mistakenly taken it out of the room? What if we had dropped the exhibit on route to and from the court? What if we had dropped the exhibit outside the police station where it was stored at night? What if we had left it behind in the police station? At this stage I had to speak to Mr Elias, he raised his right eyebrow and fixed me with the stare he kept for the most difficult of clients. 'I am sure, Mr Wilkins, that after a thorough search it will be found, if not I will have to have a very difficult conversation with the Defence.'

To cut a long story short we spent the next four days including the weekend searching CCTV footage, bins, toilets, skips, police stations and kerb sides for the missing exhibit but to no avail. Mr Elias and his team had been pre-warned when they went home on the Thursday that the exhibit was missing and he left us with the reassurance that he was sure it would turn up. Neville was going away for the weekend, but telephoned every member of the team repeatedly in the hope of good news. He didn't get it.

On our return on Tuesday, after a very stressful bank holiday break, the glove was still missing. I had made the Deputy Chief Constable aware, and I could just see the defence making hay about our meticulous handling of exhibits. I spoke to Mr Elias to inform him that we had lost the exhibit. He didn't blink and made his way to speak to Mark Evans QC.

'Mr Evans,' he said, 'Would it be possible to have a moment of your time?'

'Could you give me five minutes please, Mr Elias, I will be with you then?' Mr Evans replied.

At that moment the gods were smiling on us. As we sat in the room feeling sorry for ourselves, distraught at the fact that we had lost a key exhibit and that all our professionalism had gone out of the window, DC Mark Roach had taken it upon himself to have another look in the room. Mark opened a box file used to store statements and suddenly he let out a high-pitched screech and fell on his backside. Mark is not one to get carried away and I thought he had been bitten by a rattlesnake. He then said in an equally high-pitched voice, I've found it, the exhibit, AJM/60'. We all gasped with amazement as Mark was besieged with hugs from the team, and I have to admit to kissing a male detective in public. The outburst of elation was only interrupted by all of us simultaneously exclaiming 'Mr Elias!!' who was waiting to speak to Mark Evans. Mike Jones was told, and like a flash he was gone out the door to tell Mr Elias, just as he was about to break the news to the defence. The day was saved. Only through the tenacity of Mark Roach had we avoided the embarrassment of losing an exhibit. Neville Evans was phoned with the news and replied, 'Told you it would be there'. I could have strangled him!

Back on track our expert Roger Robson was sworn in and gave a comprehensive account of the fibre evidence. From the early days of the inquiry, when we had very little forensics, we now had a wealth of fibre evidence which corroborated a number of links to Cooper and 34 St Marys Park. Roger explained how the evidence had been recovered and its connection to key exhibits.

We had heard much about the defence's fibre expert, Mr Hodge. As is normal in Crown Court cases the defence always rely on their own experts to undermine the evidence of the prosecution's expert. We eagerly awaited his presence in the witness box to be told that he could offer no expert opinion contrary to the one given by Roger Robson. Although we had 100 per cent confidence in the fibre evidence, and its continuity and integrity, we were a little surprised to hear that Mr Hodge had left the building. The work carried out by Roger Robson had been extraordinary and his obvious expertise was impressive to say the least but I was concerned that the evidence was so complex that the jury might struggle to take it all in.

Our lock expert Mr John Crummack spent a whole afternoon describing how the 'knib wards' on the Norton Farm lock were extremely significant in comparison with the key AJM/445 discovered in Cooper's shed. Richard Thomas had visited Norton Farm on the day he was murdered and his bunch of keys, described by his farm workers were never recovered. John Crummack was adamant that the key AJM/445 had been used extensively in the lock from Norton Farm. By the end of the session and a contrary opinion from the defence expert, I think the courtroom had heard enough about the 'knib wards' and locks.

The next couple of weeks were spent by the defence exploring what's known as the 'box defence' They were trying to introduce elements of the Huntsman trial which they believed assisted their case. This opportunity had been presented to them after Mr Evans had successfully appealed their defence position. In essence he had argued that Cooper was 'dead in the water' if he could not call witnesses from the Huntsman trial. The issue was one of case management and Justice John Griffith Williams had shown considerable skill in handling the arguments.

Elements of Cooper's bad character were introduced by our counsel including the interviews from 1998 which were diligently delivered by DS 'Rambo' Rees in tandem with Mr Mike Jones, who played the part of Cooper. The Sardis trail was then examined more closely with an extraordinary claim from the defence. They said that at the end of the trail was impenetrable hedgerow and Cooper, frail at the time with his arthritis, would not have been able to negotiate it. This was the first time we had heard this new attempt to distance him from the Sardis trail. It sounded like pure desperation.

A trainer found in this location was also scrutinised by the defence as they intimated that it had been placed there days after the robbery. To assist them in this supposition they called a local man, who lived near to the Sardis robbery trail. This local character, who was known to the police, entered the courtroom during the recess because he was on crutches. When the judge returned he was already sitting in the box waiting to give his evidence, in his best Sunday T-shirt. The witness wasn't big on etiquette and it wasn't long before the judge asked him to stand when he addressed the court. Unfortunately the judge was unaware that the witness was on crutches. After a little splutter he retracted his request allowing the man to remain seated. After confirming his name he was left to answer the questions put to him by Mr Evans. Using a map on the electronic screens Mr Evans attempted to show the witness where he had discovered the trainer following the robbery. Unfortunately for Mr Evans the witness didn't agree with the account given and continued to take hold of the screen next to him in the box, running his finger down it to show the exact spot where he walked. It resembled a sketch from a pantomime, as the conversation deteriorated into: 'Oh yes you did. Oh no I didn't.' There was no doubt that the defence was attempting to introduce this man as a possible suspect to deflect blame away from Cooper as they had done during the Huntsman trial.

Cooper had clearly told lies in the Huntsman trial. A hair had been found in the balaclava abandoned on the Sardis trail and it belonged to Cooper. He had tried to suggest that the local man had DNA which resembled his. It was clearly nonsense. The fibre evidence had forced Cooper into accepting that the balaclava had belonged to him but he now insisted that it had been stolen from his boat. This local witness presented Cooper with a problem because he could not directly accuse him of the Sardis robbery because he had a very good alibi; CCTV at a local garage showed him filling his vehicle with petrol at the same time as Sheila Clarke was being attacked. It was another diversion tactic.

One of the last civilian witnesses to give evidence was the very brave Sheila Clarke, victim from the Sardis robbery. She was a lovely, gentle, kind person who, having had the trauma of giving evidence in 1998, found herself back in the witness box. The defence's intention was to challenge the description she had given on the night she was confronted by a man wearing a balaclava brandishing a sawn-off shotgun. Giving a description of an attacker in such circumstances is not an exact science and if you put ten people in a room and asked them to describe an incident the differences would be alarming. This is always a problem with recall and eye witness evidence. It was a lame attempt to cast doubt on her recollection and unfortunately for Cooper it backfired on him. Mrs Clarke had given a harrowing account of her ordeal and the unnecessary violence she was subjected to. During cross-examination by Mark Evans she was asked to describe the attack.

'I was tied up and looking at this masked man pointing a gun at me, I thought, thank god my husband will be home any minute.' She then went on to say, 'I looked at this man with the gun and thought, I really hope my husband doesn't come home.'

I felt sure that in that short exchange the circumstances of the murders of Richard and Helen Thomas flashed into the minds of the jury. What Sheila Clarke described had played itself out at Scoveston Park, only this time Richard did come home and a robbery turned into a double murder. In my mind, if the jury were still satisfied that Cooper had committed the Sardis robbery; he had just convicted himself of the Scoveston Park killings.

It was now time for the centrepiece of the defence. It is always a big question as to whether a defendant will go into the box. In Cooper's case I had no doubt that he would. The controlling element of his character meant that he would believe that he was the only person on earth able to get himself acquitted. So it was no surprise when Mark Evans uttered the words, 'Call John William Cooper!'

Throughout the trial the public gallery had been packed, but never more so than when the usher called Cooper. He stood in the box in his grey suit, white shirt, matching tie and handkerchief. The defence began their opening by portraying a man who had suffered most of his life. Cooper they said had been plagued by arthritis, wrongly accused of burglaries, wrongly convicted, had a run of bad luck, lost his fortune on bad businesses, lost his wife after being apart for so many years and was being wrongly accused again. Cooper came across as a helpful and respectful man. With his bucket of keys he would always help people in distress and he knew nothing about the crimes. Mark Evans QC skilfully led him through his evidence that no doubt Cooper had rehearsed many times in his cell. The evidence he gave was well structured and presented his life in a logical sequence.

Mr Evans had delivered his client to the jury, and had over the day teased out of him the points that he felt portrayed the real John Cooper. By now I had been allowed to sit in court and I too felt that Cooper had given a good account of himself. The court day normally finished at four thirty, and it was now four o'clock. Mr Evans concluded his evidence in chief and sat down, no doubt expecting the day to finish leaving Cooper to be cross-examined by the prosecution the next day. Having sat down the judge enquired with Mr Elias if he would like to start his cross-examination of Mr Cooper the following day. To my surprise Gerard Elias got to his feet, 'No, my lord, I would like to have twenty minutes with him this evening'. I had spoken with Mr Elias regarding his strategy to cross-examine Cooper and he had given me an outline of his plan. This did not include a quick twenty minutes with him at the end of a long day. What I, and those people who were privileged enough to be in court that afternoon, witnessed was pure genius that I will never forget for the rest of my life.

Cooper clearly thought he would be taken through his life just as Mr Evans had done. Mr Elias cut to the chase.

'Mr Cooper, during the Huntsman trial in 1998 did you

tell lies to that jury?'

'No,' came the confident reply from Cooper.

'Mr Cooper, I will ask you again, in 1998 before that jury, did you tell lies?'

Again Cooper replied, 'No, I did not.'

Gerard Elias now turned to the jury and directed his question to them: 'Well let me help you out, in that trial you never accepted ownership of the balaclava abandoned on the Sardis trail, did you?' Cooper tried to go off on a tangent as was his way. 'Answer the question, Mr Cooper, did you ever accept that that balaclava was yours? You said you had never seen it before.' Again Cooper tried to deflect the question away.

The court was silent at this exchange. I thought to myself, you clever, clever man. It was on the hoof and he had his man under pressure straight away.

'You have in this trial accepted the balaclava is yours and was stolen from your boat with other property, so you lied to that court, didn't you? Yes or no?' said Gerard Elias in a raised but controlled voice. Cooper again tried to avoid answering this simple and direct question, 'Yes or no, Mr Cooper?' repeated Elias. 'Yes or no?' Cooper was visibly squirming in the box and desperate to avoid the only answer he could give. You could have cut the atmosphere with a knife.

Justice John Griffith Williams intervened, 'Mr Cooper, the question is quite simple.'

For a few moments there was silence only broken by Cooper's response, 'Yes.'

I could see members of the jury looking at each other, recognising the significance of what they had just heard.

'My Lord, I think that will be an opportune time to call

it a day,' concluded Gerard Elias QC.

As Cooper walked back to the dock I saw him glance at the prosecuting counsel with a look of despair because he knew he had been outflanked by a man at the top of his game. In those few minutes Mr Elias had established that during his previous trial Cooper had told lies. As the court cleared I spoke to Mr Elias and congratulated him on a brilliant opening to his cross-examination and a most unexpected one. It was clear he was looking forward to the following day. As I left the court I was approached by a member of the press who exclaimed, 'Wow, that was fantastic, I didn't jot down a single word, I couldn't take my eyes off them.'

The next day Mr Cooper was back in the witness box at the mercy of Mr Elias.

'Mr Cooper, last evening we established that you told lies in your previous trial,' he announced as if to remind the jury, if they in fact needed reminding that this man was a stranger to the truth. In the following hour Gerard Elias established on a number of occasions that Cooper had told lies in his Huntsman trial. It was at that stage that Mr Elias moved onto the Ottawa offences. Cooper had changed tack during his evidence and cross-examination. He had maintained that he didn't know Richard and Helen Thomas when it had been established from a number of witnesses that he had in fact worked for them. It was also a fact that Cooper had once tried to buy land from Richard Thomas and had been refused. Gerard Elias referred Cooper to two specific documents: the first was a police 'stop-check' form completed shortly after the Scoveston Park murders. The local police had set up a roadblock to check vehicles near the entrance to Scoveston Park to see if they had passed the location on the relevant evening or had other information. When questioned at the 'stop-check' about his knowledge of the Thomas siblings, Cooper indicated that he only knew them to 'say hello to' and no more; this was another lie. The second document concerned the time when the police visited his home and he put forward a false alibi that the whole family was at home at the time of the murders; this statement was written down on a police house-to-house questionnaire. Why was he so reluctant to tell the police that he knew them well, or volunteer the fact that the blue Cortina so sought after by detectives belonged to the Cooper family?

Cooper was in trouble and you could sense it. The tension in the court was tangible and all present were transfixed on the confrontation. Gerard Elias moved onto the wedding ring and other rings sold by Cooper to the jeweller on Main Street in Pembroke. Cooper had already accepted that it wasn't his wedding ring and in interview had suggested he handled stolen property. Two receipts were produced, one signed J.W. Cooper and one signed J. Cooper with a different address from his true home at 34 St Marys Park. Cooper could give little explanation and tried to cast some doubt by suggesting that he was not convinced that the signatures were his, though he accepted they could be. He went onto say that he had a number of different signatures which he used for different purposes. His responses were cannon fodder for Mr Elias and he made every exchange even more painful for Cooper. His explanation for burying a gun under the duck run was equally unbelievable, suggesting he was getting rid of it so it wouldn't fall into the wrong hands. The fact that he had preserved it in oilcloth to be used at a later date and modified it in an identical manner to the murder weapon was not lost on the jury.

During a lighter but equally significant exchange, Cooper was asked 'You have problems with arthritis, do you, in your left arm?'

'Yes that's correct,' came the reply.

'Is it correct?' he was asked again. 'When you fixed curtain poles at your wife's clients houses, you used both arms?'

'I did,' said Cooper. 'But I would use my good arm for the drill,' he replied.

'So how would you hold the pole in place?' asked Mr Elias. 'Using the arm you can't lift up, supposedly?'

After a long pause Cooper replied, 'Well I would hold it in place with my good arm and then drill.'

'So it was a one-arm operation?' asked Mr Elias. This raised a titter in the courtroom as Cooper could clearly see he was on a slippery slope. He was then asked to account for how he would dig in the garden with one arm and how he buried the shotgun in the drainpipe with one arm. One of the significant moments for me during this cross-examination was when a piece of paper balancing on the edge of the witness box started to fall, only to be stopped in mid-flight by the quick reflexes of Mr Cooper's arthritic left arm shooting out to grab it. There were a few knowing looks from the jury.

Equally telling was his explanation for the scratches and marks on his face seen by a witness days after the Sardis robbery. He told the court that he had fallen over an old Christmas tree growing near the entrance to his caravan which was parked in his garden. Cooper insisted a blurred object seen on a photograph of the caravan was the tree. A video of the same caravan was then shown to the jury. On the video however it was clear that the blurred object was in fact a piece of wood leaning against the side of the caravan, not a Christmas tree as described by Mr Cooper. It was yet another lie.

Mr Elias spent all of that morning showing how Cooper was a compulsive liar, how his complex web of deceit had been exposed by the witnesses and forensic evidence provided to the court in the previous weeks. For the first time I could see that Cooper looked defeated. The man who thought he had all of the answers had been dismantled lie by lie. As Cooper returned to his glass cage the courtroom was set for the closing statements of Mr Elias followed by Mr Evans. This would be their last opportunity to make their prosecution and defence arguments respectively.

Gerard Elias was direct as he went through the forensics and the catalogue of other circumstantial and bad character evidence which was the Crown's case. He was calm, measured and detailed. Piece by piece he unravelled the forensic evidence and then established its significance and connectivity to Cooper. At the end of his summing up and having detailed the wealth of evidence he asked the jury, 'Is this just coincidence?' As he pieced the jigsaw together I could not help thinking that I would rather be in our camp than Cooper's. As he concluded he was equally clear in his submission. 'What you have heard is the most damming of evidence that John William Cooper is guilty.'

Mark Evans QC was brief but equally as clear in his closing speech. The Crown's case he said was all based on the fact that John Cooper was guilty of the Sardis and Huntsman offences. If the jury were persuaded that they doubted that conviction then the rest would fall like a pack of cards. The defence also doubted the value of the forensic evidence and protested that all of this evidence could be explained by cross-contamination and less than professional handling of the exhibits. I remember thinking how unfair this was when they had not established this during the trial or presented any credible evidence to undermine the forensic evidence. Our experts had been seen and heard in the court; in contrast the defence experts had been seen, but *not* heard.

The case was then summed up by Justice John Griffith Williams, he went through the almost ten weeks of evidence skilfully and in detail, maintaining a balanced and considered approach. He then concluded with the points of law he was required to deliver to the jury and agreed by counsel. As he sent the jury out he instructed them that it was the job of the Crown to prove the guilt of John William Cooper, not for the defence to prove his innocence. If we had failed to do so then they should acquit him.

As the jury filtered out from the packed courtroom I sat alone for a few minutes and pondered the last six years and in particular the last ten weeks. Could my team and I have done any more to prove the case? As I did a feeling of great satisfaction came over me: no, we could not have done any more! I had been supported by a fantastic team of officers and police staff. The chief officers and Police Authority had shown unwavering faith and support. Our partner agencies and the local community had been right behind us. All of the witnesses had attended and given their evidence in a clear and honest way and our experts had come up trumps. I looked across the courtroom and saw Lynne Harries, Glyn Johnson, Paul Jones and Gareth Rees and I could not have asked for more personal commitment from these four men who had made many sacrifices over the years. It was over. Matters were now in the hands of twelve men and women, good and true, to consider the guilt or otherwise of another human being in a process that I had placed my faith in many times over the years.

CONCLUSION

On the 26th of May 2011, John William Cooper was found guilty of all charges and told that he would spend the rest of his life in prison. On the 31st of October 2012, Cooper appealed his conviction at Cardiff Crown Court, an appeal that failed. His grounds for appeal were that the judge in his trial, Justice John Griffith Williams, had misdirected the jury in his summing up on the identification evidence. It related to the Sardis robbery case and the value of the *Bullseye* comparison with the artist's impression. Like the vast majority of his defence case, he was hanging on to his insistence that he was not guilty of the Huntsman offences and conviction. The strange thing was, in his application to appeal, he had accepted our forensic evidence, which had strengthened that very conviction.

What made John William Cooper commit the offences that he did? To me, the fact that he kept mementos of his offending gives us an insight into this controlling, evil man. He thrived on control and the items he stole served a number of purposes. When he stole keys it made the victims feel that he could return in the future to terrorise them. Some of the items he stole were worthless, like the shorts he stole from Gwenda Dixon. Again every time he wore them was reminded of the moment in time when he held their lives in his hands. The cash and jewellery he stole supported his gambling addiction, allowing him to continue and perhaps hide the full extent of his gambling from his family. Some of the property he took provided the perfect cover story. He would tell his family that he had bought it from car boot sales and the like, allowing him to use his cash for gambling. I have often been asked, why Cooper did what he did? My response is simple. I believe some people are born evil and John William Cooper is one of them.

By the end of June 2011, the vast majority of the Ottawa team had returned to their normal duties. This proved to be a very testing time for them. My team had great difficulty in re-adjusting to normal policing duties following the intensity of the investigation, trial and the national recognition they received. During the case they had been carried on a runaway train that was heading down the tracks with nothing to stop it. Suddenly they were back to investigating house burglaries and attending to more mundane administrative duties that were a world away from Ottawa. The case had consumed so much of our lives; it was where we could go to practice our art, fully focused on achieving justice.

Unfortunately some of the team experienced a certain amount of jealousy from other police officers not involved in the case. The fact that these people had the capacity and mindset to display such feelings is probably the reason I did not choose them in the first place. Within a very short space of time two of my senior management team would seek help for post traumatic stress and their lives would change dramatically. Within a month of the end of the case my wife told me that our marriage was over;

a conclusion she had come to many months before. I was so wrapped up in the case that I did not see it coming. Little did I know that months later I would fall in love with Diane, the most wonderful and courageous woman who is battling cancer for the second time. Her beauty and bravery make everything else pale into insignificance.

The difference between success and failure is small and in Ottawa we embarked on a journey which had the potential for both outcomes. Success brought with it national recognition, rewards and accolades for a fantastic, successful investigation and yes, we accepted all of those rewards. The same people were also prepared to accept failure, the disappointment that would bring, and the inevitable post-mortems from wise observers. It was my job to ensure that the team never contemplated failure; it was an option that, as the detective leading the investigation, I could not allow to enter their thoughts. As a young officer I would never accept that I would fail; I always worked on the basis that I would get a breakthrough and detect the crime. In Operation Ottawa I had like-minded people supported by a fantastic force in Dyfed-Powys Police, who then when times were difficult and with rising costs, held their nerve and supported the investigation. In the current financial climate I am not sure that I would have received the same support over such an extended period, and that I believe is a risk to justice.

I will take many memories from my thirty-three-year career; my informative years in Cheshire Constabulary and the fantastic detectives I worked with as a DC in Winsford and then on the Serious Crime Squad. Likewise, moving to Dyfed-Powys presented me with fantastic opportunities whilst living in a safe and beautiful part of the world. My two wonderful children, Emily and George, have thrived and become two individuals who never let me down and of whom I am immensely proud. It is a privilege to be a police officer and to discharge that responsibility without fear or favour, with humility and humour. A smile and a joke in the right place can defuse many situations and humour has been a large part of my life. I've met some fantastic people, like the victims and the families of the victims in this case. There are many difficult and emotional conversations I have had with them which no doubt make interesting reading, but that would betray a trust. Those conversations will remain between us as a bond that will go beyond a job or a short-term association; we will always remember and understand what went on and why. It is these moments of contact with people who have suffered the most terrible loss that I will look back on to remind myself of how privileged I was to meet such exceptional people.

As a senior detective you always hope that you get a chance to lead a 'big one' and I was given that opportunity with Operation Ottawa. Furthermore you hope that you can rise to the challenge. I was lucky on both counts. For me there were several critical elements. First and foremost the foresight of the senior investigating officers in all three investigations to retain the exhibits and material as they did. Also crucial was the remarkable investigation carried out by the Operation Huntsman team and their foresight in keeping exhibits. The energy of the new CID team in 2005, who decided to grasp the nettle and conduct a thematic forensic review of undetected serious crimes in Pembrokeshire, was also a key element in the story. Bringing together a handpicked team who were not involved in the original investigations set us on the right course, as did the decision to locate all evidential material before any efforts were made to recover it. Our attention to detail when recovering the old exhibits negated any challenges in court. We only dealt in fact and were not swayed by the many myths and legends which had grown up around the case, and we were honest with ourselves, warts and all, even this made our work more challenging. The relationship with the scientists enabled us to question their thinking without compromising their independence and my decision-making was always scrutinised by senior management. We had a first-class media strategy and my team always displayed the utmost professionalism. Finally, Lynne Harries and Glyn Johnson, Gareth Rees, Paul Jones and myself were supported by an excellent police force.

At the end of the investigation I was asked whether Cooper might have committed further crimes. I fear we will never know. There was much speculation in the press regarding other murders and unexplained deaths. What we do know is that even faced with the most damming of forensic and circumstantial evidence, John Cooper admitted and accepted nothing. From work I have carried out there is very little in the way of material to be examined on which informed comment can be made. However, the death of Florence Evans in 1989 troubles me and I have spoken to her family, but again that is a conversation that will remain between us. As we now know, John Cooper made a big mistake in his interviews. He anticipated what we had and in doing so put forward defences and introduced vulnerabilities which he felt he needed to explain away. In fact, he actually offered us direction. It was John Cooper who introduced Florence Evans into his interviews on more than one occasion and that worries me deeply.

As I now contemplate life after retirement, I will look back on Operation Ottawa as a time when I could practice my skills as a detective and lead a fantastic team of officers and staff. The feeling when the word 'Guilty' rang out in Swansea Crown Court on the 26th of May 2011 will remain with me forever, nothing will ever come close.

POSTSCRIPT

I had time to think long and hard about writing this book before I eventually decided to do it. I have read books by retired police officers and I have questioned the appropriateness of such a venture. At the conclusion of this case I was quite clear in my own mind that I was not going to become an author. Soon after though, I was contacted by a number of journalists who were intending to write a book about the Pembrokeshire murders and asking me to take part. I started to question the value of someone else telling a story that others and I had lived and breathed over the previous six years. I mentioned it to my chief constable, Ian Arundale, a very shrewd and forward-thinking senior officer, whose response was simple: 'Do it yourself, Steve.' The more I thought about it the more his words made sense.

This was a story of how a police force with the fewest officers and the largest geographical area in England and Wales had demonstrated why it has consistently been top of performance charts for crime investigation for many years. Now some cynics will say, that's all well and good, but nothing happens in Dyfed-Powys. Frankly that is nonsense. Some six weeks after I retired my former colleagues were facing the critical and at times unforgiving eye of the world's media as they investigated the sad circumstances around the disappearance of five-year-old April Jones. Had I still been Head of CID I would probably have been the senior investigating officer. I know only too well the kind of pressure they will be under but I also know the calibre of excellent officers and support staff that will be totally committed to achieving justice for the family and local community. The public will have seen the total commitment and professionalism demonstrated by those tasked with leading and conducting such an investigation. Our communities are small and close-knit; everyone *does* know everyone else, and their fathers and their fathers' fathers. Most of the officers are born and bred in the areas they police and I believe that is our strength.

Operation Ottawa is the story of those kinds of officers and their dedication to duty. It is a story of how a small police force carried out an investigation into a serial killer and through their skill and attention to detail achieved justice. The feeling that justice had been done and a sense of relief shared by many, from the victims and their families to the communities of North Pembrokeshire. In telling this story I wanted to take the reader on a journey which spans twenty-five years of detective work. Many processes and procedures have changed over the years in line with national best practice and advances in forensic science. Murder investigations are far more structured and scientific compared with years ago. I have been fortunate enough to have worked in both eras and what has not changed is the quality of detective work and that good old-fashioned 'gut feeling', and in this story there is plenty of that. In leading Operation Ottawa the investigation captured the old and the new and in doing so developed its own best practice.

I have presented the story of the case to a wide range of audiences, including senior detectives. A common observation from them is the attention to detail that characterised the case and the huge demands made on people to get things right. My response is simple; that is what we do. If we cannot get that right, then we have no right to represent the victims and their families. It was my motto, right up until the day I walked out of my office for the last time. In this investigation I was blessed with a like-minded team who shared those values. This has been the true account, based on my personal records, recollections and discussions with a handful of people. In the light of the Leveson inquiry I have not spoken to serving police officers, to avoid any possible conflict with their senior officers.

As an observation, professional relationships between senior police officers and members of the media should continue to flourish, as long as they are exactly that: professional. Leveson has triggered a certain amount of paranoia in the chief officer ranks, which risks us going back to the 'bad old days' when police and journalists treated each other with mistrust. Leveson was about members of an industry who were out of control and corrupt police officers who took money for information that put people and investigations at risk. There is no better example for me how this relationship should work, than my relationship with Jonathan Hill. A chance conversation and a snap decision on trust, started a professional relationship which had clear boundaries and I will be forever indebted to him for not breaking that trust. Our collaboration on this project has been a rewarding and enlightening experience.

I would like to thank my team, many of whom are mentioned in the pages of this record. They were truly magnificent. There are many who could be singled out for a special mention but this would be unfair to others. Those who shared this investigation know who they are and will recognise their contribution, which is detailed in these pages. Having said that, Lynne Harries and Glyn Johnson were superb and the people of Wales owe them a great debt of gratitude for their unwavering commitment and devotion to duty. They made it happen. Tom Atherton, from the Crown Prosecution Service, was also superb and his selection of Gerard Elias QC to prosecute on behalf of the Crown was inspired. The work of LGC Forensics, under the watchful eye of Dr Angela Gallop, was quite brilliant. I would also like to thank retired police officers Aldwyn Jones, Don Evans, Derek Davies and Clive Jones, men who led those early investigations and whose foresight enabled me to finish the job. In particular I am so glad that I had the chance to meet and spend time with retired Detective Chief Superintendent Dave Davies, or D.M. to his friends and colleagues. Sadly D.M. passed away shortly after the conviction of John William Cooper. I know that he told his close friends that he would go to his maker a happy man, knowing Scoveston Park was detected.

It was a privilege to have met such wonderful people during this investigation, in particular the victims of the Milford Haven attack and the families of Richard and Helen Thomas and Peter and Gwenda Dixon. Their dignity and strength was truly amazing and their support was unwavering. The conversations and discussions I had with Tim, Keith and Julie always left me with a feeling of total admiration for them as a family. Peter and Gwenda would be very proud of the people they have grown to be. I also had the pleasure of meeting members of the Thomas family, Angela, Robert and Richard James who are good Pembrokeshire people. Sadly, shortly before the court case 'Maria' one of the Milford Haven victims passed away and never saw justice. She never really recovered from the ordeal. This book is dedicated to her and the rest of the victims and family members.

THE AUTHORS

Steve Wilkins moved to Pembrokeshire from the North West when he was seventeen and worked locally in the area before joining Cheshire Police in 1980. He transferred to Dyfed–Powys Police in 1992 and has extensive experience in CID, thirty years of his thirty-three years' service has been as a Detective. He was seconded to the National Criminal Intelligence Service as Head of Region for the North West of England and prior to returning to force he was the head of intelligence for the UK. Wilkins returned to Dyfed-Powys Police as a detective superintendent to work as senior investigation officer on numerous cases. He has also worked closely with the Foreign and Commonwealth Office in trying to secure justice for the family of Kirsty Jones who was murdered in Thailand in 2000. Steve retired in 2012, having been promoted to Detective Chief Superintendent, Head of Crime. He is now married to Diane and lives in his family home in Cheshire.

For more than twenty-five years Jonathan Hill has been the main presenter of *ITV News* in Wales. As an award-winning journalist he has covered some of the biggest news stories in Wales, from the Gleision mining disaster to the murder of April Jones, and also presents the ITV network news at weekends. Jonathan was an executive producer on the recent ITV drama *The Pembrokeshire Murders*, which is based on this book.